AF735129

Reaganomics Goes Global

Reaganomics Goes Global

What Can the EU, Russia and Other Transition Countries Learn from the USA?

Edited by

Wojciech Bieńkowski,

Josef C. Brada

and

Mariusz-Jan Radło

palgrave
macmillan

Selection and Editorial Matter
© Wojciech Bieńkowski, Josef C. Brada and Mariusz-Jan Radło 2006
Individual chapters © contributors

All rights reserved. No reproduction, copy or transmission of this publication may be made without written permission.

No paragraph of this publication may be reproduced, copied or transmitted save with written permission or in accordance with the provisions of the Copyright, Designs and Patents Act 1988, or under the terms of any licence permitting limited copying issued by the Copyright Licensing Agency, 90 Tottenham Court Road, London W1T 4LP.

Any person who does any unauthorised act in relation to this publication may be liable to criminal prosecution and civil claims for damages.

The authors have asserted their rights to be identified as the authors of this work in accordance with the Copyright, Designs and Patents Act 1988.

First published 2006 by
PALGRAVE MACMILLAN
Houndmills, Basingstoke, Hampshire RG21 6XS and
175 Fifth Avenue, New York, N.Y. 10010
Companies and representatives throughout the world

PALGRAVE MACMILLAN is the global academic imprint of the Palgrave Macmillan division of St. Martin's Press, LLC and of Palgrave Macmillan Ltd. Macmillan® is a registered trademark in the United States, United Kingdom and other countries. Palgrave is a registered trademark in the European Union and other countries.

ISBN-13: 978–1–4039–9941–2
ISBN-10: 1–4039–9941–4

This book is printed on paper suitable for recycling and made from fully managed and sustained forest sources.

A catalogue record for this book is available from the British Library.

Library of Congress Cataloging-in-Publication Data
Reaganomics goes global : what can the EU, Russia and other transition countries learn from the USA? / edited by Wojciech Bieńkowski, Josef C. Brada and Mariusz-Jan Radło.
p. cm.
Includes bibliographical references and index.
ISBN 1–4039–9941–4 (cloth)
1. United States—Economic policy—1981–1993—Congresses. 2. European Union countries—Economic policy—Congresses. 3. Former communist countries—Economic policy—Congresses. I. Bieńkowski, Wojciech II. Brada, Josef C., 1942– III. Radło, Mariusz-Jan.
HC106.8.R422 2006
338.9—dc22 2005051547

10 9 8 7 6 5 4 3 2 1
15 14 13 12 11 10 09 08 07 06

Printed and bound in Great Britain by
Antony Rowe Ltd, Chippenham and Eastbourne

Government's view of economy can be summed up in a few short phrases. If it moves, tax it. If it keeps moving, regulate it. And if it stops, subsidize it.

Ronald Reagan

Contents

List of Figures x

List of Tables xi

Foreword by William A. Niskanen and Leszek Balcerowicz xii

Preface xv

List of Contributors xviii

Acknowledgements xx

Part I The US Economic Model

Section 1: Foundations of the US Economic Model

1 Lessons from America's Founding Fathers and US Experience 5
Steve H. Hanke

2 Lord Acton on the Origins of American Liberty and Prosperity 12
Krzysztof Łazarski

3 The Cultural Roots of the American Business Model 28
Małgorzata Durska

4 Constitutional Foundations of American Capitalism 44
Clifford A. Bates

Section 2: Character and Effectiveness of US Economic Policy

5 The Evolution of US Economic Policy in the 1980s 53
Steven F. Hayward

6 Economic Policy during the Clinton Administration 64
William A. Niskanen

7 The Economic Policy of George W. Bush: a Continuation of Reaganomics? 69
Wojciech Bieńkowski

Part II Applicability of the US Economic Model

Section 3: The US Economic Experience and Its Applicability to Countries in Transition

8 Successes and Failures in Catching Up: the Post-Communist Case 85
Leszek Balcerowicz

9 The American Economic System: a Model for Poland? 104
William A. Niskanen

10 What Has America to Offer? 109
David Lipton

11 American Economic Experience: Russian Perspective, Possibilities and Limits of Application 114
Ruslan Khasbulatov

12 Why Russia Cannot Abide the American Economic Model: Round Peg/Square Hole 125
Steven Rosefielde

13 China versus the Orthodoxy: State and Ownership Reforms in Transition Economies 137
Jeffrey B. Miller and Stoyan Tenev

Section 4: The US Economic Experience and EU Economic Policies

14 Economic Reform in the European Union: Will the 'Lisbon' EU Catch Up with the US? 155
Mariusz-Jan Radło

15 The EU Concept of Cohesion: Is It Compatible with the Anglo-Saxon Model? 170
John Bradley

16 Ireland's Delayed if Spectacular Convergence 180
Daniel McCoy

17 Convergence and Divergence of the European Union: Are the European Economies to be 'Americanized'? 192
Tadeusz Kowalik

18 Political Integration and Fiscal Federalism in the American Dollar Area and Eurozone 205
Sławomir Bukowski

19 Toward an Efficient Labor Market Model in the EU: To Centralize or not to Centralize 217
W. Stan Siebert

Section 5: Economic Policy Choices in Europe: Perspective on the US Model Performance

20 Discussion by Jan Krzysztof Bielecki, John Bradley, Marshall Goldman, Stanisław Gomułka, Ruslan Khasbulatov, Andrzej K. Koźmiński, William A. Niskanen 235

Conclusions 256

Index 259

List of Figures

8.1	Value added in industry per worker, various dates	87
8.2	Life expectancy at birth, 1989	88
8.3	Secondary school enrollment, the ratio of total enrollment to the population of age that officially corresponds to the level of secondary education, 1990	88
8.4	Real GDP, 2004	90
8.5	Inflation, 2004	91
8.6	Change in labor productivity in industry, 1992–2003	91
8.7	Cumulative per capita FDI inflows, 1989–2003	92
8.8	GDP/unit of energy use, 1989 and 2001	92
8.9	Life expectancy at birth (1990, 2002)	93
8.10	Gini coefficient of income per capita, 1987–90 and 2000–01	93
8.11	Kyrgyz Republic vs Moldova (private sector share in GDP and GDP level)	94
8.12	EBRD liberalization index vs growth in real GDP	95
8.13	General government expenditure	97
8.14	Domestic credit to private sector and market capitalization of listed companies, 2002	97
8.15	Average value of the EBRD liberalization index and average rating of political and civil liberties, 1991–2004	99
14.1	Average working time vs income transfers and tax rates on low-wage earners	158
14.2	Employment rate vs regulation of product markets and labor protection	158
14.3	Unemployment and income transfers in the EU-15, 1970–2000	161
14.4	Public spending and GDP growth, 1990s	161
16.1	Employment share by sector in Ireland, 1961 and 2002	183
16.2	Output (GDP) share by sector in Ireland, 1961 and 2002	183
16.3	Ireland: GNP compared to EU, 1960–2010	184
16.4	Ireland's dependency ratio, 1960–2010	185
16.5	Ireland's real output growth performance, 1990–2005	187
16.6	Decomposition of Irish GNP per capita growth, 1970–2020	189
19.1	Bargaining coordination reduces wage inequality	221
19.2	Supply and demand	227
19.3	Union density increase is positively linked to unemployment increase	227
19.4	Employment protection laws reduce FDI	228

List of Tables

7.1 Reagan and Bush tax cuts in historical perspective 71
7.2 Reagan and Bush tax cuts compared to other budget items 72
8.1 Empirical studies reviewing experiences of transition countries 96
14.1 Structure of public spending in 2000 in the EU and the US 159
14.2 Changes in the structure of public spending in the EU-15, 1963–2000 160
17.1 FDI inflow and GDP growth of eight new EU members' economies, in 1994–2001 196
19.1 Determinants of unskilled worker job opportunities 219
19.2 Corporatism and labor markets in France and the UK 222
19.3 UK–France comparisons of pay, labor costs, and productivity (averages over 1992–95) 224
19.4 UK–France measures of unskilled job opportunities (samples taken 1994–95) 225
19.5 Union density and real wages 230

Foreword

Reaganomics has now become a global message about how to increase economic growth: reduce the growth of government spending, reduce *marginal* tax rates, reduce regulatory and trade barriers and rely on monetary policy to control aggregate demand.

Twenty-five European governments, including that of Poland, have now delegated trade policy and monetary policy, respectively, to the European Union and the Economic and Monetary Union. This is all the more reason to pay special attention to those fiscal and regulatory policies that remain at the discretion of the member governments. For the governments of many poor nations, the four key elements of Reaganomics are policies to which they can only aspire because their highest priority should be to establish an effective rule of law with secure property rights and uncorrupt courts. Notwithstanding all these exceptions, some or all the elements of Reaganomics have been adopted by Chile, Britain, Ireland, New Zealand and the new governments of Eastern Europe. Often they were adopted or have been maintained by center-left governments, all of which have achieved a higher rate of economic growth than the European average.

So it is important for all governments to understand the major lessons learned from the experience with Reaganomics in the United States.

- Monetary policy is *very* much more effective than fiscal policy in controlling aggregate demand and reducing inflation. Tight monetary policy, for example, reduced the inflation rate from 13.5 percent in 1980 to 3.2 percent in 1983.
- There is *no* long-term trade-off between inflation and unemployment. Over the full eight years of the Reagan administration, for example, the inflation rate declined from 13.5 percent to 4.1 percent and the unemployment rate declined from 7.1 percent to 5.5 percent.
- An increase in the government deficit has *no* significant effect on either inflation or interest rates in nations with an independent central bank and an open capital market. This reduces the short-term incentive to control the deficit, but deficits should still be a focus of concern because they represent an involuntary transfer from future taxpayers to current taxpayers.
- A reduction of marginal tax rates significantly increases long-term economic growth.

During the Reagan Administration, for example, the top income tax rate was reduced from 70 percent in 1981 to 28 percent in the Tax Reform Act of 1986, providing one basis for the significant increase in economic growth in the subsequent years. In contrast with other assertions by supply-side advocates, however, a reduction of tax rates does *not* pay for itself, and an increase in the deficit does *not* lead to a reduction in spending. A policy focus on tax rate cuts alone has unfortunately led to a casual attitude toward the government deficit.

Like any Administration, the Reagan Administration also distributed a lot of special favors in the form of spending, tax, regulatory, and trade preferences. There is no special lesson from this experience other than that a generally principled economic policy was not immune to the normal incentives of democratic government. The global message of Reaganomics is how economic growth is increased by reducing the role of government even though the implementation of these policies by any government will be somewhat less than perfect.

William A. Niskanen
Cato Institute, Washington, June 2005

It is generally believed that modern economic growth only began around the year 1800 and that such growth occurred for a long time only in Western Europe and its offshoots, not becoming a global phenomenon until the 1950s. In the last half century, however, there have been vast differences in the speed with which living standards in various countries have improved, and this has raised the question of where the fundamental sources of economic success or failure lie.

In answering this question, Adam Smith and his followers and successors stressed the positive role of market competition – one of the products of economic freedom – and were very critical of monopoly. They viewed trade barriers and high or distortionary taxation as being among the major obstacles to a nation's progress. They emphasized the 'unproductive' nature of the public sector and were skeptical of state regulation of the economy.

But then the statist view reappeared. Its supporters regarded the free market and the related limited state as harmful for economic development, and consequently recommended the expansion of state prerogatives as the key to growth. Such an approach to the sources of economic growth was a return to the mercantilist tradition that Adam Smith had so much criticized. It found its most vocal and somewhat paradoxical exponent in Karl Marx. While praising the technological dynamism of capitalism, he predicted its demise, pointing out, among other faults, the allegedly destructive role of the 'anarchy of production,' that is, of market competition.

Soviet growth in the pre-war period and during the Great Depression infused the statist idea with seductive power. However, in practice, the growth of state-imposed restrictions on economic freedom did not ensure economic success. On the contrary, the more radically a government expanded, the greater was the economic damage. By the 1980s, with the crisis and subsequent breakdown of Soviet socialism, it became entirely clear that government-led development was an illusion. Moreover, a government's failure very often turned out to be two-fold: the government that tried to be ubiquitous and omnipotent witnessed not only poor economic results, but also tended to fail in performing its proper task, that is, in providing public goods.

Based on these experiences and on the intellectual contributions of Hayek and other thinkers, economic policies in the world started to change. In the West, this change was initiated by Ronald Reagan and Margaret Thatcher. Reagan proved in practice that, in spite of powerful lobbies, limiting the scope of government involvement is possible. To the surprise of many people, such a policy turned out to be compatible with electoral success, as it improved economic performance quite rapidly. A far deeper change has been seen in post-communist countries, most of which have moved away from anti-market dictatorships toward democratic capitalism. The same tendency can be viewed in the Third World. However, the global transition toward prosperity is far from complete. The sources of economic development and the nature of policies conducive to growth still need to be thoroughly studied. It is all too easy to find examples of poor countries that have failed to embark upon the path of lasting convergence. An important research and policy question is to discover which partial reform packages can be introduced successfully, and which are likely to fail.

The topic of this book is Reaganomics and its counterparts in other countries. The book begins with a description of the US economic system and an assessment of its efficiency. Then it searches for those aspects of Reagan's economic policies that could be of use for transition economies and the EU. Since 'beneficial' does not necessarily mean 'achievable,' Reaganomics is analyzed from different perspectives, with the possible economic outcomes being only a starting point.

LESZEK BALCEROWICZ
National Bank of Poland, Warsaw, June 2005

Preface

The conference from which the papers in this volume are drawn was held in the fall of 2004. At the time, the EU had successfully expanded to encompass new members, and the euro was rising against the dollar. There was great confidence that the European economic model was not only successful, but also ascendant, extending its reach to more and more countries. As this preface is being written, in June, 2005, the European project is in disarray, and the European economic model is under sharp attack. On the surface, it would seem that a stark choice between the European and American economic models now faces the peoples of Europe. In fact, this choice has long existed, as we point out below, although it has been submerged somewhat by the EU's seemingly successful expansion and the deepening of the integration process. What is new is that the emerging European debate on statism and free market philosophies will now have to be based on a deeper understanding of the American model, an understanding that is not based on clichés such as 'jungle capitalism' or 'creating jobs at starvation wages' but rather on a clear understanding of the philosophical foundations of the American model and of the real, rather than imagined, differences between the US and EU economies. It is toward that understanding that this book strives.

Because of the superior performance of the American economy, many countries imitate the US when framing their own economic policies. Many economists outside the US analyze US economic policies and economic structures in order to assess the sources of American competitive advantage, and many governments try to adjust their economic policies accordingly. However, we believe that there is more to be done in this respect.

The economic success of the United States and the sources of that success are all too often not fully understood, especially by academics and policymakers seeking to make their own countries more efficient and competitive. The purpose of this book is to help address this failing by providing an accessible analysis of all aspects of the US economic model and to widen the discussion on economic policy choices in many countries, especially in Continental Europe and the post-communist states.

The EU, when planning its own economic policies, usually compares itself to the US in order to set economic goals or implement reforms. The most notable set of EU goals is the so-called Lisbon Strategy. In formulating this strategy, the leaders of the EU declared that they want to make the Union the most competitive economy in the world, even more competitive than the US. The crucial reason for the Lisbon Strategy was the fact that the United States in the 1990s was experiencing significant economic growth, while, at the same time, economic growth in the EU was relatively low. As a result, the GDP per capita gap between the EU and US in 2000 reached its highest level since the beginning of the 1970s. This meant that the European effort, started after World War II, to achieve parity with, or even to surpass, the US economically, totally collapsed in the 1990s. The Lisbon Strategy was partly based on the assumption that the marvel of the American 'new economy' was the result of market flexibility, entrepreneurial climate and various tax, regulatory, and so on, incentives. These helped accelerate the spread of information technologies and enabled the United States to increase its competitive advantage over other nations. This situation made the EU's economies appear insufficiently dynamic and entangled in policies that limited the EU's growth. Also, EU members were facing the results of failed policy objectives that encouraged low labor market flexibility, high unemployment rates, over-regulated product markets, the lack of a single market for services, and the retention of strong monopolies, including those connected with the spread of new technologies, transport, gas and electricity. Therefore the EU planned many economic reforms that sought to emulate, in varying degrees, the US deregulation of the 1980s.

Rapid US economic growth was not the only reason why EU economists desired to understand the nature of the US economy. Comparisons of the US and the EU are also useful for assessing the viability of the Economic and Monetary Union and of the euro as a currency that competes in international financial markets with the US dollar.

Apart from the EU's efforts to form a single economic unit, there are some European countries that want to change their internal economic policies by incorporating more Anglo-Saxon solutions based on US experience. The most successful case is Ireland. Starting in 1986, the Irish government started a process of reform that made its economy the most similar to the US in all of Europe. The reform brought public spending in Ireland to US levels and deregulated product and labor markets. Thanks to these changes, the Irish economy became the most successful European economy in the 1990s in terms of economic growth. There is also a visible growing interest in the American model in Spain, Portugal, the Netherlands and even in Germany and France. It is worth noting that some elements of the American model have been successfully incorporated in Australia, New Zealand and Chile with visible and lasting positive results, becoming another important reference point of our discussion on the applicability of Reaganomics worldwide.

The US economic model is also relevant to economists dealing with transition countries, especially those in transition away from the Soviet model. Economists from new EU member states, most of which have made or are making the transition to a market economy, seeing the various and entrenched economic problems faced by many old EU member states, prefer to base their national economies and policies not on the European economic model but on the US model.

In other words, the editors of this book, which is a collection of assessments presented by policy-makers and academics from the US, Europe and post-communist countries and which were first delivered at a conference on the 'American Economic Way: Its Character, Effectiveness and Applicability' in Warsaw in October 2004, would like to achieve several goals. The first is to analyze the character of the American economic model, its historical background, evolution and current status. The second is to assess the effectiveness of US economic policy and its current impact on the global economy, while explaining America's competitive advantage over the advanced economies of Europe and Asia. Finally, the authors of several chapters investigate the applicability of the US economic model as a policy guide for other countries, with emphasis on selected applications of the model in the EU and in post-communist countries.

The first part of the book is devoted to the analysis of the US economic model. It starts with chapters focusing on the role of America's Founding Fathers, Constitution, philosophy and culture. Next, US economic policy is analyzed. The second part of the book is dedicated to the applicability of the US economic model. Special attention is paid to the applicability of the US economic experience to shaping the economic policy of the European Union as well as of its member states. We hope that this broader interpretation of the American experience and its sources can make a positive contribution to the debate now beginning in Europe.

WOJCIECH BIEŃKOWSKI
JOSEF BRADA
MARIUSZ-JAN RADŁO

List of Contributors

Leszek Balcerowicz is Professor of Economics and Governor, National Bank of Poland, as well as the former Minister of Finance of Poland.

Clifford A. Bates is Professor of Political Science, American Studies Center, Warsaw University, Poland.

Jan Krzysztof Bielecki is President of Pekao SA, as well as former Prime Minister of the Republic of Poland.

Wojciech Bieńkowski is Professor of Economics and Director, US Economy Research Center, Warsaw School of Economics, Poland.

Josef C. Brada is Professor of Economics and Director, College of Business International Programs, W.P. Carey School of Business, Arizona State University, and Executive Secretary, Association for Comparative Economic Studies, USA.

John Bradley is Research Professor, Economic and Social Research Institute, Ireland.

Sławomir Bukowski is Professor of Economics, Economic Faculty, Technical University of Radom, Poland.

Małgorzata Durska is Associate Professor, American Studies Center, Warsaw University, Poland.

Marshall Goldman is the Associate Director of the Davis Center for Russian Studies at Harvard University and Professor of Economics at Wellesley College, USA.

Stanisław Gomułka is Professor of Economics, London School of Economics, United Kingdom.

Steve H. Hanke is Professor of Applied Economics, Johns Hopkins University, USA, as well as a former member of the Council of Economic Advisers in the Reagan Administration.

Steven F. Hayward is Resident Scholar and F.K. Weyerhaeuser Fellow, American Enterprise Institute, USA.

Ruslan Khasbulatov is Professor of Economics and Director, World Economy Department, Russian Plekhanov Academy, as well as a member of the Russian Academy of Sciences, and former speaker of the Russian Parliament.

Tadeusz Kowalik is Professor of Economics, Polish Academy of Sciences, Poland.

Andrzej K. Koźmiński is Professor of Economics and Rector, Koźmiński Academy of Entrepreneurship and Management, Poland.

Krzysztof Łazarski is Professor of History and Political Philosophy, Faculty of Economics and Management, Łazarski School of Economics and Law, Poland.

David Lipton is a former US Under Secretary of the Treasury, USA.

Daniel McCoy is Senior Research Officer, Economic and Social Research Institute, Ireland.

Jeffrey B. Miller is Professor of Economics, Department of Economics, University of Delaware, USA.

William A. Niskanen is Professor of Economics and President of the Cato Institute, USA, as well as former Acting Chairman of the Council of Economic Advisers in the Reagan Administration.

Mariusz-Jan Radło is Associate Professor, Warsaw School of Economics, as well as Research Fellow and Vice President for Research of the Polish Lisbon Strategy Forum, Gdańsk Institute for Market Economics, Poland.

Steven Rosefielde is Professor of Economics, University of North Carolina, Chapel Hill, USA.

W. Stan Siebert is Professor of Labour Economics, University of Birmingham, United Kingdom.

Stoyan Tenev is an Economist at the International Finance Corporation, World Bank, USA.

Acknowledgements

We would like to thank all of those who provided us with assistance in the creation of this book. Without their assistance, helpful comments, suggestions and criticism, this book would not exist. First we thank those who played a key role in helping to bring about the conference from which the volume emerged, especially Jerzy Koźmiński, Leszek Balcerowicz, Radek Sikorski, Clifford Bates, Stanisław Gomułka, Robert Koński, Sławomir Sikora and Piotr Freyberg.

Next we would like to thank all the authors for their contributions, without which there would be no book. We also would like to thank John Bradley, Jan Krzysztof Bielecki, Marshall Goldman, Stanisław Gomułka, Ruslan Khasbulatov, Andrzej K. Koźmiński and William A. Niskanen, for their lively participation in the conference's closing panel, which brilliantly captured and summarized what the conference was all about and which, in transcribed form, serves as the last chapter of this volume.

We would also acknowledge the support of the Warsaw School of Economics, especially the committee in charge of commemorating the 100th Anniversary of the School, as well as the American Enterprise Institute, our co-partner in the conference. Also the National Bank of Poland played a very important role in giving patronage to the conference and helping with the logistics. Let us also not forget the important financial, logistical and media support given by the Harvard Club of Poland, the US-Polish Fulbright Commission, Hewlett-Packard Poland, Citibank Handlowy, the Westin-Warsaw, KPMG Poland, 3M Poland, the US Embassy in Warsaw, Rzeczpospolita, TVN24, Newsweek Polska, and Polish Radio 1.

Most important we would like to thank the editors' wives and families, who put up with our departures for trips abroad, lost weekends, and odd working hours.

Part I

The US Economic Model

Section 1

Foundations of the US Economic Model

1
Lessons from America's Founding Fathers and US Experience

Steve H. Hanke

In the aftermath of World War I, President Woodrow Wilson set out to make the world safe for democracy. Since then, US Presidents have marched to the drumbeat of Wilsonian idealism. Indeed, most US foreign policy is carried out under the pretext – and in some cases perhaps the genuine belief – that America is delivering democracy to the rest of the world. President George W. Bush's rationale for foreign engagements is, therefore, not new or unusual.

Most people, including most Americans, would be surprised to learn that the word 'democracy' does not appear in the Declaration of Independence (1776) or the Constitution of the United States of America (1789). They would also be shocked to learn the reason for the absence of the word democracy in the founding documents of the USA. Contrary to what propaganda has led the public to believe, America's Founding Fathers were skeptical and anxious about democracy. They were aware of the evils that accompany a tyranny of the majority. Not surprisingly, the Framers of the Constitution went to great lengths to insure that the federal government was not based on the will of the majority and was not, therefore, democratic.

The Constitution divided the federal government into legislative, executive and judicial branches. Each branch was designed to check the power of the others because the Founders did not want to rely only on the voters to check government power. As a result, citizens were given very little power to select federal officials. Neither the President, members of the judiciary nor the Senate were elected by direct popular vote. Only members of the House of Representatives were directly elected by popular vote. But even in this case, the franchise was restricted to white males who owned property. Moreover, state governments had the right to place further restrictions on the citizens' franchise.

If the Framers of the Constitution did not embrace democracy, what did they adhere to? To a man, the Framers agreed that the purpose of government was to secure citizens in John Locke's trilogy of the rights to life, liberty and property. The Framers wrote extensively and eloquently on liberty. John Adams, for example, wrote that 'the moment the idea is admitted into society, that property is not as sacred as the laws of God, and that there is not a force of law and public justice to protect it, anarchy and tyranny commence' (Adams, 1851, p. 9).

The Founders' actions often spoke even louder than their words. Alexander Hamilton, a distinguished lawyer, took on many famous cases out of principle. After the Revolutionary War, the state of New York enacted harsh measures against Loyalists and British subjects. These included the Confiscation Act (1779), the Citation Act (1782) and the Trespass Act (1783). All involved the taking of property. In Hamilton's view, these Acts illustrated the inherent difference between democracy and the law. Even though the Acts were widely popular, they flouted fundamental principles of property law. Hamilton carried his views into action and successfully defended – in the face of enormous public hostility – those who had property taken under the three New York state statutes.

The Constitution was designed to further the cause of liberty, not democracy. To do that, the Constitution protected individuals' rights from the government, as well as from their fellow citizens. To that end, the Constitution laid down clear, unequivocal and enforceable rules to protect individuals' rights. In consequence, the government's scope and scale were strictly limited. Economic liberty, which is a precondition for growth and prosperity, was enshrined in the Constitution.

After European settlement, America consisted of thirteen English colonies. They benefited from a rather light administration from London and salutary neglect. This contrasted with the French colonies, which were controlled from Paris, and the Spanish colonies, which had entire institutional superstructures imposed from Spain.

Everything did not go well in the American colonies, however. One major colonial problem centered on money. Officially British silver coins were the coin of the realm in America. But there were problems. The Navigation Acts prohibited the export of silver coins from England. There was also a prohibition against any of the colonies establishing mints. As a result, there was an endemic shortage of silver coins in the colonies. To fill this large gap, bills of credit were issued and circulated freely during the first half of the eighteenth century.

This resulted in high inflation, which forced most of the colonies to abandon fixed exchange rates and a specie standard. Things finally deteriorated to such an extent that the British Board of Trade imposed the Currency Acts of 1751 and 1764. These prohibited the issuance and use of bills of credit not fully backed by specie. The prohibitions against paper money created an enormous source of resentment in the colonies. Coupled with the better-known Stamp Act of 1765, the prohibitions on bills of credit set the stage for the Declaration of Independence and the ensuing Revolutionary War.

The Revolutionary War added to America's money problems. The best estimates place the cost of the Revolutionary War at about 15 to 20 percent of the colonies' GNP. Roughly 85 percent of it was financed with fiat money. During the 1775–80 period, annual inflation was about 65 percent. Subsequently – and prior to the Constitutional Convention (1787) – the economic situation was one in which individual states increased taxes and regulations dramatically and money remained unstable. In addition, there was a great deal of political corruption and scandal. And to top it off, the economy was in a general slump which was punctuated by the crisis of 1787.

As a reaction to the overall political-economic situation, the Constitutional Convention convened in 1787 in Philadelphia. In due course, the Constitution was crafted and ratified in 1789. It is a short, clear, intelligible document. The Constitution's preamble contains only 52 words which are followed by seven short articles and ten amendments known as the Bill of Rights (1791). The original Constitution established the rule of law and limited government. About 20 percent of the Constitution itemizes things that the federal and state governments may not do. Another 10 percent of the Constitution is concerned with positive grants of power. However, most of these were simply a reaffirmation of powers that had been previously exercised under the Articles of Confederation or by the states. In total, the legitimate powers granted by the Constitution were less than those that had existed. The bulk of the Constitution – about 70 percent – addresses the Framers' conception of their main task: to bring the United States and its government under the rule of law.

The Constitution is primarily a structural and procedural document that itemizes who is to exercise power and how they are to exercise it. A great deal of stress is placed on the separation of powers and the checks and balances in the system. It was not a Cartesian construct or formula aimed at social engineering, but something to protect the people from the government. In short, the Constitution was designed to govern the government, not the people.

The Bill of Rights establishes the rights of the people against infringements by the State. The only claim citizens have on the State, under the Bill of Rights, is for a trial by a jury. The rest of the citizen's rights are protections from the State. For roughly a century after the Constitution was ratified, private property, contracts and free internal trade within the United States were kings. The scope and scale of the government remained very constrained. All this was very consistent with what was understood to be liberty.

A remark about the Framers and the public is in order. There were 55 Framers and 35 had attended college. The college entry standards in those days were very high and strict. At the age of 14 or 15, the normal college entry age, students were required to be fluent in both Latin and Greek and proficient in classics. They were skilled at the art of rhetoric and were keenly aware of the necessity of garnering public support for their constitutional project. The Framers knew that policies needed to be developed from the bottom up.

At the time, Americans were literate and well informed, via pamphlets and manuscripts, about the political debates of the day. There were four times as many newspapers in the United States as there were in France, which was the center of continental thinking and debate on many constitutional and philosophic matters. The Federalist Papers were actually published in 1787 and 1788 in New York City's *Independent Journal*, an ordinary newspaper. These important essays, written under pseudonyms by Alexander Hamilton, James Madison and John Jay, were of very high quality and set the stage for the Constitutional Convention and the resulting product. In passing, it is worth mentioning that Hamilton organized this project, wrote most of the essays, and of all the Founding Fathers, performed the most intellectual work for the least historical credit. That said, two notable economists have given Hamilton his due. Milton Friedman wrote in 1972 that Federalist Paper 15, written by Hamilton, 'contains a more cogent analysis of the European Common Market than any I have seen from the pen of a modern writer' (Friedman, 1972, p. 92). And if that were not enough, Lionel Robbins (1998, p. 240) thought the Federalist Papers were 'the best book on political science and its broad practical aspects written in the last thousand years.'

After the Constitution was ratified and George Washington was elected President, the new federal government lacked credibility. Public finances hung like a threatening cloud over the government. Recall that paper money and debt were innovations of the colonial era, and that once the Revolutionary War began, Americans used these innovations to the maximum. As a result, the United States was born in a sea of debt. A majority of the public favored a debt default. Alexander Hamilton, acting as Washington's Secretary of the Treasury, was firmly against default. As a matter of principle, he argued that the sanctity of contracts was the foundation of all morality. And as a practical matter, Hamilton argued that good government depended on its ability to fulfill its promises.

Hamilton won the argument and set about digging the country out of its financial debacle. Among other things, Hamilton was what would today be called a first-class financial engineer. He established a federal sinking fund to finance the Revolutionary War debt. He also engineered a large debt swap in which the debts of individual states were assumed by the newly created federal government. By August 1791, federal bonds sold above par in Europe, and by 1795, all foreign debts had been paid off. Hamilton's solution for America's debt problem provided the country with a credibility and confidence shock.

The state of economic affairs in the United States, roughly until World War I, was in the spirit of the Constitution. The economy flourished, with large increases in labor and capital inputs as well as strong productivity growth. There was, of course, one near fatal interruption during this period: the Civil War. The war consumed 15 to 20 percent of GNP, about the same proportion as during the Revolutionary War. War finance was somewhat similar in the Confederacy (the South) as it was during the Revolutionary War. About 60 percent of the financing for the southern effort was paper money. The North also resorted to fiat money financing, but at only a 13 percent rate. Consequently, there was inflationary surge. In addition to the major disruption caused by the Civil War, it is worth mentioning one major anomaly in the US economy: lands were owned by the federal, as well as state and local, governments.

Alexander Hamilton, the first Secretary of the Treasury, wanted to sell the public lands as fast as possible. This did not happen. In consequence, the government still owns a lot of real estate. Its surface area is about ten times larger than the total area of Poland. This is a huge state-owned enterprise. As you might expect, it is also very unproductive. Detailed studies of SOE lands indicate that they are only about 25–30 percent as productive as comparable private ones.

America's SOE lands have been the center of repeated debates about the free market system in the United States. Indeed, even the American Economic Association put itself at the center of one of these debates. One of the major motivations for establishing the American Economic Association was as a protest against laissez-faire attitudes in the United States. Not surprisingly, therefore, the May 1885 *American Economic Review*, contains three papers justifying the retention of government-owned timberlands!

On the eve of World War I, government expenditures were less than 2 percent of GNP and 99 percent of the population paid no income tax. Income tax had just been introduced, but the top rate was only 7 percent and applied to incomes exceeding $500,000. The federal government had around 400,000 employees, less than 1 percent of the labor force. About 165,000 troops were on active duty. No federal regulations of capital or labor markets existed. Agricultural production and distribution were also unregulated. There was no minimum wage rate and no social security. One area where there was a rather aggressive interference in the economy concerned the rates and tariffs the railroads charged. Antitrust was also strong.

World War I marks a violent break with the letter and spirit of the Constitution. Property rights were suspended on a large scale. There were wide-scale nationalizations of rail, telephone, telegraph and to a lesser degree ocean shipping. Over 100 manufacturing plants were nationalized. The government got involved in labor–management relations under the Adams Act in 1916. Conscription was instituted. The Espionage Act was passed in 1917. The Sedition Act of 1918 imposed penalties for anti-government expression, subverting the Bill of Rights. Upton Sinclair was actually arrested for reading the Bill of Rights and Roger Baldwin was arrested for reading the Constitution. President Woodrow Wilson accomplished all this under emergency powers granted to him by Congress in 1916.

Much of this anti-Constitutional apparatus was scrapped after the war. However, residues remained and eventually resurfaced. All it took was another national emergency – the Great Depression, World War II, the Vietnam War, and so on. With each, laws were enacted, bureaus created and the budgets enlarged. In many cases, these changes turned out to be permanent. The result is that crises acted as a ratchet, shifting the trend line of government size and scope up to a higher level.

It comes as no surprise that governments spend more money and regulate more actively during crises – wars and economic bail-outs are expensive and complicated. But a more active government also attracts opportunists, who perceive that a national emergency can serve as a useful pretext for achieving their own objectives.

The US and other countries seem no more aware of this today than they were in the past. And yet history has provided many examples to illustrate how damaging it is. Take the Great Depression. At that time, the organized farm lobbies, having sought subsidies for decades, took advantage of the crisis to pass a sweeping rescue package, the Agricultural Adjustment Act, whose title declared it to be 'an act to relieve the existing national economic emergency.'

Almost 70 years later, the farmers are still sucking money from the rest of society and agricultural policy has been enlarged to satisfy a variety of other interest groups, including conservationists, nutritionists and friends of the Third World. Then, during World War II, when government accounted for nearly half the US GDP, virtually every interest group tried to tap into the vastly enlarged government budget. Even bureaus seemingly remote from the war effort, such as the Department of the Interior (which is in charge of government lands and natural resources), claimed to be performing 'essential war work' and to be entitled to bigger budgets and more personnel.

Within the US government, the latest emergency – the war on terrorism – has given cover to a multitude of parochial opportunists, whose proposals range from bailing out the airlines to nationalizing vaccine production. As a result, President George W. Bush – a so-called conservative – has blessed a record-setting expansion of government. That is where we are now.

What lessons can we learn? First, 'democracy' and 'freedom' are not interchangeable words. Second, only the first century of the American experience represents a standard for freedom. Expanding democracy is a slogan which requires great caution. It can easily result in elected tyranny. Freedom is the concept. Our challenge is to persuade every citizen that benefits flow from freedom's practical applications. Freedom might then flourish in very diverse and unexpected forms in different parts of the world.

References

Adams, John (1851), *The Works of John Adams, Second President of the United States*, edited by Charles Francis Adams, Vol. VI, Boston, MA: Charles C. Little and James Brown.

Friedman, Milton (1973), 'Alexander Hamilton on the Common Market', *Newsweek*, 4 June.

Robbins, Lionel (1998), *A History of Economic Thought, the LSE Lectures*, edited by Steve G. Medema and Warren J. Samuels, Princeton, NJ: Princeton University Press.

2
Lord Acton on the Origins of American Liberty and Prosperity

Krzysztof Łazarski

> Power tends to corrupt, absolute power corrupts absolutely.
> Great men are almost always bad men.
> Liberty is ancient and it is despotism that is new.
>
> Lord Acton

For about three centuries, ever since colonial times, America has amazed the world with the extent of its liberty, stability of its political institutions, prosperity and dynamic economic growth. Trying to understand and explain the American phenomenon, historians and political thinkers usually turn their attention to English political heritage and the religious roots of American order, to the legal equality of the colonists and their participation in self-government, to the nature of the American Constitution, to the abundance of land for the settlers and to equality of opportunity.

Modern historiography has questioned many of those traditional premises: not all colonists were free or equal, or particularly religious. African slaves at times constituted the majority of new arrivals. North America was penetrated not only by the British but also by the French, Dutch, Spanish and Russians, hence focusing on New England as the source of American order is not justified. The Framers of the Constitution suppressed democratic impulses coming from below and established an order that served mainly their own interest and that of their class. Furthermore, America was not an empty continent but had an indigenous population that was deprived of its land and largely exterminated, mostly through diseases brought from Europe, maltreatment and outright slaughter.[1] This approach denies any exceptional quality to the American past: it sometimes substitutes occultism, witchcraft and religious hysteria for Puritanism; slavery for freedom; inequality for equality; and violence and cruelty for order. Ultimately, this approach is not far from the commonplace view in certain quarters that America is the source of most evil in the world.

Lord Acton's view on America could certainly be placed among 'favorable' interpretations of American history, and the purpose of this chapter is to present his perspective on the American past until the end of the eighteenth century, in particular on the origins of American freedom and prosperity. As America is a major, if not the foremost, element in Acton's theory of liberty, and as his admiration for America originates in his passion for liberty in general, the chapter also presents a brief summary of his history of freedom. To fully appreciate the value of Acton's opinions and to place them in certain perspective, the chapter begins with a short recollection of who he was and why his views might still be relevant in our time.

John Emerich Edward Dalberg-Acton (1834–1902) was born into an Anglo-German aristocratic family.[2] At sixteen he was sent to Munich because both Oxford and Cambridge denied him entry, probably on account of his Catholicism. The eight years he spent in Munich (1850–57) were formative. He studied at the University of Munich, or to be precise, he underwent a rigorous tutoring under Father Professor Ignaz von Döllinger, one of the leading German historians of that time. Hard work under Döllinger evolved into a life-long habit of reading and studying, on average, a book a day, the proof of which are tens of thousands of index cards with his notes, now stored at the Cambridge University Library. His area of study was, first of all, history, particularly modern European history. However, he was interested and extremely well-read in theology and philosophy, especially in political philosophy.

After his Munich years, Acton became the editor of, and chief writer for, several influential periodicals he founded, and one of the leading figures among English liberal Catholics. That work brought him close to papal excommunication after the First Vatican Council (1869–70). Briefly a Member of Parliament (1859–65), he later became an intimate friend of Liberal Prime Minister William Gladstone, and through him, he had some direct influence on British politics. At the end of his life (1895) he was appointed Regius Professor of Modern History at Cambridge University, one of the two most prestigious academic posts in Great Britain in the field of history. Since Acton never gained any academic degree, except for several honorary doctorates he received late in his life, and published no book, that honor was a public recognition of the fame he had already enjoyed as one of the best educated men of his time and perhaps of all time.

From his earliest writing, it is clear that Acton was fascinated by the idea of freedom. In time, liberty became his predominant interest. He came to the conclusion that the idea of liberty is 'the central thread of all history' that gives history unity and meaning.[3] As Tocqueville found divine Providence behind the idea of equality, so Acton discovered liberty as yet another Providential idea that seems higher even than equality itself.[4] 'Liberty is not a means to a higher political end. It is itself the highest political end.'[5] As such, it is a mighty force; it crushes empires, abolishes kingdoms, breaks rulers and overcomes powerful groups and individual interests. It grows over millennia and ages. Yet, liberty is also 'a delicate fruit of mature civilization' that has many enemies among the powerful as well as among the poor and destitute. To flourish, it must be carefully cultivated and guarded, yet it cannot be fully erased for a long period of time.[6]

Acton's research on ideas and his conviction that they are the moving forces of the world's history was prescient of the much later birth of a new field of study, the history of ideas. With his warnings against 'the crimes of majorities and the fury of uncontrolled democracy,'[7] and the threats they pose to liberty, Acton seems to have been a prophet for posterity rather than for his time.[8] At least the generation that witnessed the horrors of German Nazism and Soviet Communism judged so. Increased interest in his writing in recent years indicates that he has not been forgotten by the current generation either.

Acton had not always liked America. His first and only personal encounter with it in 1853 shows no sign of future high regard. '[The] Yankee type of countenance... is not a very intelligent face, and a selfish face. They are generally thin, and their hair turns white early, perhaps partly by the quantity of drink and profuse perspiration. They are seldom fine men.' He also noted a common 'custom of chewing and spitting at N.Y.'[9] He was not impressed by Harvard University either: 'a couple of red brick buildings of rather tumbledown appearance' and a student body of 600 paying tuition of $80 a year. At Harvard '(n)othing is studied for its own sake, but only as it will be useful in making a practical man... There is no demand for learning' as in America 'money is the great object of life.'[10] Listening to the proceedings of one of the State Legislatures, he disliked the informal manners and the rough language as well as the content: 'A half-madman... made a speech suggesting equality of all things' including 'votes for women and such-like.'[11] Those remarks typify the opinion of any casual and superficial observer of America and young Acton – he was nineteen years old at that time – obviously belonged to that category of observers. What altered Acton's view on America was his research on the development of freedom in history. And as said before, since America plays an eminent role in his concept of the growth of liberty, this chapter will now present a summary of Acton's history of liberty.

The dawn of freedom, according to Acton, began in Israel. Through Moses and the prophets the Israelites received a divine law. In politics that translated into a limited government and equality of the Jews. Rulers were not lawgivers; they only executed the God-given and thus unchangeable law. For the first time in history there appeared a theoretical curb on political power. But the Babylonian captivity destroyed 'the sanctuary of freedom in the East, and a new home was prepared for it in the West.'[12]

That new home in the West was Greece in general and Athens in particular. As a result of reforms instituted by Solon (594 BC), Athens became a limited democracy. In accordance with the principle that 'political power ought to be commensurate with public service,' only taxpayers had the right to rule and the obligation to serve in the army without pay, but the poor gained the right to elect magistrates from higher classes. This small concession to the poor 'completely inverted the notion of human authority... Government by consent superseded government by compulsion.'[13] Soon after the Persian Wars (490–480 BC), the poor were granted full political rights because they served in the victorious fleet. Furthermore, they also began to be paid for participation in the Popular Assembly. Thus the Athenian regime changed from limited democracy into unlimited democracy, which rapidly degenerated into a tyranny of the majority.[14]

Athens did not have anything similar to US constitutional law, and the Assembly could vote upon anything, even a law that contradicted one voted a day earlier. In consequence, the Assembly was turbulent and easily manipulated by demagogues, and what was worse, those who lost had no recourse; the Assembly's decisions were final. During the Peloponnesian War (431–404 BC) when state revenues decreased and expenses increased 'the policy of making one class give, that another might receive' drove the rich minority to treason and, finally, the state to collapse. Athenian democracy survived only about one generation of this madness and never recovered its power.[15]

Commenting on those events, Acton pronounces the following maxims: 'It is bad to be oppressed by a minority, but is worse to be oppressed by a majority. For there is a reserve of latent power in the masses which... the minority can seldom resist. But from the absolute will of an entire people there is no redemption, no refuge but treason.'[16] The Athenian lesson 'teaches that the government by the whole people, being the government of the most numerous and most powerful class, is an evil of the same nature as unmixed monarchy, and requires... institutions that shall protect it against itself.'[17]

The Romans also had some merit in the development of liberty, depending mainly on the spread of Greek civilization and of local self-government throughout the vast Empire. For the Empire was a sort of confederation of former city-states which preserved a lot of internal autonomy and citizens' participation in self-government. In time, their inhabitants gained Roman citizenship. So, while the Emperor's power was absolute in Rome and evolved into despotism, municipal self-government and provincial assemblies were not crushed but rather spread.[18]

Concluding his remarks on antiquity, Acton turns his attention to two unresolved problems relating to power and the state. The first was a practical question, namely the division of power. Although the ancients knew that undivided power leads to excess, monarchy degenerating into tyranny, aristocracy into oligarchy and 'democracy into the supremacy of numbers,' the only solution they came up with was the theory of mixed government, that is, of monarchy, aristocracy and democracy mixed together, which in practice never worked.[19] The second problem was even more difficult because it touched a fundamental question of political philosophy, namely by what principle can political power be circumscribed and put within definite limits? The Stoics contributed to the doctrine of a divine-given, natural law standing higher than any written law; Christianity resorted to Christ's words 'Render unto Caesar the things that are Caesar's, and to God the things that are God's' (Mark 12:17) which reduced political authority within certain limits, but, in practice, the government remained omnipotent and Christian Emperors never intended to give up their arbitrary powers.[20] That problem Acton characterizes in the following powerful words:

> [T]he vice of the classic State was that it was both Church and State in one. Morality was undistinguished from religion and politics from morals... What the slave was in the hand of his master, the citizen was in the hands of the community... The passengers existed for the sake of the ship. By this disregard for private interest, and for the moral welfare...both Greece and Rome destroyed the vital elements on which the prosperity of nations rests.[21]

The Middle Ages were crucial in the growth of liberty, says Acton. Primitive German rulers were not able to absorb the despotic political tradition of the late Roman Empire and their authority was much weaker. Furthermore, they needed churchmen, who were the only literate men with some knowledge of Roman law, so the Church rapidly gained privileges it had never enjoyed under Rome, such as exemption from taxation and from civil jurisdiction. As an institution it became powerful. But the growth of feudalism – the investiture struggle – began to threaten its independence. In the context of that struggle Acton forcefully pronounces:

> To that conflict of four hundred years we owe the rise of civil liberty. If the Church had continued to buttress the throne of the king whom it anointed... all Europe would have sunk down under a Byzantine or Muscovite despotism. For the aim of both contending parties was absolute authority. For although liberty was not the end for which they strove, it was the means by which the[y] ... called the nation to aid. The towns of Italy and Germany won their franchises, France got her States-General, and England her Parliament out of... the contest; and as long as it lasted it prevented the rise of divine right [of kings].[22]

That conflict of Church and State resulted in gradual recognition that the people are the ultimate source of power and that they have the right to resist against unlawful conduct of their ruler, which in fact meant a limited government.[23] The advancement of liberty, both in practice and theory was thus amazing:

> Representative government, which was unknown to the ancients, was almost universal. The method of election was crude; but the principle that no tax was lawful that was not granted by the class that paid it – that is, that taxation was inseparable from representation – was recognized . . . as the right of all . . . The political produce of the Middle Ages was a system of states in which authority was restricted by the representation of powerful classes, by privileged associations, and by the acknowledgment of duties superior to those which are imposed by man.[24]

The rise of the modern (nation-) state, Machiavelli's doctrine and, finally, the Reformation reversed the process that had began in the High Middle Ages. Nation-states created powerful monarchs; Machiavelli 'released government from the restraint of law,' while Luther subordinated the Church to civil authority.[25] Taken together that led to modern absolutism in almost all of Europe. The torch-bearers of liberty were the Dutch, who enjoyed old liberties, self-government and the right to tax themselves. They revived their right to resist against unjust authority and freed themselves from Spanish domination (1566–87). That torch moved in the seventeenth century to England during the struggle with the Stuarts, which ended with the Glorious Revolution (1688) and the establishment of a state based on contract.[26] Strangely, however, Acton pays little attention to those events and makes some disparaging remarks about it and about its main actors, including John Locke.[27] He pays much more attention to Protestant sects, mainly in England, the Puritans, Baptists, Quakers, Anabaptists, and others. And those sects finally bring us to America.

The spread of Protestant sects coincided with the reign of the Stuarts, who were happy to rid themselves of troublemakers and permitted them to emigrate to America; further granting them liberal royal charters. Self-rule in the new colonies allowed the immigrants to enjoy the religious freedom whose absence had prompted the sectarians to leave England in particular and Europe in general. For the Puritans and others, the Established Church of England was not much better than the Catholic Church. It persecuted them, and they viewed it as a state church; they called it 'Babylon.'[28] Thus they brought to the New World a deep-seated repugnance of state religion. Although the 'Pilgrims' in New England and other colonists elsewhere did not entirely avoid the temptation of imposing their particular creed on others, gradually religious tolerance took root everywhere in the American colonies. But Acton claims that for the advancement of a more mature notion of liberty there occurred in America something much more important than mere tolerance, namely the concepts of religious freedom based on conscience and of limited state power.

Liberty of conscience was 'a dream of great Christian writers' from the late Roman Empire to Erasmus and Thomas More, but it remained an idea and was never put into practice.[29] Since the sectarians had no designs on gaining state power, they paid much more attention to the value of an individual.

An individual has a soul that is immortal, and that is therefore infinitely more valuable than the State and Church, which are temporal. As there is no proportion in value between mortal and immortal, the State must not interfere with the individual's relation to God. State power must, therefore, be restricted and religion should be committed to human conscience.[30] In this context, Acton pronounces another of his maxims that 'religion was the mother of freedom (and) that freedom was the lawful offspring of religion.'[31]

Another powerful impact of the Puritans on the shape of American order was their Church government. It was not controlled by the State, or the bishops, or the presbyters, but by all the faithful: each congregation was governed by its members. 'It was an ideal of local self-government and of democracy,' and as such it could not be ignored in state administration.[32] That influence and close links between religious and civil freedom are clearly visible in the following statement by a Connecticut preacher quoted by Acton. As early as 1638 he said that: 'The choice of public magistrates belongs unto the people, by God's own allowance. They who have the power to appoint officers and magistrates, it is in their power, also, to set the bounds and limitations of the power and place unto which they call them.'[33]

Finally, the colonists were privileged with very liberal royal charters, which, together with their notions of religious liberty, Church self-government and its influence on civil government created a remarkably free society: almost all colonists were free, legally equal and participated in the election of their self-government on a local and colonial level, and they taxed themselves. Rhode Island was a democracy in which elections were held every year, and that system lasted until 1842. Connecticut had well-developed local self-government which served as a model for the federal system included in the American Constitution. The Quakers in Pennsylvania – whose order Acton particularly liked – knew no slavery, oppression nor privilege. After all, they left England and 'went to the desert' in order 'to enjoy freedom, liberty of conscience, and the right to tax themselves.'[34]

In the seventeenth century, the colonies were already more advanced than England so far as free institutions and individual liberty were concerned.[35] But that was not their only advantage vis-à-vis the mother country. Acton notes that English colonies in America were not state enterprises, initiated, supported and directly managed by the State, as were the colonies of Spain and France, but that they were ventures of various elements of English society over which the State exercised very limited control. Furthermore, the nature of colonial life required self-reliance, independence of spirit and an ability for self-organization, that is, qualities which became essential for American national character.

> That is why...(the) habit of expecting all things from the government...is so fatal to colonists. That is why the English and German succeed, and the French fail, except when, like the Canadians,

> they flourish under English government. The Frenchman is so little independent, so extremely sociable, that he sinks to the level of the society about him when he lives in a savage country.[36]

And since the American colonists did not have to deal with the remnants of feudalism which plagued Europe, did not pay high taxes – another plague that torments Europe until today – knew almost no permanent poverty, nor idleness, nor bureaucratic hindrance in running their business, they began to experience rapid growth, even in the seventeenth century, and that process continues, we may add, until today.[37]

In this context it is worth examining Acton's view on the relations between the colonists and the native American population, the Indians, and on slavery. The problem has become very sensitive in recent decades and Acton's view might easily be dismissed as racist. There is no question that he regards the treatment of Indians and slavery as evil, yet not as absolute evil. He says that whenever two groups of people of unequal civilization live side by side, they cannot exist as equals. Inevitably, the group which has much lower skills, inferior tools and represents a much more primitive culture 'would have been quickly reduced to pauperism . . . fallen into bondage, and . . . exposed to unmitigated cruelty.'[38]

> By themselves the laws of trade and economy must ruin the natives as soon as they come in contact with us, and establish an exchange between us. The promotion of our trade requires us to awaken new desires in them; indeed, these new desires are the inevitable consequences of new knowledge and new ideas. Their old manner of life does not suffice to satisfy these new ideas – to purchase spirits, weapons, gunpowder, domestic animals and medicine. As hunters they are destitute of stored wealth. The craving for the new commodities . . . must gradually exhaust their means. So the missionaries just dread the contact. But they cannot prevent it without the closest alliance and support of the civil power.[39]

And that brings us to Acton's main point, that the natives could have been protected only by an arbitrary government. Such was the case in the Spanish colonies in America. The absolute government in Madrid gave certain protections to the Indians and supported the Catholic Church's missionary works among them, but at the cost of arbitrary rule over the colonies. However, when the Spanish Government's power waned in South America, 'there have been wars of blood, of colour, and of race.'[40] The case of English colonies in America was different. The colonists were free and governed themselves. And however unpleasant Acton's conclusion is, the fact remains that because they were free they did not care about the natives. They treated them as not fully human, did not attempt to convert them to Christianity and used every opportunity to expel them from their land.[41] In short, the Indians were not incorporated into the new society. Yet, that was the necessary condition for preserving freedom for the colonists.

The situation with African slaves was similar. Acton condemns slavery, yet he says that 'the introduction of the Blacks [to America] fails to be a fatal evil because they are slaves. If they were free, there would be an end of freedom for both, for them and for the whites.'[42] In colonial America there was no other way: either tyranny for both groups or freedom for one and slavery for another. On the other hand, he implies that by the time of the Revolution, America had outgrown slavery and its retention is considered as one of the weaknesses of the American Constitution.[43]

From the outset, Acton notes, the relations between England and its American colonies were mutually advantageous. Unlike Spain, England did not establish its American colonies for fiscal purposes. Even such mercantilist devices as the Navigation Acts, the first of which was enacted in 1651, which required that all international trade between England and its colonies be conducted on British ships, did not hurt them. That began to change after the Glorious Revolution, when new regulations on industrial production and trade were made for the benefit of England and to the cost of the colonies. At the same time, in the eighteenth century, colonies grew increasingly rich, became more self-reliant and gained in self-respect, produced more goods and became less dependent on British imports. Their interest required trade with others and throwing off the barriers that the British imposed.[44]

There is an ongoing discussion among political thinkers and historians as to the causes and nature of the American Revolution. We cannot go into details of that discussion but for our topic suffice to say that some deny that it was a revolution. Unlike the French Revolution, it had no ambition for radical social, economic and legal changes, hence it was not a revolution but a war for independence. Others say that since Americans fought to retain the traditional liberties of Englishmen, it was a revolution and not a war for independence, although backward-looking and conservative, rather than radical. Still others turn their attention to the Declaration of Independence – which was certainly not backward-looking and proclaimed universal rights of men, inalienable to all, without regard for national traditions and laws – and conclude that it was a revolution after all.

Acton does not fit well to any of those views. He says it was, in fact, 'the greatest Revolution that had ever broken out among civilized men.'[45] And its greatness and uniqueness lies in that:

- It broke out for no compelling and tangible reasons but for an abstract and theoretical end – liberty; therefore, it set an example for others.
- It had to find new principles to justify the revolt against authority which was not arbitrary but based on representation of the people, and by doing so it created new limits on state power and broadened the boundaries of liberty.

- It ended not with disorder, destruction and centralization of power, like the French Revolution, but it established a powerful democracy by the division of power that was able to preserve freedom, and, as such, it is a model for posterity.

As for the first point, Acton reminds us that Americans did not live under tyranny. 'The colonists were in many ways more completely their own masters than Englishmen at home.'[46] Their grievances against the British authorities were trifling compared to those Frenchmen had against their king.[47] British insistence on raising more taxes on Americans after the Seven Years War (1756–63) was not unreasonable in view of its huge cost and in view of the benefits it brought to the colonies. Yet, Americans were not thankful. First of all, until 1765 the colonists had paid no other taxes than those voted by their representatives. No wonder they did not wish to lose that privilege. Furthermore, the conquest of Canada had eliminated the main reason for the need of English military protection, and now that this was no longer necessary, the mercantilist policies that benefited England and injured the colonies looked less tolerable than ever.[48] On constitutional grounds, they did not claim that the Parliament had no right to tax them, and on practical grounds, '[t]he suffering that would be caused by submission was immeasurably less than the suffering that must follow resistance... The utilitarian argument was loud in favour of obedience and loyalty.'[49]

In view of that quotation, Acton's assertion, that the Revolution was in fact radical, fought at great risk for a principle as impalpable as liberty, becomes more evident. Beginning with the Stamp Act (1765), Parliament attempted several times to impose taxes on the colonies, each time withdrawing them under protests, yet claiming to preserve the right to taxation. The colonists each time protested: as Englishmen, they claimed that they could not be taxed without their consent, that is, without having their representation in the Parliament. Then, as Acton says, the British Government decided to bribe Americans by lowering taxes in order to enforce the right of taxation. In 1773, it suspended the Navigation Act and permitted tea to enter the colonies without paying toll in England. As a result, Americans would have paid a toll of threepence instead of fifteen. 'How could it be a grievance to pay less?' asks Acton. Yet, 'that threepence broke up the British empire.'[50] The Americans put aside their local interest: in some cities they did not allow tea to be unloaded and in Boston they threw it into the harbor. The conflict between Great Britain and the colonists was, therefore, much more than mere selfish interest: it was a clash between 'liberty and authority, government by consent and government by force.'[51] Its object was thus, 'liberty, not independence,' and it was for liberty that the colonists resolved to give up everything, to 'honour a precept of unwritten law. That was the transatlantic discovery in the theory of political duty, the light that came over the ocean. It represented liberty not as a comparative release from tyranny, but as a thing so divine that the existence of society must be staked to prevent even the least constructive infraction of its sovereign right.'[52]

The second of Acton's points is that the Revolution had to wrestle with and resolve very difficult political questions with no precedent in modern history. For when he noted that English rule in America was not oppressive he meant that the government did not abuse power, and that it was a legal government. The British Government was limited and constitutional, not absolute; and it was Parliament's prerogative – or to be exact, that of the House of Commons – as the representative of the nation, to impose taxes. And the House of Commons was particularly sensitive about that right. Therefore, the colonists had to find entirely new theoretical principles to challenge the power of the Parliament, and those principles were not readily available. Political theories relating to the Glorious Revolution were irrelevant. For it is an entirely different thing to question the legality of arbitrary power and that of the nation itself, acting through its representatives:

> The old European criteria for good government were found insufficient protection against parliamentary oppression... The political problem raised by the New World was more complicated than the simple issues dealt with hitherto in the Old. It had become necessary to turn back the current of the development of politics, to bind and limit and confine the State, which it was the pride of the moderns to exalt. It was a new phase of political history.[53]

Originally, the early Fathers of American independence admired British constitutionalism as based on immutable laws of nature.[54] Yet, when they found that appeals to its fundamental principles did not help, when they realized that the Parliament as it should have been existed only in theory, was only 'virtual,' while the real one was corrupt, bribed by the king, and had no regard for English fundamental laws, they decided to put aside arguments from old parchments, charters and constitutions: 'The case was fought out on the ground of the Law of Nature, more properly speaking, of Divine Right.'[55] That law was higher than any written law; furthermore, it implicitly set limits on any authority, even that established by the people themselves. James Otis, whom Acton quotes, expressed it in the following words:

> By the law of God and nature, government must not raise taxes on the property of the people without the consent of the people or their deputies. There can be no prescription old enough to supersede the law of Nature and the grant of God Almighty, who has given all men a right to be free.[56]

A few years later Thomas Jefferson expressed similar ideas in the Declaration of Independence (1776) in a language that is abstract but whose phrases are dear to any advocate of freedom: 'We hold these truths to be self-evident, that all men are created equal, that they are endowed by their Creator with certain unalienable Rights, that among these are Life, Liberty, and the pursuit of Happiness.' Those universal rights stand above any human authority and their encroachment renders it illegal. And since the British Government, the king and Parliament, had violated them repeatedly, American colonists renounced their allegiance to the British Crown and declared themselves free and independent.

The final and most important reason for the greatness of the American Revolution in Acton's eyes is its last phase, the period of construction, that is, the drawing up of the Constitution. The Constitutional Convention which gathered in Philadelphia in 1787 faced manifold difficulties, including the most fundamental, such as erecting one sovereign state or a union of several sovereign states, and dividing powers between central and state governments and among various branches of the government. The Convention in Philadelphia was cautious, sensible, not swayed by abstractions.[57] Those present at the Convention were 'the most eminent men in America,' and, 'Franklin, indeed, appears to have been the only very foolish man among them, and his colleagues seem to have been aware of it.'[58] At the Convention, as Acton notes, 'every effort was made, every scheme was invented, to curb the inevitable democracy.'[59]

It might look strange that of all the problems that the Framers of the Constitution had to deal with, Acton singled out the threat of democracy. To understand why he took that position let us recall his statement on Athenian democracy: that unlimited democracy leads to tyranny. He elaborates on the question of democracy in his essay 'Political Causes of the American Revolution' and reveals deeper reasons for his fear. According to him, both monarchies and republics can be either absolute – when they are governed by the will of the ruler or the will of the people – or constitutional, when they are governed by law. But monarchy is surrounded by many opposing powers, interests and opinions which resist or seek to share power, and eventually they overcome the resistance of the king. Absolute royal power is, therefore, gradually eroded and the rule of will is replaced by the rule of law. With republics, the direction is just the opposite:

> Democracy tends naturally to realize its principle, the sovereignty of the people, and to remove all limits and condition of its exercise; whilst monarchy tends to surround itself with such condition. In one instance force yields to right; in the other might prevails over law...in a democracy the power is already in the hands of those who seek to subvert and to abolish the law. The process of subversion is consequently irresistible, and far more rapid...Hence monarchy grows more free, in obedience to the laws

> of its existence, whilst democracy becomes more arbitrary. The people is induced less easily to abdicated the plenitude of its power, because it not only has the right of might on its side, but that which comes from [the right of] possession, and the absence of a prior claimant.[60]

When the will of the majority is not constrained by law, 'the minority can have no permanent security against the oppression of preponderating numbers [majority]...and the moment will inevitably come when separation will be preferred to submission.' But the ensuing disruption of the state, either by emigration or secession, will not end when the majority wins. For the majority comprises of many future minorities, which are afraid of a new future majority. 'The strict principle of popular sovereignty must therefore lead to the destruction of the state.'[61]

Acton saw that direct democracy can easily became prey to powerful groups, party machinery and 'wire-pullers.' For example, he says that what is recognized as the majority is often nothing else but a party which succeeds 'by force or fraud' in elections. He does not regard elections as free if electoral districts are too large and people are obliged to vote for unknown candidates. Democracy cannot subsist if its constituency is not educated and includes illiterate voters. He also sees a threat of manipulating electoral law by existing authorities.[62] As we see, those vices of democracy, so common in our time, were already visible in Acton's time.

Acton indicates that the Framers of the Constitution were aware of the danger of 'direct democracy,' and that is why they put so many checks on it. He approves each of them: the division of powers between three branches of the Federal Government; a strong and independent Supreme Court with the right of annulling unconstitutional law; the two-chamber Congress in which the Senate represents the states and the House of Representatives the citizens of the Union, as well as the indirect election of the President.[63] But what he admires most is the federal system that regulates the relation between the central (federal) authority and that of the states. The Federal Government received important powers, but they all were enumerated in the Constitution. That left the states, whose powers were limited, a powerful tool with which to defend themselves against encroachment by central government.[64] Acton considers federalism the most effective and congenial of all the checks on democracy, and he comments as follows:

> The true natural check on absolute democracy is the federal system, which limits the central government by the powers reserved, and the state governments by the powers they have ceded. It is the one immortal tribute of America to political science, for state rights are at the same time the consummation and the guard of democracy.[65]

And two more of Acton's powerful comments on American federalism:

> The Federal Constitution did not deal with the question of religious liberty. The rules for election of the president . . . proved failure. Slavery was deplored . . . and was retained. The absence of a definition of State Rights led to the most sanguinary civil war of modern times. Weighted in the scales of Liberalism the instrument, as it stood, was a monstrous fraud. And yet, by the development of the principle of Federalism, it has produced a community more powerful, more prosperous, more intelligent, and more free than any other which the world has seen.[66]

> [Americans] had solved with astonishing and unexampled success two problems which had hitherto baffled the capacity of the most enlightened nations: they had contrived a system of federal government which prodigiously increased the national power and yet respected local liberties and authorities; and they had founded it on the principle of equality, without surrendering the securities for property and freedom. I call their success unexampled, not because it is a forcible term, but because it exactly indicates the peculiar character of the history of the American Constitution, and its special significance for ourselves.[67]

Acton deeply respected and admired America. His disparaging remarks written in 1853 during his visit to the US can be treated as youthful indiscretion. Although it may sound like a common cliché, Acton considered America to be a land of freedom, and because it was a land of freedom, it was also a land of opportunity. In colonial America, persecuted dissidents and other restless spirits found refuge in America's wilderness. Because they had self-rule and freedom of religion, and were not plagued by old, irrational social arrangements, corporate interests, vested powers and the like, they quickly grew in freedom and prosperity. The arrangements of their order contributed much to our better understanding of the principles on which liberty rests.

When America decided to cut the cord linking it with its mother country England, it stood at a crossroads. It could have taken the road of direct, pure democracy, when according to Acton, the 'sovereignty of numbers' would have built up equality and, at the same time, unparalleled tyranny. Instead, America chose another path. Faithful to its past, it chose freedom over equality; and secured it via checks and balances on various powers of the government, and by an original federal system that reinforced its strength, preserved freedom and fundamental equality, and secured prosperity for ages to come.

Notes

1. For example, Jon Butler, *Awash in a Sea of Faith: Christianizing the American People* (Cambridge, MA: Harvard University Press, 1990); Alan Taylor, *American Colonies* (New York: Viking, 2001).

2. The most exhaustive of his biographies, based on thorough research of primary sources as well as literature on Acton is a recently published book by Robert Hill, *Lord Acton* (New Haven & London: Yale University Press, 2000).
3. Acton Papers, Cambridge University Library, Add. Mss, 4991, p. 1, quoted in J. Rufus Fears (ed.), *Selected Writing of Lord Acton*, 3 vols (Indianapolis: Liberty Classics, 1985–88) III, 494, hereafter referred as SWLA; James Bryce, *Studies in Contemporary Biography* (London, 1903), 396.
4. Lord Acton, *Lectures on Modern History*, 3rd edn (Cleveland and New York: Meridian Books, 1967), 26–7, 194–5.
5. Lord Acton, 'The History of Freedom in Antiquity,' first published in 1877, reprinted in SWLA, I, 22.
6. Acton, 'The History of Freedom in Antiquity,' 5 and passim, 5–28. For a very short but excellent summary of Acton's political philosophy, see, Owen Chadwick, *Acton and History* (Cambridge: Cambridge University Press, 2002), 231–6
7. Lord Acton, *The History of Freedom and Other Essays*, edited with an introduction by John Neville Figgis and Reginald Vere Laurence (London: Macmillan, 1907), xxviii. The quote is by Figgis and Laurence.
8. Gertrude Himmelfarb, *Lord Acton: a Study in Conscience and Politics*, 2nd edn (Chicago: University of Chicago Press, 1962), vii. 'He is of this age, more than of his. He is, indeed, one of our great contemporaries.'
9. 'Lord Acton's American Diaries,' *Fortnightly Review* CX (1921): 728–33.
10. 'Lord Acton's American Diaries,' CX (1921): 929–31.
11. 'Lord Acton's American Diaries,' CXI (1922): 74.
12. 'The History of Freedom in Antiquity,' SWLA, I, 8.
13. 'The History of Freedom in Antiquity,' 10.
14. 'The History of Freedom in Antiquity,' 10–11, 14; Acton, 'Sir Erskine May's Democracy in Europe,' first published in 1878, reprinted in SWLA, I, 59–61.
15. 'The History of Freedom in Antiquity,' 13–14; 'Sir Erskine May's Democracy in Europe,' 60–1.
16. 'The History of Freedom in Antiquity,' 13.
17. 'The History of Freedom in Antiquity,' 14–15.
18. 'The History of Freedom in Antiquity,' 16; 'Sir Erskine May's Democracy in Europe,' 68.
19. 'The History of Freedom in Antiquity,' 20.
20. 'The History of Freedom in Antiquity,' 23–7.
21. 'The History of Freedom in Antiquity,' 17–18.
22. 'The History of Freedom in Christianity,' first published in 1877, reprinted in SWLA, I, 33.
23. 'The History of Freedom in Christianity,' 34–5.
24. 'The History of Freedom in Christianity,' 36–7.
25. *Lectures on Modern History*, 19, 188–9.
26. *Lectures on Modern History*, 152, 221.
27. Compare *Lectures on Modern History*, 208, 220–1; 'Sir Erskine May's Democracy in Europe,' 72.
28. *Lectures on Modern History*, 192.
29. 'The History of Freedom in Christianity,' 46–7.
30. 'The History of Freedom in Christianity,' 47; *Lectures on Modern History*, 24–5.
31. *Lectures on Modern History*, 25.
32. *Lectures on Modern History*, 192.

33. Quoted in *Lectures on Modern History*, 292, and in Lord Acton, *Lectures on the French Revolution* (London: Macmillan, 1910), 21.
34. *Lectures on Modern History*, 292–3; *Lectures on the French Revolution*, 21.
35. Compare *Lectures on the French Revolution*, 21.
36. Acton, 'Colonies,' first published in *Rambler* 6 (March 1862), reprinted in SWLA, I, 183–4. His remarks on Spanish colonies, ibid. 180–3.
37. 'Colonies,' 186; *Lectures on the French Revolution*, 21; 'Sir Erskine May's Democracy in Europe,' 72. Commenting on taxes paid by the colonists, an American historian wrote: 'No other people in the world (except the Poles) paid so little.' See John P. McKay, Bennett D. Hill and John Buckler, *A History of Western Society*, 3 vols (Boston: University of Illinois at Urbana-Champaign), II, 671.
38. 'Colonies,' 179–80.
39. 'Colonies,' 183.
40. 'Colonies,' 180, compare 178–84.
41. 'Colonies,' 180–2.
42. 'Colonies,' 180.
43. *Lectures on Modern History*, 295; Acton, 'The Civil War in America: its Place in History,' first published in 1866, reprinted in SWLA, 273–4. The question of Acton's view on slavery is outside the scope of this chapter.
44. 'Colonies,' 186–7; *Lectures on Modern History*, 288.
45. *Lectures on Modern History*, 292.
46. *Lectures on Modern History*, 291.
47. *Lectures on the French Revolution*, 31–2.
48. *Lectures on the French Revolution*, 21; *Lectures on Modern History*, 287–8.
49. *Lectures on the French Revolution*, 24.
50. *Lectures on Modern History*, 291–2.
51. *Lectures on Modern History*, 290.
52. *Lectures on the French Revolution*, 24–5.
53. *Lectures on Modern History*, 290–1.
54. *Lectures on the French Revolution*, 23–5; *Lectures on Modern History*, 289–90.
55. *Lectures on the French Revolution*, 23–4; *Lectures on Modern History*, 292.
56. *Lectures on the French Revolution*, 24.
57. *Lectures on the French Revolution*, 34.
58. Acton 'Political Causes of the American Revolution,' first published in 1861, reprinted in SWLA, 219. Acton does not explain his remark on Franklin but perhaps he alludes to the latter's ideas of a single-chamber congress and a weak executive, which were rejected.
59. *Lectures on the French Revolution*, 34.
60. 'Political Causes of the American Revolution,' 217.
61. 'Political Causes of the American Revolution,' 218. In Acton's opinion, the American Civil War (1861–65) was developing just according to that principle, compare Acton, 'The Civil War in America,' 265–6.
62. 'Sir Erskine May's Democracy in Europe,' 82–4.
63. *Lectures on Modern History*, 295; *Lectures on the French Revolution*, 35; 'Sir Erskine May's Democracy in Europe,' 82.
64. *Lectures on Modern History*, 295.
65. *Lectures on the French Revolution*, 37. Also compare 'Sir Erskine May's Democracy in Europe,' 84.
66. *Lectures on Modern History*, 295.
67. 'The Civil War in America: its Place in History,' 264.

3

The Cultural Roots of the American Business Model

Małgorzata Durska

Introduction

American business culture is strongly individualistic, masculine, with weak uncertainty avoidance and moderate power distance (Hofstede, 2001; Inglehart, 1997; Hall and Hall, 1990). It is also strongly universalistic, with monochronic approach to time and low context. All these traits determine values, norms and social behavior patterns in the economic sphere and make American business exceptional. They also correspond with a specific and very stable institutional structure – many institutions have functioned in an unchanged form for decades or even centuries. They have been modified, but their basic logic has not been changed. Such strong persistence proves that the institutions mirror basic values and norms accurately and that certain patterns of behavior have strong social acceptance.

Individualism

In American social thought, belief in the indispensability of individual rights crystallized in the period of the struggle for independence. In the creation of the American state, the Founding Fathers were guided by the thinking of Locke and the Magna Carta. The ideas of the social contract in Hobbes' or Rousseau's version were rejected in favor of its Lockeian version. Jeffersonian 'indispensability' of individual rights and protection of these rights against the state were, in the opinion of Americans, more attractive than resignation from these rights in exchange for security and social welfare. Institutions and customs were shaped by the tradition of Enlightenment 'disengagement,' by the belief in the power of the instrumental mind, by – unlike in disestablishment France – Christian ideas, and by a strongly-held conviction about American exceptionality. American character, American credo, or American exceptionalism have traditionally been associated with the idea of liberal individualism.

God's way for fallen man

The development of the American capitalist economy is commonly linked with Calvin's theological doctrines. The concept of predestination gave a special meaning to work. Calvin taught that work is everybody's duty – even that of the rich – since it is not the possession of goods or an easy life that are the purposes of work, but the constant reinvesting of profits in future ventures. As indicated by Weber, Calvinism set the spirit of capitalism free. It is due to this spirit that the structure of individual motivation and behavior, as well as the ways of picturing the world, changed.

Men of action – men of God

The fact that Puritans treated work as a blessing, a calling and a warrant of eternal life, contributed to the development of hard and systematic work habits accompanied by an ascetic personal life. Social pressure from other members of the community imposed behavior that overcame weaknesses. At the same time, as stressed by Ossowska (1985, pp. 198–200), religion legitimized individual entrepreneurship. The desire for possessions was sanctioned while consumption was restrained. The change in the approach toward business activities began at the end of the seventeenth century. Then 'talk of trade rather than the Bible dominated conversations in Boston... A capitalist spirit and a merchant elite gradually superseded the authority of the pulpit' (Pusateri, 1988, p. 59). The imperative of hard work became secularized but it kept its status as one of the basic cultural norms.

'Qualitative change and quantitative expansion' of modern, rational capitalism, as described by Weber, were made possible by two factors: a lifestyle that was based on self-control and a new moral system that favored the accumulation of capital. A prototype of the modern capitalist and utilitarian individualist who attained self-realization through work was Benjamin Franklin. He changed American thinking about business and established the image of an individual entrepreneur. In his numerous works (*Autobiography, Poor Richard's Almanack*) he created the ethos of a self-made man and made work a measure of all value. In Franklin's opinion, 'making money' was a proper calling for a man; it gave real independence, it made people virtuous (in accordance with the proverb 'an empty bag cannot stand upright') and it provided high social position. This strong pursuit of material gain ('nothing but money is sweeter than honey') and openly-advised ruthlessness in conducting business ('bargaining has neither friends nor relations') can be regarded as manifestations of typical masculine traits. Individual getting-on has been identified with 'the American dream.'

Franklin shares the title of the 'father of American entrepreneurship' with Adam Smith. Probably not many American businessmen have waded through the one thousand or so pages of Smith's *An Inquiry into the Nature and Causes of the Wealth of Nations* but all of them know about the invisible hand of the market and are aware that 'it is not from the benevolence of the butcher, the brewer, or the baker that we expect our dinner, but from their regard to their own interest' and that 'we address ourselves, not to their humanity but to their self-love, and never talk to them of our own necessities but of their advantages' (Smith, 1977, p. 119). The idea that in a free market economy an individual egoistic interest turns into a social good and that the best economic policy of the government is laissez-faire became the main motto of the American business world. Many American historians of economic thought emphasize that no other idea and no other single author had a bigger influence on the development of the American economy and society. Taylor argues that the development of free market relationships and individualistic thinking were mutually dependent; on the one hand, individualistic thinking paved the way for the development of free market relationships, while on the other hand, the growth of trade exchange made people think that an individualistic perspective was natural (Taylor, 2001, p. 385).[1]

In contrast to many other countries, where running business was an occupation hardly commendable or refined, suitable only for those who could do nothing else, in America, entrepreneurship acquired a mythical, heroic dimension. 'The world of trade in England has always been an underworld, precisely that everything that is light, gay, disinterested, personal, artistic has held aloof from it, has been able to form a self-substituting world which is beyond it, while trade itself is only a dull residuum. The cream has risen to the top, and the world of business is perfectly conscious that it is only skimmed milk' (Brooks, 1975, p. 136). In America, the division was less striking. Although American cultural and artistic circles contested the 'culture of money,' for the majority of the population, business was definitely something more than a dull and superficial way of life. Successful people were held in esteem rather than envied.

The low context of the American culture made business a separate sphere of life with its own rules. At the same time, business activities involved a moral obligation set against the selfish attitude of people concerned solely with their spiritual or intellectual self-realization (Brooks, 1975, p. 32). The idol of the middle class became the 'Captain of Industry' who combined the qualities of an independent entrepreneur with the role of a successful pioneer of industry: 'he was the first national image of the middle-class man as a businessman, and no one has ever supplanted him' (Mills, 1956, p. 5).

Self-interest properly understood

Today, nobody is surprised that a businessman strives for higher profits, that an employee goes after higher pay or that a customer looks for a lower price. This highly utilitarian attitude manifests itself in the labor market, in managerial practices, in the highly competitive systems of evaluating and promoting employees, in co-workers' relationships and even in consumer rights. Among the seven essential traits of the American, Novak (1973, p. 111) lists self-sufficiency, nervous activity and egoism ('It is all right just to think of themselves, to go after exactly what they wanted, to give free rein to avarice and ambition'). At the end of the nineteenth century, in a book entitled *American Nervousness and Neurasthenia*, the author George Beard claimed that 'in all classes there is a constant friction and unrest – a painful striving to see who shall get higher' (Beard in Bellah, 1986, p. 118). Bellah argues that although Americans have a relatively strong sense of community and express willingness for cooperation with others, the real meaning of their life is to become their own person, as Bellah puts it, 'to give birth to oneself' (Bellah, 1986, p. 82). Utilitarian individualism tells them to succeed in the sphere of work, to prove that they are able to stand on their own feet and provide for themselves. This results in a duality as they strive to initiate cooperation with others while at the same time keeping a distance from the group and treating it as a vehicle to achieve their goals. One of the reasons for this is that American society has never functioned as a single community with a uniform vision of a good life and a good society. Social mobility has always been high and was often connected with a lack of acceptance.

Especially in the sphere of business, cooperation and unselfish actions are not the result of an idealistic faith in the idea of sacrificing something for others or helping others, but rather as Tocqueville (1969, pp. 525–8) put it, are carried out in the name of a self-interest properly understood. 'In America not the virtue is big, but the temptation small, which proves to be the same. Not the unselfishness is big but the self-interest big, which again proves to be almost the same' (Tocqueville in Aron, 1997, p. 35). According to Franklin, good intentions do not matter because the virtue of deeds lies in their utility. Franklin used to say that 'self-denial is not the essence of virtue.' The virtue simply pays off ('honesty is the best policy'). And it has to pay off since, as Merton (2002, p. 230) noted, 'in America no other definition gains such a common acceptance as the one that identifies success with making money.' In Ayn Rand's novel *Atlas Shrugged*, which is the second most-read book in America after the Bible, we read that:

> If you ask me to name the proudest distinction of Americans, I would choose – because it contains all the others – the fact that they were the people who created the phrase 'to make money'. No other language or nation had ever used these words before; men had always thought of wealth as static quantity – to be seized, begged, inherited, shared, looted or obtained in favor. Americans were the first to understand that wealth has to be created. The words to 'make money' hold the essence of human morality.
>
> (Rand, 1957, p. 391)

Such a strong fascination for and acceptance of material achievements are interpreted by the influence of Protestant ethics and the affluence of resources that has been so typical for America throughout the centuries. The success of ventures was identified with tangible gains and did not deprive others of a chance for success. Americans think positively about successful people because those who failed probably did not try hard enough.[2] This conviction manifests itself in treating success as an entirely individual achievement. Success in America always has an individual hero even when it is an outcome of collective effort. As Galbraith put it (1986, p. 54): 'The individual has far more standing in our culture than the group. An individual has a presumption of accomplishment; a committee has a presumption of inaction.'

Masculinity

The fact that success is so strongly identified with material achievement is also a derivative of the strong masculinity of American culture. In the process of institutionalization of the business sphere, the role of this dimension is profound, both in the normative and cognitive senses. On the one hand, it defines values and expectations connected with gender norms and justifies them with moral rationale, while on the other hand, it shapes categories, clarifies structures and defines scenarios of behavior.

In the American business world, despite many changes, there is still a clear-cut distinction between female and male roles – which means that soft and caring roles are assigned to women while the strong roles of bread-winner and conqueror are assigned to men. The logic of work, and life, is dominated by hard values that are traditionally associated with men; the norm is to be competitive, to strive for material success and to give priority to professional life over private life. Personality profiles of managers, standards of professional life, images of proper business conduct or professionalism, as well as the meanings ascribed to organizational space, time and body, including its sexuality, are all formulated in typically masculine categories.

I live to work

Asked to draw a picture of an ideal person, almost half of American adolescents drew a man being busy at work (Hofstede, 2001, p. 301). Work was presented in the pictures as a source of success, achievement and wealth. 'However we define work,' writes Bellah (1986, p. 66), 'it is very close to our sense of self. What we do, often translates to what we "are".' This ubiquitous rule – that 'one is what one does' – seems to dictate that Americans be constantly active and involved in work affairs. 'The typical employee is expected to give his best to the corporation and usually he does' (Galbraith, 1969, p. 78).

In 2003, an average working day in American business was 9.6 hours. On average, people worked 50 hours a week and rested 20 hours a week. In 1973, they worked 41 hours and rested 26 hours. The data from 1979–98 show that in the group of developed countries, the US is the country in which people work the longest hours and the only country in the world where year after year people work more. In all other countries, except Sweden, people spend less and less time working (Mishel et al., 2003, pp. 400, 403).

American systems of employee evaluation and compensation comply with the principle of equity. The idea of fair compensation in America has, however, a different meaning than in more feminine cultures where the salaries are determined with consideration for social matters, and where solidarity and egalitarian attitudes dominate. In the masculine US, fairness means payment consistent with individual abilities and achievements. The principle of equity is superior to the principle of equality. Typically masculine categories define what is expected from employees and how their work is evaluated. It means that rewards go to those who subjugate their private and family life for work and career. The National Study of the Changing Workforce from 1997 shows that cultural factors are perceived by employees as a basic obstacle for the reconciliation of professional career with family duties.

Masculine business practices are executed by equally masculine managers who follow the tradition of American masculine heroes. Frontier heroes, historical war heroes, movie stars, famous politicians (all American presidents and vice presidents have been men), cartoon characters (also until quite recently only men) and managers have a lot of 'masculinity' in common. It is not a coincidence that a lot of managerial expressions use military rhetoric. Strategy, target, mission, guerrilla attack, counter-offensive, defense, strategic alliances, flank attack or bullet questions are just a few examples of business language. Many of these expressions have become a part of international business jargon – often keeping their English form because it was impossible to translate them into other languages. The authors of American management bestsellers also use a military rhetoric. The titles of some management bestseller books could make us think that there is a war going on. The very word 'aggressive' has positive connotations. An aggressive employee, aggressive seller, aggressive advertising campaign or aggressive candidate for work sound like superlatives. In more feminine cultures they seem dangerous, pathetic or ridiculous.[3] In American business, aggressive attitudes are considered to be a virtue. In 1952, the National Organization of Manufacturers monthly was warning readers against 'intellectual theorists' who offered the delusive 'dream of an inanimate heaven,' a non-competitive system. It was stressed that 'the only time when the competitive spirit of a human being is stilled is when the human heart ceases to beat' (Sutton et al., 1956, p. 40). Numerous studies presented by *Harvard Business Review* in 2002–04, show that the aggressiveness and assertiveness of American business is constantly growing.

Defining professionalism in typically masculine categories also includes the approach to time. Time is one of the most significant determinants of business behavior. Americans treat time in a typically masculine, sequential way. Time-and-motion studies, time management, time-to-market, just-in-time or the assumptions about product lifecycles in which products are born, mature and get old – all these are based on the sequential approach to time. Monochronic time is, as pointed out by Hall and Hall (1990, p. 13), as tangible as money; it can be 'spent, saved, wasted or lost.' Time schedules, precisely stated times of meetings, impassable deadlines, focusing on one activity at a time – these are just some examples of the sequential approach that is considered by most Americans as universally professional.

This approach is related to the concept of 'time thrift' that emerged in the beginnings of the seventeenth century on tobacco plantations in Virginia. The idea was to increase the number of working hours and raise work effectiveness. In Franklin's time, time thrift was captured in a famous phrase 'time is money.' Individual, methodical, systematic and precisely-planned schedules popularized by Franklin, a meticulous set-up of sleep-time, work-time, rest-time and entertainment-time, turned into a piece-rate system under industrialization. In the famous McGuffey readers that served as reading primers from the 1830s, effective time management and punctual completion of tasks were presented as basic moral obligations.

The sequential approach to time is usually accompanied by a tendency to overestimate the role of the present and the future while consistently ignoring the past – 'History is good for cowards and losers' – which is why so many aphorisms from well-known business bestsellers can be reduced to one statement: to learn is to forget. Management guru Drucker says that the past and the future are in conflict. In the future results are achieved, in the past problems existed. There is an ongoing 'slaughter of the past' – memory retains only those elements which can be used as ideas for tomorrow (Drucker, 1985, p. 24). Attention is focused on current and short-term goals. Treating the future not as an abstract category of time but as a form of anticipated consequences of today's actions is an American cultural innovation (Stewart and Bennett, 1991, p. 36). Academic management textbooks and magazines are full of discussions on the role of strategic planning and long-term plans. Most American managers would like to think about themselves as future-oriented people. Actually, in practice they are extremely present-oriented – all companies' efforts are concentrated on achieving short-term goals.

Female roles, male roles

In an international study conducted in 1996, the respondents were asked to attribute traits to three categories: women, men and successful managers (Schein et al., 1996). All American respondents, regardless of sex, gave descriptions of men and successful managers that were strongly correlated. The correlation between the descriptions of women and successful managers was zero in the case of American male respondents, and positive but relatively weak in the case of American female respondents.

In American history, social norms determining what was feminine and what was masculine were not so unambiguous. In colonial times the family was the main source of affiliation for both men and women. On family farms, women's work was a warrant of economic security on a par with men's work. In the eighteenth century, traits such as courage, strength, boldness or toughness could have been associated with both men and women. In pre-industrial America, small towns and villages were 'a metaphor of a moral ecology in which the polarities of public and private, masculine and feminine, were integrated... American character oscillated between the instrumental orientation of the masculine world of work achievement and the values of feminine spheres of nurturing domesticity' (Bellah, 1986, p. 46).

The development of a market economy and then the industrial revolution separated the sphere of money and work from the home. The formation of an urban middle class sanctioned the division of feminine and masculine roles not only socially but also legally. 'The cult of true womanhood' encouraged women to guard their 'natural' place – the home – with their 'natural' virtues of piety, purity and submissiveness (Powell, 1993, p. 16). Franklin's ideas about female roles were consistent with this approach. He was famous for having a 'tender heart for women' but his ideas about the social roles of women were limited to working at home, bringing up children and attending church services. From the middle of the nineteenth century – except in the West where the categories of femininity and masculinity overlapped for longer – the norms defining masculinity and femininity became even clearer. Traits that earlier were common for women and men became polarized. Strength, aggression and pugnacity became 'natural' attributes of men, while weakness, caring and sensitivity were perceived as 'natural' for women. The phenomenon was labeled by Sandra Bem as 'gender schematism,' understood as a learned readiness to perceive the polarized categories of gender as natural determinants of reality (Bem, 2000, p. 122).

Nowadays in America, women make up almost 50 percent of the workforce. In the sphere of business every other employee is a woman, but 88 per cent of managers are men (Becker, 2002). This discrepancy is even bigger if we take into consideration the positions of the CEOs. *Business Week* research from 2000 indicates that in 825 companies surveyed, women held only 171 out of the 4341 best-paid positions, which is just 3.9 percent of top managerial positions, and less than 1 percent of CEOs were women (Lavell, 2001).

The results of a study conducted by Bridges and Nelson (2001, pp. 167–87) in four big American companies indicate clearly that pay differentials between men and women are culturally determined. The authors state that in American private business gender inequality operates predominantly at the managerial/professional level. At lower-level positions, compensation is structured by the job, and gender differences in pay are a result of differences between jobs. At upper-level positions companies pay for the person rather than for the job. The apparent certainty of organizational wage structures is based not on defensible, objective criteria (as managers and officials tend to believe) but on convention.

Weak uncertainty avoidance

American entrepreneurship, innovativeness and openness to everything that is unknown, new and different, indicate that Americans have weak uncertainty avoidance. It manifests itself in institutional solutions accepted on the American labor market, in the American legal system, in the dynamics of economic development, and at a lower level in the mobility of employees, openness for education, ability to adjust and to requalify. Americans have a gift for reforging uncertainty into gold and using it for their own benefit.

New is beautiful

'New, different and unknown' are epithets that have shaped American culture. Puritans lived in hope of the arrival of 'the new' and the creation of a New World with God's help. Immigrants coming to America gave up their past and relied on the future. The world's first democratic revolution was an exemplification of these hopes in the sphere of politics. Inventions, geographical expansion, industrial and technological revolutions were subsequent stages on the road to progress. According to Turner, the American mentality is characterized by traits typical of the frontier: creativity, shrewdness, risk-proneness, vitality, pragmatism and determination (Turner, 1996, p. 37). When in 1890, the US Census Bureau announced that there was no more borderland to settle, the habits of mobility and changeability were preserved in the development of technology. In *American Business Creed* one may read that 'the businessman or the citizen who finds a new and effective way of doing things is a hero' and that what made America great was not 'security' but 'flexibility, daring, and imagination' (Sutton et al., 1956, p. 260). Americans were supposed to adjust an unfriendly environment to their own requirements. What differentiated the American working class from the European was their 'constant curiosity, skeptical and iconoclastic mindset, and ability to improvise and innovate' (Lasch, 1997, p. 63).

Sources of uncertainty and anxiety

Institutional order in America and the mechanisms for dealing with risk and uncertainty were shaped by specific cultural factors. In the American vision of 'order,' threats are defined as all those things that may bound individual rights and freedom. The definition of risk supports and consolidates a strongly individualistic culture.

It should be emphasized that individual rights and freedoms are considered to be superior only if an individual supports 'a social order of individual success.' The very moment this order is disturbed, for instance by inability, weakness, sickness or financial crisis, a phenomenon called 'individualization of social risk' occurs (Beck, 2002, p. 149). It means that all social problems and blame are passed on to an individual. That is why American employees take responsibility for problems at work (lay-offs, lack of promotion and so on) much more easily than employees from other cultures.

Ways of dealing with uncertainty: trust

Weber pointed out that belonging to a same-faith community was perceived as a guarantee of moral qualities that were important both in public life and in conducting business (Weber, 1946, pp. 302–22). Sectarian religious communities were especially significant. Affiliation with this type of community was more evidently voluntary than in the case of more institutionalized churches and the members were more closely knit.

With the process of secularization, this role was taken over by associations, fraternities, clubs and even prestigious universities. A careful selection of new members assured that everybody who got accepted was 'a gentleman patented after investigation and probation' (Weber, 1946, p 308). The trust placed in the co-members was not based on blood ties or inherited aristocratic titles but on the qualities that each member had to demonstrate.

Many contemporary business institutions are a legacy of Protestantism. The traditional solutions based on trust were replaced by formal, legal or organizational structures that helped to reduce uncertainty. Lipset and Lenz observe that a low level of corruption in America is a result of attachment to specific procedures. Observance of 'the sacred rituals,' typical for Protestants, and the readiness to conform to rigid principles even at the expense of weaker authority, significantly raises the chances of revealing abuse (Lipset and Lenz, 2003, p. 194).[4] It should be emphasized that in the sphere of norms and laws the dominant regulations are those that are moderately demanding and feasible for execution and that do not therefore create barriers to development and innovation. Between extreme levels of morality – altruism marked with high ideals and standards, and sinister morality marked with disdain for the rights of others – there exists a level of morality that can be called, after Aron, 'a reasonable egoism.' Most Americans are 'reasonable egoists,' who 'neither aspire to the roles of saints, nor are criminals, but just desire their own good within the frameworks marked out by the law and by the responsibility toward a society' (Grondona, 2003, p 107).

Ways of dealing with uncertainty: praise to the heresy

Americans seek sources of wealth in things that do not exist yet, and not in what they possess. 'The main sources of wealth ... are innovations that have not been started yet' (Grondona, 2003, p. 107). This approach is strongly connected with the rejection of orthodoxy, with the openness to innovation and with the boldness to reinterpret received ideas. Barzini says that:

> national traits of Americans that are most bothering for Europeans stem from a deeply rooted conviction that they are obliged to do experiments that no one before them dared to do. Americans do not have respect for

> the experiences of other nations and the past generally. On the grand seal of the Republic which appears on the back side of one-dollar bill, there is a motto which proudly proclaims: *Novus ordo seculorum*, which means more or less that the world and the history starts with us. Most Americans are convinced that every problem 'just occurred this morning.'
>
> (Barzini, 2001, p. 250)

Many authors emphasize that Americans have a strong inclination for rejecting dogma. This reluctance of Americans to take up ideologies and impractical theories was also described by Tocqueville. He argued that although 'the strength of mind and its restless activity' do not raise Americans 'toward the higher spheres of the intelligence,' their pragmatism still performs wonders and changes the face of the world. 'For people in this frame of mind every new way of getting wealth more quickly, every machine that lessens work, every means of diminishing the cost of production, every invention which makes pleasures easier or greater, seems the most magnificent accomplishment of human mind' (Tocqueville, 1969, p. 462).

The American system of education promotes individualistic attitudes and independent thinking. It focuses more on interpretation and 'heresy' than on reproducing the imposed truth. In a way, the ambition of the system is to educate innovators and heretics. The role of the teacher is more of a consultant than of an expert or guru. This perception of the teacher–student relationship shapes future workplace relationships. In order to be a good manager one does not have to know all the answers. The ability to help employees in finding solutions is appreciated more than expert knowledge. In the opinion of Americans, providing easy answers to employees weakens their initiative and stifles their creativity.

All this reminds us of Schumpeter's creative destruction process – a continuous cycle of destroying older, less effective products and services and replacing them with new and more effective ones. As Tocqueville (1969, p. 453) put it, for Americans 'even the best of boats would be almost useless if it lasted more than few years.'

Moderate power distance: equal because free

Everybody who has experience with American business has experienced its informality. Although addressing each other by first names and the proverbial patting on the back are just very superficial evidence of egalitarianism, still they convey a deeper conviction that first of all, the main source of authority is not in external attributes of power but in competence, and second of all, that hierarchical structures primarily provide an organizational formula that allows for coordination of actions and the facilitation of problem-solving, and that they are not authority structures.

The cultural dimension of power distance illustrates the extent to which the less powerful members of institutions or organizations expect and accept the fact that power is distributed unequally (Hofstede, 2001, p. 98). In American business culture it is assumed that achievement in one sphere should be also visible in other spheres: '*winner-take-all*.' This attitude is a result of strong individualism linked with universalism, masculinity and low context.

Members of colonial society were not equal in terms of their positions or social status, but the absence of institutions that were commonly associated with hierarchical society did not allow for the traditional social stratification. The colonial upper class never became an aristocracy in the British sense. Europeans visiting America were surprised by the materialization of the ideal of classless society. Universality of belonging to the 'middle class' was in sharp contrast with the strongly hierarchical class system of Europe.

In the nineteenth century, foreign commentators were astonished that 'ordinary Americans had opinions on every imaginable subject and few of them seemed to have any sense of their proper place' (Lasch, 1996, p. 58). Egalitarianism was apparent not only in the distribution of wealth but also in the distribution of knowledge and skills. It was said that 'American mechanics are not untaught operatives, but enlightened, reflective people, who not only know how to use their hands, but are familiar with principles' (Lasch, 1996, p. 60).

One of the foundations of classless American society was its social mobility understood as a territorial expansion (Lasch 1996, p. 50). When the possibilities of settling on new territories started to shrink, the idea of mobility was reformulated and resolved itself to the idea of social advance, upward movement, 'ascending.' The end of the 'borderland times' coincided with the rapid development of modern industrialism and the creation of 'wealth aristocracy.' Classlessness was replaced by hierarchy. This hierarchy, however, was not a hereditary social stratification but rather a highly dynamic, constantly redefined configuration of social positions. The pace of change in American society had no precedent in other countries. It was social mobility that became a redemption of a hierarchical world (Lasch, 1997, pp. 56–9). Baudrillard described America as a country where 'freedom ... has no static or negative definition. Its definition is spatial and mobile ... Just look at this girl who serves you in the guest-room: she does so in total freedom, with a smile, without prejudice or pretentiousness, as though she was sitting opposite you ... democracy presupposes equality at the outset' (Baudrillard, 1988, pp. 93–4).

Tocqueville emphasized the role of the equality of condition. In his opinion, it was the defining factor in the creation of modern American society (Tocqueville, 1969, p. 9). This equality stemmed from freedom, social mobility, the American work ethos and the commonness of earning. 'Payment, enjoyed by all, gives them all a family resemblance ... American servants do not feel degraded because they work, for everyone around them is working. There is nothing humiliating about the idea of receiving a salary, for the President of the United States works for salary. He is paid for giving orders, as they are for obeying them' (Tocqueville, 1969, p. 551).

It should be stressed that American perceptions of equality are based on the principle of equal treatment but not on the assumption that everybody is literally equal or on the idea of equalizing people. American individualism is not – as Hayek (1998, p. 39) put it – 'aligning.' Inequalities in hierarchical structures (corporations, organizations), authority structures, or huge discrepancies in incomes are generally accepted because people believe that success is not a result of a predetermined ascription but of individual achievements and efforts. Many studies indicate that if Americans have to choose between freedom and equality, they will choose freedom (Hofstede, 2001; Inglehart, 1997).

It is also worth noticing that marketing strategies in American business have always carried the elements of egalitarian thinking. The American economy was traditionally associated with mass production and universal consumption patterns. Most of the 'universal' easily accessible products and services were invented in America. America is not famous for haute couture or haute cuisine, but for an identical pair of jeans for everybody and for fast-food restaurants, also for everybody. As Chałasiński notes, one of the crowning achievements of the social liberation of the individual was the Ford car: 'Masses of immigrants that arrived in America in order to quit poverty, gained in their cars a proof of citizens' equality. A proof obvious to them and to all the others, an American testimony' (Chałasiński, 1962, p. 210).

Final note

All these cultural traits are reflected in institutions that characterize the American business environment. Relationships between business and the government are based on liberal principles that promote individualistic and masculine attitudes. The free market is considered to be the most effective way of providing favorable conditions for both business and society. Controlling and correcting functions are performed to some extent by lobbying groups, public interest groups and labor unions, but they do not disturb the integrity of the whole system and do not question its institutional set-up or the system itself. The government is expected to facilitate the conquest of the markets and the evaluation of its performance is based on how well it fulfills these expectations. 'This state role was not an inevitability dictated by the market, however, and emerged from a historically developed vision about the "correct" state/industry relation' (Hamilton and Biggart, 2001, p. 469).

The American labor market is a clear exemplification of such traits as individualism, masculinity and weak uncertainty avoidance. This system assumes individual responsibility for work and career; promotes typically masculine attitudes (being focused much more on competing with others and on effectiveness than on the welfare of all employees), and expects from the employees initiative, mobility and ability to adjust.

Law is the linking element for all institutions of the economic sphere. The facilitation and improvement of the conditions for conducting business, rather than controlling and correcting, seem to be the major functions of American economic regulations. Law is also a very important tool for conducting a game or even a fight between the market actors. This approach to law promotes masculine attitudes and low uncertainty avoidance. The financial institutions are also characterized by strong individualism, masculinity and weak uncertainty avoidance. To obtain funds for new ventures is much easier than in other countries.

Notes

1. This innate or universalistic nature of the individualistic approach is only a specific cultural preference. In America strongly individualistic and competitive attitudes are promoted while in many other cultures the main focus is on collective security. John Gray emphasizes that 'there is no credible theory in which the particular freedoms of deregulated capitalism have the standing of universal rights. The most plausible conceptions of rights are not founded on seventeenth-century ideas of property but on modern notions of autonomy. Even these are not universally applicable; they capture the experience only of these cultures and individuals for whom the exercise of personal choice is more important than social cohesion, the control of economic risk and any other collective good' (Gray, 1998, p. 108).
2. It is assumed that 'success or failure depends totally on an individual – if one fails, it must have been his own fault. Un-self-made man is a derivative of a self-made man' (Merton, 2002, p. 232). It is significant that today no one talks about a calling to serve God or a community or about being chosen. Centuries ago, hard work and achievements were a sign of being called to fulfill God's intentions. Today it is said that 'a rich person cannot be completely bad – or else the person would not be rich' (Stewart and Bennett, 1991, p. 82).
3. In Polish business circles this aggressive terminology was accepted because of the appeal of the American way of doing business, and also because of the lack of national patterns. It would be interesting to investigate the cultural conditioning of this rhetorical takeover. A lot of evidence may indicate that this is a result of a similar level of masculinity.
4. Aron notices that contrary to France 'in America... new institutions emerged parallel to society and they were not based on the sense of privileges or aristocratic pride but on religious spirit. A citizen who is a subject to rules, gives the respected authorities hearing regardless of who is in power... There is a huge difference between the obedience of an aristocrat toward a worshiped lord, and the obedience of a citizen toward the law which he co-created' (Aron, 1997, p. 34).

References

Aron, R. (1997), *Esej o wolnościach*, Warszawa: Fundacja Aletheia.
Barzini, L. (2001), *Europejczycy*, Warszawa: Muza, S.A.

Baudrillard, J. (1988), *America*, New York: Verso.
Beck, U. (2002), *Społeczeństwo ryzyka*, Warszawa: Wydawnictwo Naukowe Scholar.
Becker, E. (2002), 'Study Finds a Growing Gap between Managerial Salaries for Men and Women', *New York Times*, 24 January, Section A, p. 24.
Bellah, R.N. (ed.) (1986), *Habits of the Heart*, New York: Harper & Row.
Bem, S.L. (2000), *Męskość i kobiecość*, Gdańsk: Gdańskie Wydawnictwo Psychologiczne.
Bridges, W.P. and R.L. Nelson (2001), 'Economic and Sociological Approaches to Gender Inequality in Pay', in M. Granovetter and R. Swedberg (eds), *The Sociology of Economic Life*, 2nd edn, Boulder, CO: Westview Press, pp. 163–90.
Brooks, V.W. (1975), *America's Coming-of-Age*, New York: Octagon Books.
Chałasiński, J. (1962), *Kultura amerykańska*, Warszawa: Ludowa Spółdzielnia Wydawnicza.
Drucker, P.F. (1985), *The Effective Executive*, New York: Harper & Row.
Franklin, B. (1982), *The Autobiography and other Writings*, New York: Bantam Books.
Galbraith, J.K. (1986), *The New Industrial State*, 4th edn, New York: Penguin Books.
Galbraith, J.K. (1969), *The Affluent Society*, Boston: Houghton Mifflin Company.
Gray, J. (1998), *False Dawn*, New York: The New Press.
Grondona, M. (2003), 'Kulturowa typologia rozwoju gospodarczego', in L.E. Harrison and S.P. Huntington, *Kultura ma znaczenie*, Poznań: Zysk i S-ka, pp. 101–15.
Hall, E.T. and M.R. Hall (1990), *Understanding Cultural Differences*, Yarmouth, ME: Intercultural Press Inc.
Hamilton, G.G. and N.W. Biggart (2001), 'Market, Culture, and Authority', in M. Granovetter and R. Swedberg (eds), *The Sociology of Economic Life*, 2nd edn, Boulder, CO: Westview Press, pp. 444–78.
Hayek, F. (1998), *Indywidualizm i porzadek ekonomiczny*, Kraków: Znak.
Hofstede, G. (2001), *Culture's Consequences*, 2nd edn, London: Sage Publication.
Inglehart, R. (1997), *Modernization and Postmodernization. Cultural, Economic and Political Change in 43 Societies*, Princeton, NJ: Princeton University Press.
Lasch, Ch. (1997), *The Revolt of the Elites*, New York: Norton.
Lavell, L. (2001), 'For Female CEOs, It's Stingy on the Top,' *Business Week*, 23 April.
Lipset, S.M. and G.S. Lenz (2003), 'Korupcja, kultura i funkcjonowanie rynków', in L.E. Harrison and S.P. Huntington (eds), *Kultura ma znaczenie*, Poznań: Zysk i S-ka, pp. 188–205.
Merton, R.K. (2002), *Teoria socjologiczna i struktura społeczna*, Warszawa: PWN.
Mills, C.W. (1956), *White Collars. The American Middle Classes*, Oxford: Oxford University Press.
Mishel, L., J. Bernstein and H. Boushey (2003), *The State of Working America 2002/2003*, Ithaca: Cornell University Press.
Novak, M. (1973), *The Rise of the Unmeltable Ethnics*, Toronto: Macmillan Publishing.
Ossowska, M. (1985), *Moralność mieszczańska*, 2nd edn, Wrocław: Ossolineum.
Powell, G.N. (1993), *Women and Men in Management*, 2nd edn, Newbury Park, CA: Sage.
Pusateri, C.J. (1988), *A History of American Business*, 2nd edn, Arlington Heights, IL: Harlan Davidson, Inc.
Rand, A. (1957), *Atlas Shrugged*, New York: The New American Library.
Schein, V.E., R. Mueller, T. Lituchy and J. Liu (1996), 'Think Manager, Think Male: a Global Phenomenon', *Journal of Organizational Behavior*, 17, 33–41.
Smith, A. (1977), *The Wealth of Nations*, New York: Penguin Books.
Stewart, E.C. and M.J. Bennett (1991), *American Cultural Patterns. A Cross-Cultural Perspective*, Yarmouth, ME: Intercultural Press, Inc.

Sutton, F.X, S.E. Harris, C. Kaysen and J. Tobin (1956), *The American Business Creed*, Cambridge, MA: Harvard University Press.
Taylor, Ch. (2001), *Źródła Podmiotowości*, Warszawa: PWN.
de Tocqueville, A. (1969), *Democracy in America*, trans. G. Lawrence, New York: Harper & Row.
Turner, F.J. (1996), *The Frontier in American History*, Minneola, NY: Dover Publications.
Weber, M. (1946), 'The Protestant Sects and the Spirit of Capitalism', in H. Gerth and C.W. Mills (ed. and trans.), *From Max Weber. Essays in Sociology*, New York: Oxford University Press, pp. 302–22.

4
Constitutional Foundations of American Capitalism

Clifford A. Bates

Introduction

To what degree does the nature of the American economic system depend upon the political environment created by the US Constitution? Marxists claim that the political system is a superstructure to economic reality, a post hoc justification of the existing economic system. Such a view cannot explain how politics can lead to a change in economic systems, as the countries of Central and Eastern Europe have experienced since 1989. This chapter suggests that the political choices made in the creation and ratification of the US Constitution created an environment that allowed or encouraged the development of the American economy. I do not mean to deny the role of social and cultural factors which also played a role in the creation of the economic dynamic, but rather I argue that the Constitution of 1787 gave shape to a specific environment that made possible the fertile ground by which a transnational interstate market emerged, developed and prospered. Over 20 years ago the American Enterprise Institute published a collection of essays asking the question 'How Capitalistic is the Constitution?' In that volume several leading American scholars on the US Constitution attempted to tackle the question asked. Some looked at the history of the Constitutional text or its historical background, whereas others addressed current questions of policy and used the occasion to criticize the then Administration's economic and social policy. This chapter asks a slightly different question and therefore will look at the various specific provisions of the Constitution of 1787 and show how they provide for an environment that allows for, but also provides for the regulation and security of, a transnational interstate market. The architects of the current European project could, if they wished, learn much from the American Constitution.

Background to the Constitution of 1787

Up to the time of the US Constitution, political systems tended to be either centralized unitary systems, relying on mercantilism to help aggregate state power, or decentralized confederated systems, such as the Holy Roman Empire and the various confederations of Europe (for example, the Swiss and the Dutch) where most political and economic control was retained by the members of the confederation. What the Constitution of 1787 created was something unprecedented in the history of political thought, a political system of shared ultimate authority, where the whole and the parts, to various degrees, accepted differing areas of control based upon their differing abilities, as understood in the terms set forth in the Preamble: 'to form a more perfect Union, establish Justice, insure domestic Tranquility, provide for the common defense, promote the general Welfare, and secure the Blessings of Liberty to ourselves and our Posterity.' It is important to remember that the American states are not mere administrative units, but retainers of vast political power to this day, even if that power has been increasingly restrained by the national government.

It is perhaps easy to forget the problems plaguing the thirteen states in their first decade of independence – the strife between debtors and creditors, the actions of state legislatures to benefit their supporters and penalize their opponents, no common currency, thirteen different sets of rules governing commerce, and state excise that frustrated interstate trade. Also, given the dependency of the government upon the various state legislatures under the Articles of Confederation, interstate trade disputes made doing such business costly. The political arrangement under the Articles of Confederation did not provide for effective means to address interstate issues. Nor did it provide ways to effectively facilitate commerce between the states that did not depend upon the willingness of state legislatures not to interfere with such commerce.

These failures contributed to the general insecurity felt by many people at the time, not at all aided by the fact that the newly independent America was surrounded by the empires of England, France and Spain. The fear of many of the Founders was that those large powers might be all too willing to take part in the domestic disputes by siding with one faction over another, thus undermining American independence. What was needed was a stronger central government, one that could protect the nation from outside forces, and that was also strong enough to be an equitable arbitrator between states, so that disputes among them could not be taken advantage of by external actors.

The Founders saw not only the immediate connection between the need for stable and equitable interstate commerce and the national security of the nation, but also the connection between domestic tranquility, economic prosperity, and political liberty. There was much agreement that the current government under the Articles of Confederation was insufficient to secure not only the nation's security but also its liberty, that either a reform of the Articles or the creation of a new constitution was needed. This agreement led to the Annapolis Convention's recommendation calling a constitutional convention, to be held in Philadelphia in the summer of 1787, which was to reform the Articles. History records that in Philadelphia, there was general agreement that the Articles needed to be scrapped and a new constitution formulated, but there was much disagreement over the specifics. Madison, along with most members of the Virginia delegation and Hamilton from New York and allied with Governor Moris from Pennsylvania, came to Philadelphia with plans for a strong and unified national government, the so-called Virginia plan. This plan provided for a highly centralized national government which alarmed many of the smaller states who saw it as little more than a ruse by which larger states would dominate the smaller.

Reaction to the Virginia plan led to the New Jersey plan which was little more than an attempt to maintain the status quo of political power as it existed under the Articles. This division between large states and small states led some, such as Roger Sherman of Connecticut, to see that the only way out of this dilemma was through compromise. He therefore proposed a compromise that would create a powerful national government to meet the needs that only such a government could deliver and at the same time would protect the states as the guarantor of rights that a national government would be unable to deliver, given the diversity of communities that formed the nation.

Constitutional provisions and shaping of the economy

Let us look at the various specific provisions of the Constitution and see how they help shape what we understand to be the American economic way. The Constitution gives vast power to Congress. Article I, which vests legislative power in the Congress, clearly spells out the powers of the Federal Government. It is especially in section 8 of Article I that the powers of the Federal Government are enumerated. Let us look at how these powers have a role in shaping the economic environment, starting with the first paragraph of section 8:

> The Congress shall have Power To lay and collect Taxes, Duties, Imposts and Excises, to pay the Debts and provide for the common Defence and general Welfare of the United States; but all Duties, Imposts and Excises shall be uniform throughout the United States.
>
> (Art I, sec 8, par 1)

Although giving the power of taxation to the national government seems quite normal for a state actor, one must recall that the United States was at the time a union of thirteen states which had previously reserved the taxing power to themselves and only paid into the national government a common contribution. So the creation of a uniform tax policy for the national government had a significant impact over the commerce and trade of what had been thirteen separate state actors with thirteen separate sets of import and export rules and taxes. The first paragraph specifically requires that import and export rules and taxes are uniform. This created a common import and export market and equalized market access across all states. In the next two paragraphs of section 8, the Constitution gives to Congress the power to 'To borrow Money on the credit of the United States' and 'To regulate Commerce with foreign Nations, and among the several States, and with the Indian Tribes' which again centralizes and creates greater efficiencies for commerce than if one had to negotiate with what was thirteen then and is now fifty different states.

Another way in which the Constitution helped to create the American economic way is seen in the second half of paragraph 4 where the text requires 'uniform Laws on the subject of Bankruptcies throughout the United States.' The fact that there must be uniform rules of bankruptcies both in New Mexico and New York not only reduces the risk of operating from one state to the next, but also insures an equal playing field for those who fail, giving them another chance.

The first half of paragraph 4, dealing with the need to establish 'an uniform Rule of Naturalization' also played no little role in shaping the US economy, since naturalization rules in US history have often shaped and reacted to the needs of the labor market. The fact that the Constitution required a uniform naturalization policy created a level playing field for the inflow of new labor to respond to the needs of the economy.

Something should be said about paragraph 7, which authorizes the creation of 'Post Offices and post Roads.' The role of the post office in the spreading of commerce to remote areas is something that cannot be dismissed. The role that the Sears' catalogue played in increasing consumer power would not have been so effective had it not for the existence of an effective, safe and inexpensive way to deliver goods, which post offices provided. Also the creation of post roads, followed by interstate highways, assisted in the creation of an interstate transportation infrastructure that greatly helped commerce and the economic development of many areas of the US. The post office and the post roads played a very important part in the development of the national economic infrastructure of pre-Civil War America.

From the infrastructure offered by the post offices and post roads, we turn in paragraph 8 to encouragement of the promotion of science and the useful arts by the authorization of a national copyright for intellectual property. The Constitution authorized Congress to grant copyright to secure 'for limited Times to Authors and Inventors the exclusive Right to their respective Writings and Discoveries' (Art 1, sec 8, par 8). This protects the property rights of ideas and inventions, so such ideas and inventions will be encouraged. But at the same time the Constitution limits the time of exclusivity of such property rights, so as not to prevent other inventors and authors from improving upon those ideas.

Shaping things by restricting government

If the Constitution fertilized the ground so that economic prosperity would be encouraged, it also restrained the Congress in Art I, sec 9. In paragraph 5, the Constitution prohibits Congress from enacting national export taxes. This provision encouraged the growth of export sectors of the US economy, and the history of pre-Civil War America demonstrates the important role that exports played in the development of the American economy.

The Constitution 'navigation acts' also prohibited laws that privileged any port in any one state over another. Here is what the Constitution says:

> No Preference shall be given by any Regulation of Commerce or Revenue to the Ports of one State over those of another; nor shall Vessels bound to, or from, one State, be obliged to enter, clear, or pay Duties in another.
> (Art I, sec 9, par 6)

This provision arose from the reaction to the Navigation Acts passed by the English Parliament that led to the American Revolution.

Aside from restraining the power of the national government as a way of encouraging economic activity, Article I, section 10 paragraph 1 has the 'Contracts clause' which prohibits states from creating any law 'impairing the Obligations of Contracts.' This clause must be seen in the context of attempts by various state legislatures to pass laws that forced creditors into actions that would greatly disadvantage them, such as the requirement in the state of Rhode Island to accept the highly inflated paper money of the state as payment of debts or else face criminal penalties. The 'Contracts clause' gave a powerful tool to contracting parties to restrain the interference of state legislatures.

Protecting individual states while still unifying the nation

Article IV of the Constitution deals with the states. The Constitution of 1787 did not wholly abolish the sovereignty of the states in the creation of the national government. It recognized the inherent sovereignty of the states in many realms of activity. One must remember that the Constitution created a stronger and more powerful union, not a unified, unitary state.

Rather, the Constitution of 1787 is innovative in that its system of shared sovereignty between the national government and the states gave birth to federalism, a wholly new system of government that balances between a unitary state and a confederacy. Because the Constitution and the Founders wanted to preserve the sovereignty of the states, citizenship and voting rights to national offices were defined by one's state citizenship. State governments had better competencies in areas such as issuing of documents or licensing for various activities, regulation of marriage, creation of commercial firms and so on. Thus it was thought best to require all states to recognize valid documents, licenses and the like issued by other states. This was done was by Article IV, section 1:

> Full Faith and Credit shall be given in each State to the public Acts, Records, and judicial Proceedings of every other State. And the Congress may by general Laws prescribe the Manner in which such Acts, Records and Proceedings shall be proved, and the Effect thereof.
>
> (Art IV, sec 1)

The 'Full Faith and Credit' clause makes it possible that the documents or judicial proceedings of one state will be accepted in another. When this is tied to section 2, paragraph 1, which reads 'The Citizens of each State shall be entitled to all Privileges and Immunities of Citizens in the several States,' it secures the rights of citizens of another state while in another state to exercise the same rights and privileges as citizens of the state they are in. These two provisions thus greatly encourage the greater development of interstate commerce.

Conclusions

While only looking at the main text of the Constitution of 1787 and not at amendments to it, we already can see the provisions of this document to be favorable to commercial activity and an environment where greater trade and commerce will flourish and prosper. Without such provisions, it would be doubtful whether the commercial character of the American Republic would have been sustainable or that future developments could have evolved from less hospitable soil. No, the Constitution of 1787 must be seen as a significant factor that helped to shape what we understand to be the political landscape that directed so much of America's economic history. And it is that very history that has given many people the faith to pursue the opportunities that other societies or political systems fail to offer.

Section 2

Character and Effectiveness of US Economic Policy

5
The Evolution of US Economic Policy in the 1980s

Steven F. Hayward

The evolution of US economic policy in the 1980s may be more properly regarded as a revolution, so dramatically did policy break from past practices and economic orthodoxy. With the passing of Communism in Eastern Europe, current economic reform is taking a no less revolutionary path. However, the path of reform is far from smooth. Painful dislocations and setbacks will occur along the way, as happened in the US in the 1980s. The lessons from this era are worth keeping in mind.

Both the United States and Poland were suffering from dismal economies in the late 1970s. One unappreciated aspect of the economic scene in the late 1970s is that the economies of the United States and Poland were suffering from the same root problem. On the surface this sounds surprising and unlikely, given that the US was a capitalist market economy while Poland was a centrally planned socialist economy. But the poor performance of the two economies was rooted ultimately in the fallacy of economic mastery that had been in the ascendance since the middle of the twentieth century. Although it took different forms on the surface, both nations suffered from the same hubristic belief, or 'fatal conceit' in Friedrich Hayek's famous phrase, that governments could overmaster the economy. Although in Poland and other post-communist countries the belief in economic mastery took the form of socialism, the market economies of the West, especially the United States, were not all that different in some respects. The doctrines of Keynesian economics provided the illusion of mastery over the business cycle, and western governments thought they had unlocked the secret to consistent and stable economic growth. This robust, confident Keynesianism might well be thought of as 'socialism lite.'

For a number of years after World War II it did seem as though state control and direction of the means of production could achieve economic growth comparable – and occasionally superior – to the market economies of the West, but by the mid-1970s stagnation had gripped the economy of Poland and other Eastern European nations. Prime Minister Edward Gierek's 'great leap forward,' which included large state-directed investments in steel, shipbuilding, petrochemicals, and heavy equipment manufacturing, was a great leap backwards, characterized, in Timothy Garton Ash's words, by 'breathtaking incompetence.'[1] Inflation, rising foreign debt, and falling productivity contributed to the discontent and crisis from which flowed the Solidarity movement.

But the market economies of the West were stagnating as well, generating a crisis and political upheaval that, while less dramatic, was nearly as fundamental as that which took place in Poland. As with the apparent early success of the command economies of the East, in the 1960s Keynesian economics seemed to have unlocked the key to perpetual prosperity for the US which enjoyed an unprecedented economic boom. 'Economists proclaimed themselves high priests of social engineering,' economist James W. Dean wrote, looking back in 1980, 'claiming in their Keynesian wisdom credit for the sustained boom.'[2] But in the 1970s the United States began to experience slow growth with simultaneous high inflation and high unemployment, along with slow productivity growth and declining capital formation and investment. This was contrary to what Keynesian theory taught. On top of this condition came the 'energy crisis' – a shortage of energy supplies along with sharp and disruptive price increases. 'By any economic standard,' economist Michael Boskin wrote, 'the decade of the 1970s was the worst relative performance since the Great Depression.'[3] Allan Meltzer delivered the verdict: 'Economists trained in the heyday of Keynesian economics were responsible for the major policy failures of the 1960s and 1970s.'[4]

In the mid-1970s it was still widely thought, especially among the economists trained in Keynesian doctrines, that the answer to America's economic difficulties was increased government control of the economy. Among American liberals in the mid-1970s the idea that open markets and economic liberalization could better solve economic problems was still held in disdain, while the idea of national management of the economy, if not a national economic planning that verged on socialism, was still very much alive. In the summer of 1975 *Time* magazine expressed the doubts of liberalism with a cover story asking 'Can Capitalism Survive?' 'National economic planning is an idea whose time has come,' the socialist Michael Harrington (who at that time was a Democratic congressman from Massachusetts) wrote in *Harper's* magazine. Harrington thought national planning should be the central issue of the 1976 presidential campaign. And indeed the 1976 Democratic platform included a plank that read: 'Of special importance is the need for national economic planning capability.'

There was a powerful intellectual current among a few economists in favor of centralized economic planning. Wassily Leontief had been awarded one of the first Nobel prizes for economics for his work on 'input–output' models, a technique by which the overall economic effects of changes in investment and output from a single sector of the economy could be estimated. It seemed like the ultimate refinement of Keynesian general equilibrium theory, promising to provide government with the long-sought 'black box' by which to perfect 'fine-tuning' of the economy.

A good example of how this thinking played out can be seen in the debate over several proposals for federal employment programs. One of President Franklin Roosevelt's last campaign promises in 1944 had been to guarantee the right to a job to every American worker. In 1975 a group called the 'Initiative Committee for National Economic Planning' convinced Senator Hubert Humphrey and liberal Republican Senator Jacob Javits to introduce a bill to achieve this goal at last by instituting a federal economic planning board that would produce six-year plans every two years. While this bill went nowhere, the prospects seemed more realistic for the 'Full Employment and Balanced Growth Act of 1976,' more popularly known as the Humphrey-Hawkins Act because of its two chief sponsors, Senator Humphrey and Representative Augustus Hawkins of California. There was already a 'Full Employment Act' on the statute books dating back to 1946, but it set full employment as a 'goal,' and not as firm or enforceable commitment. Humphrey-Hawkins promised to change that. It set a goal of achieving 3 percent unemployment within four years through a coordination of government programs and a guaranteed federal job for each worker if the private economy failed to achieve the 3 percent goal. The original draft of Humphrey-Hawkins included a clause allowing a worker to sue the federal government if the government did not find or create a job for him or her.

Some form of Humphrey-Hawkins would likely pass, and would be, in the approving words of investment banker Felix Rohatyn, 'the first step toward state planning of the economy.' The enthusiasm for national economic planning was not limited solely to liberal Democrats. John Sawhill, President Gerald Ford's director of the Federal Energy Administration, had publicly endorsed the idea of national economic planning in 1975. Most Republicans, though, were naturally aghast at Humphrey-Hawkins; the chairman of Ford's Council of Economic Advisers, Alan Greenspan, strenuously opposed it. Ford would have vetoed Humphrey-Hawkins if it had passed in anything close to its original form. A few orthodox liberal economists were worried about the inflationary potential of a full employment program along the lines of Humphrey-Hawkins, but others dismissed this concern. Walter Heller, President John F. Kennedy's chief economic adviser, said the bigger budget deficits necessary to bring about full employment would not risk inflation because the new money would only be putting idle men and machines back to work. A much watered-down version of Humphrey-Hawkins finally passed in 1978 with the crucial compromise of giving inflation an equal priority with unemployment.

At the same time as American policy-makers were tackling slow employment and productivity growth, inflation began to soar. A series of oil price shocks early in the 1970s became a scapegoat for inflation, but monetary policy mistakes were a more dominant cause of the sustained inflation of the latter half of the decade. President Jimmy Carter came to office in 1977 wanting both to balance the budget and to stimulate the economy. Since he did not want to stimulate the economy with the old-fashioned Keynesnian elixir of more deficit spending, he instead encouraged the Federal Reserve to lower interest rates by expanding the money supply. The money supply had already been growing at the rate of about 11 percent a year by 1977, a rate of money growth that monetarist economists warned was too high, up from 7 or 8 percent in 1974–75. A parade of liberal economists, along with the Joint Economic Committee of Congress, was trotted out to argue that the money supply wasn't growing fast enough. 'We need faster monetary growth,' said economist and Carter adviser Lawrence Klein. 'Government programs to stimulate the economy do not need to contribute to inflation.'[5] *Time* magazine had recommended that the Federal Reserve 'should pump out as much money as might be needed to keep interest rates relatively stable.' Carter's first Federal Reserve chairman, G. William Miller, obliged. The result was accelerating inflation.

Taking note of this monetary indiscipline, *National Review* predicted in 1975: 'Nobody is even talking, any more, about getting inflation below 6 or 7 percent. Having established that level as a politically viable floor for inflation, the discussion now centers on how rapidly we should take off from that point toward double-digit rates – and, of course, another big recession.'[6] Inflation rose from 7 percent in 1977 to 9 percent in 1978 and the dollar began to plunge in the international currency exchanges. Polls in 1978 found that Americans now rated inflation as the most important national problem. Liberals had a blind spot for the dangers of inflation, as well as deep confusion about its source. Senator McGovern argued that 'the principal source of inflation now is oligopolies such as the oil and steel cartels which can raise prices regardless of demand or supply.' True to form, Carter tried to explain inflation as a moral problem afflicting the people: 'It is a myth that the government itself can stop inflation.' Rather, inflation was a reflection of 'unpleasant facts about ourselves,' of 'a preoccupation with self' that retards the willingness of Americans 'to sacrifice for the common good.'[7] The chairman of the White House Council on Wage and Price Stability, Barry Bosworth, echoed Carter in blaming inflation on the private sector: 'If government has any part to play in fighting inflation, it must have a role in private wage and price decisions.'[8] At no time did Carter mention the money supply, or the government's role in running the treasury printing press. The Carter administration proceeded to fight inflation through 'jawboning,' which meant giving an official scowl to businesses and labor unions who sought price and wage increases. In 1979, inflation soared further, to more than 12 percent. With the prime rate nearing 20 percent and signs that inflation might begin spiraling to Latin American levels,

Carter was forced to dismiss Miller and replace him with Paul Volcker, who immediately raised interest rates to curb monetary growth.

Carter's approach to the disrupted energy market of the mid-1970s was equally disastrous. He decided that the troubled energy sector should be regarded as a national crisis of the highest order, verging on 'national catastrophe' unless drastic steps were taken. In a televised address Carter declared that 'We must face the fact that the energy shortage is permanent,' and described the imperative of an ambitious energy policy as the 'moral equivalent of war.' If the energy crisis was the 'moral equivalent of war,' just who was the moral equivalent of the enemy? For most ordinary Americans it was the Arab oil sheiks and their OPEC cartel, but the conventional wisdom of liberalism in the 1970s held fast to Pogo's observation: the American people were the enemy, because of our profligate, energy-wasting lifestyle.

One ironic aspect to this picture of economic policy confusion was that the movement to deregulate basic industries began to pick up speed. In other words, policy-makers were incoherently advocating more and less government involvement with the economy at the same time. President Carter advanced several deregulation initiatives, starting with the airline industry. To be sure, the momentum for deregulation began under the Ford administration, but Carter carried it through with equal enthusiasm. Prior to 1978, the federal government dictated routes and fares to any airline that flew interstate, which covered all airlines except a couple of small carriers who operated only in California and Texas. The Civil Aeronautics Administration (CAB), the regulatory agency that oversaw the airline industry, sometimes took several years to approve an airline's request to begin service on a new route. The CAB itself noted the irrationality of this scheme, and became perhaps the first regulatory body ever to advocate it own abolition. Carter also set in motion the deregulation of the trucking industry, which would culminate in the eventual abolition of the Interstate Commerce Commission. Senator Ted Kennedy was curiously one of the co-sponsors of the legislation to deregulate trucking. His rhetoric sounded like Adam Smith. 'The problems of our economy,' Kennedy said in 1978, 'have occurred not as an outgrowth of laissez-faire, unbridled competition. They have occurred under the guidance of federal agencies, and under the umbrella of federal regulations.'[9]

But like his fiscal policy, where Carter's rhetoric ran ahead of his performance, on the whole the Carter Administration ushered in a wholesale expansion of regulation. The *Federal Register*, the US Government's catalogue of new regulations, grew from 63,629 pages when Carter took office to 87,012 by the end of 1980 – an all-time record high that was not matched again until the regulation-happy closing days of the Clinton Administration. The regulatory burden would have been even higher had not Congress rejected Carter's proposal for a cabinet-level consumer protection agency and several other regulatory proposals. In 1978, General Motors grabbed headlines when it claimed that it spent more in a single year ($1.6 billion) to comply with federal regulations than it cost to run the entire US Government for the first 75 years of the nation's existence. GM added that the paperwork alone required 20,000 'person-years' to fill out.[10]

This extended look at the economic difficulties and confused policy of the 1970s is necessary to understanding the complete reversal of policy that occurred in the 1980s. The catastrophic economic record of the 1970s was prominent among the reasons that American voters turned to Ronald Reagan in the election of 1980. Reagan's campaign promised a wholesale change in the direction of American policy, nowhere more so than the economy. Reagan took office in early 1981 amidst an atmosphere of economic crisis that was perceived to be very nearly as serious as that which faced Franklin Roosevelt upon taking office in 1933. A memo to President-elect Reagan warned: 'No American President since Franklin Roosevelt has inherited a more difficult economic situation... 1980 may well have been the most critical year for the American economy in half a century.' Although Reagan had campaigned for office on a wide range of issues, including confronting the Soviet Union, his chief of staff James Baker and others described the three top priorities of the Reagan Administration in those early months of 1981 as 'the economy, the economy, and the economy.'

Reagan's new economic policy contained four main elements: tax cuts, restraining the growth of government spending, reducing government regulation, and sound monetary policy. Taken together this policy quartet became known as 'Reaganomics.' The latter three parts of his policy – spending restraint, deregulation, and sound monetary policy – had become more or less accepted by the time Reagan took office, but the first element – tax cuts – was and remains today highly controversial. Reagan's tax cuts derived from 'supply-side economics.' The specific proposal Reagan backed was a three-year, 30 percent cut in income tax rates across the board. At the time, the top income tax rate in the US was 50 percent on 'earned' income, and 70 percent on 'unearned' income (that is, interest and dividend income).

Supply-side economics is a yeasty confection. It is no less controversial today than it was then, even though its proponents represent it as no more than a restatement of neoclassical economics.[11] A variety of succinct definitions were offered; several economists described supply-side economics as merely microeconomics applied to macroeconomic aggregates.[12] This formula will mean little to non-economists. In its simplest formulation, supply-side economics can be summed up in two words: taxes matter. Taxes matter to each individual decision to save, invest, produce, or consume. And the sum of individual decisions adds up to whether the economy is robust or stagnating.

By whatever definition supply-side economics is understood, it represented an audacious break with existing economic thought, and its advocates, who quickly became known as 'the supply-siders,' were nothing if not audacious in their representation of its promised effects. 'Nothing like them had appeared on the national scene since the early New Dealers,' the *Washington Post*'s Haynes Johnson wrote of the brash tax-cutting insurgents. Lawrence Lindsay, who would later serve as President George W. Bush's chief economic adviser, wrote that 'The supply-side challenge of [1981] was the greatest challenge to a reigning economic dogma since the overthrow of classical economics in the 1930s.'[13] Herbert Stein, senior economic adviser to President Nixon and President Ford and a critic of supply-side economics (it was Stein who first came up with the label, in fact, back in the mid-1970s), wrote that Reagan 'has chosen a rather eccentric school of economics and economists and has eschewed the opportunity of reducing responsibility for error by staying close to the mainstream.'[14]

The breathtaking audacity of supply-side economics can be best appreciated by reference to the simple theoretical construct explaining how taxes matter that became almost a household phrase: the 'Laffer Curve.' Economist Arthur Laffer, the legend goes, drew an inverted U-shaped curve on a restaurant napkin over lunch in 1975 to depict how lowering income tax rates might produce higher tax revenues. The drawing on a restaurant napkin, supposedly for then-White House chief of staff Dick Cheney, may not have actually happened (neither Laffer nor Cheney recall this taking place), but it made for a great image of an 'ah-ha!' moment.

It also led to a major misconception about the core idea of supply-side economics. High income tax rates had two main distorting effects. First, high tax rates discouraged productive investment, and caused wealthier taxpayers to invest in unproductive tax shelters. This represented a massive misapplication of capital. High tax rates along with inflation also raised the cost of capital significantly, and in the latter half of the 1970s both productivity growth and the rate of new business start-ups fell sharply. Second, with inflation pushing more and more middle-income taxpayers into higher tax, tax rates were causing people to reduce their supply of labor. Cutting income tax rates across the board, as the Kemp-Roth proposal would do, would surely induce changes in investment behavior by wealthy taxpayers that would cause those in higher-income brackets to report higher income. This had already occurred among higher-income brackets in Britain following Margaret Thatcher's reductions of the even higher income tax rates there. Cutting rates would also provide incentives for people to supply more labor. But income tax revenue would fall in the short run from taxpayers in the lower brackets whose tax liability is not determined by investment choices and other discretionary factors. The question was whether increased overall economic growth, and changes in investment behavior by upper income taxpayers, would immediately result in higher revenues at lower rates.

In their exuberance for their idea, Laffer, Kemp, and a few other supply-siders suggested that cutting tax rates would indeed produce higher tax revenues through faster economic growth. In other words, tax cuts would pay for themselves. At one point Laffer wrote that 'each of the 10 percent reductions in tax rates would, in terms of overall tax revenues, be self-financing in less than two years. Thereafter, each installment would provide a positive contribution to overall tax receipts.'[15] In fact, few if any of the economists advising Reagan found Laffer's scenario to be plausible. Milton Friedman sensibly pointed out that if tax revenues increased after a tax cut, then tax rates had not been cut far enough. Alan Greenspan estimated that only about 20 percent of the lost revenue would be made up by higher economic growth. Other estimates were higher, though still nowhere near Laffer territory. The Chase Econometrics model projected that 41 percent of the tax cut would be recovered the first year, rising to 72 percent by the seventh year.[16] Even if Laffer was not precisely right about tax cuts immediately paying for themselves, he was right about a broader point: government revenue estimates of changes in tax policy were wholly static, and made no allowance for changes in economic behavior in response to different tax rates. In other words, the government's revenue models assume that taxes do not matter. This had been proven wrong in the late 1970s, when the capital gains tax cut in 1978 – the first supply-side breakthrough – had generated increased revenue. The government models all assumed that the cut would lose revenue.

There was much more to the supply-side theory than simply stimulating higher economic growth. Contrary to the conventional wisdom that saw a large tax cut as a powerful inflationary force leading to still higher interest rates, supply-siders thought that lower tax rates would be deflationary and help reduce interest rates. This argument was simply breathtaking, but the logic of this insight goes to the core of supply-side theory. Following the classic definition of inflation as 'too much money chasing too few goods,' it was thought that increasing the supply of goods would serve to lower inflationary pressures. There was a second part to this argument, however, that was more tantalizing. The high inflation and high taxes of the 1970s had caused a disproportionate investment in tangible assets as an inflation hedge whose tax liability could be postponed indefinitely. Lower income tax rates would lead to a shift away from tangible assets and to greater investment in financial assets, such as stocks and bonds, since financial assets would be more attractive in a lower tax environment. This process would bid down the yields on stocks and bonds. The expansion of productive capital investment and the total capital stock and the shift to financial assets would make it possible to support a larger budget deficit and still have falling interest rates. The supply-siders also correctly anticipated that the American economy would become a more attractive destination for foreign capital; as one supply-sider told Robert Bartley, the Saudis would finance America's higher budget deficit. This prediction turned out to be exactly correct.

Congress approved most of Reagan's tax cut agenda, but embraced only some of his spending restraint, with the result that the US had large budget deficits throughout the 1980s, contrary to Reagan's intent. The economy also suffered a severe recession in 1982, with unemployment reaching nearly 11 percent, the highest level since the Great Depression of the 1930s. The chief cause of this recession was the tight money policy of the Federal Reserve, which was determined to wring inflation out of the economy even at a high cost in diminished economic activity. In this respect, monetary policy and supply-side tax policy acted at cross-purposes to each other. Monetary policy throughout the first half of the Reagan presidency was highly erratic, and did not settle down into Reagan's preferred range of steady, predictable growth until Alan Greenspan became chairman of the Fed in 1987. Throughout the deep recession in 1982, Reagan faced mounting pressure to reverse course on both tax cuts and spending. For the most part, he held the line, and led his party in the elections of 1982 under the slogan, 'stay the course.' It is highly unusual for an American politician to make a direct appeal to virtue amidst difficult circumstances, and although Reagan's party suffered large losses in the 1982 elections, it is arguable that they could have lost by an even bigger margin had they not stayed true to their principles. This is an important lesson for economic reformers everywhere to contemplate.

A second wave of tax reform in 1986 brought the top income tax rate in the US down to 28 percent from 50 percent when Reagan took office, and soon most of the industrialized world followed the US in reducing marginal income tax rates. Even the Scandinavian social welfare states of Sweden, Norway, and Finland got in on the act. Norway cut its top tax rate from 75 percent to 54 percent, Finland cut rates from 71 percent to 54 percent, and Sweden from 83 percent to 75 percent.[17] Supply-siders suggest Sweden's relatively poor economic performance relative to her neighbors is explained by the fact that Sweden did not cut its tax rates enough.[18]

But once the recession of 1982 was out of the way and the inflation spiral broken, the US economy enjoyed the longest peacetime boom in its history. The economy expanded for a record 92 months from 1982–90; real GDP grew by 31 percent – an amount larger than the entire economy of then-West Germany. Over 20 million new jobs were generated – twice the number as in Europe and Japan combined. Real after-tax per capita income grew by 15.5 percent, and median real after-tax income grew by 12.5 percent, giving the lie to the charge that only the wealthy benefited from the economic growth of the 1980s.

With only the mildest of recessions in 1990–91, the economic boom rolled on into the 1990s, when even a change of party did not see a significant rollback in any of Reagan's major policies. Although President Bill Clinton did push through a small increase in income taxes, he reversed course by 1997, signing a major cut in the capital gains tax. In fact, President Clinton built upon and brought to completion several of Reagan's ideas, including most significantly the consummation of the North

American Free Trade Agreement (NAFTA), an idea Reagan first proposed in the late 1970s.

The successful revival of the American economic powerhouse after a period of decline and self-doubt in the 1970s has had major consequences for economic liberalization around the world in the aftermath of the end of the Cold War. Although counterproductive government regulation and subsidization of industry continues in the US and elsewhere on a large scale, the idea of centralized economic mastery has been shattered once and for all. The most important element in the story, however, is less the particular policy details than the determination of the nation's leadership – in the case of the US, the determination above all of one man, Ronald Reagan – to stick with the course of reform through the difficult and often painful transitional phases that reform necessarily brings with it.

Notes

1. T.G. Ash (2002), *The Polish Revolution: Solidarity*, New Haven: Yale University Press, p. 17.
2. J.W. Dean (1980), 'The Dissolution of the Keynesian Consensus', *The Public Interest*, special issue, 1980, 21.
3. M.J. Boskin (1989), *Reagan and the Economy: the Successes, Failures, and Unfinished Agenda*, San Francisco: Institute for Contemporary Studies, p. 27.
4. A.H. Meltzer (1980), 'Monetarism and the Crisis of Economics', *The Public Interest*, special issue, p. 39.
5. W. Brookes (1982), *The Economy in Mind*, New York: Universe Books, p. 85.
6. *National Review*, 24 October 1975, 1160.
7. *National Review*, 28 April 1978, 510.
8. *National Review*, 26 May 1978, 637.
9. Brookes, *The Economy in Mind*, p. 153.
10. *National Review*, 6 January 1978, p. 11.
11. Arthur Laffer, for whom the 'curve' is named (see below), wrote: 'Supply-side economics is little more than a new label for standard neoclassical economics.'
12. William Niskanen's formulation (*Reaganomics: an Insider's Account of the Policies and the People*, New York: Oxford, 1988, p. 18) is: 'Supply-side economics is most accurately described as the application of microeconomic theory to the effects of fiscal policy on the incentives to work, save, and invest and on the allocation of resources in the economy.' Economist Norman Ture, one of the leading supply-side proponents, wrote: '"Supply-side" economics is merely the application of price theory – widely and tastelessly labeled "microeconomics" – in analysis of problems concerning economic aggregates – widely and tastelessly labeled as "macroeconomics"' (in Robert Bartley (1992), *The Seven Fat Years. And How to do it Again?*, New York: Free Press, p. 56).
13. Lawrence B. Lindsay (1990), *The Growth Experiment: How the New Tax Policy is Transforming the US Economy*, New York: Basic Books, p. 5.
14. Stein, in William Fellner (ed.) (1981), *Essays in Contemporary Economic Problems*, 1981–1982 Edition, Washington DC: American Enterprise Institute, p. 57.
15. Cited in Martin Feldstein (ed.), *American Economic Policy in the 1980s*, Chicago: National Bureau of Economic Research, p. 25.

16. Bartley, *The Seven Fat Years. And How to do it Again?*, p. 74.
17. Others include Australia, which cut its top tax rate from 62 percent to 49 percent; New Zealand from 60 percent to 33 percent; Israel from 66 percent to 48 percent; Canada from 58 percent to 45 percent; Austria from 62 percent to 40 percent; Japan, 75 to 50 percent; Singapore from 55 to 33 percent; South Korea from 89 to 48 percent.
18. Lindsay, *The Growth Experiment*, pp. 129–35.

6
Economic Policy during the Clinton Administration

William A. Niskanen

Economic policy during the Clinton Administration reflects a complicated record, in part a consequence of Republican control of Congress from 1995 through 2000, but the general performance of the US economy was outstanding. Real GDP per person increased at a 2.5 percent annual rate, up from a 0.9 percent annual rate during the prior Bush Administration. Productivity growth increased sharply beginning in 1996, a trend that continued during the second Bush Administration. The unemployment rate fell from 7.5 percent to 4.0 percent. The average annual inflation rate was 1.8 percent, down from the 3.4 percent rate during the prior Bush Administration. And the interest rate on long-term government bonds fell from 7.67 percent to 5.94 percent. There is not yet a consensus about how much the economic policies of the Clinton Administration contributed to these remarkable conditions. Former Treasury Secretary Robert Rubin has continued to attribute these conditions to the major tax *increase* approved in August 1993 without a single Republican vote, but, in fact, interest rates continued to increase until the Republicans controlled Congress beginning in 1995. So let us try to sort out these issues.

Spending

Over the entire Clinton Administration, the rate of growth of real per capita federal spending was the lowest of any Administration in the years since World War II, a condition characteristic of divided government. But that was not destined to be the case. Clinton's first budget called for 'economic stimulus to create jobs while laying the foundation for long-term economic growth; [and] long term-public investment to increase the productivity of our people and businesses . . . .' After hard bargaining, however, with a Congress controlled by his own party, Clinton withdrew the stimulus package and the proposed infrastructure spending was largely abandoned.

Clinton's major legislative initiative was the Health Security Act of 1994, the plan for which was drafted by a special task force headed by his wife. The main features of this act were the following:

- Universal health insurance;
- Mandates on employers and individuals to pay the insurance premiums, with some fiscal subsidies for small firms and low-income families;
- All firms except the largest had to purchase insurance from a regional pool. Insurers would have to offer standard plans and enroll all who applied; rates would be the same for everyone in the pool.

It was never quite clear what the total cost of this proposal would be. A small part of the cost would be covered by the proposed increase in the federal excise tax on cigarettes from 24 cents a pack to 99 cents a pack. But most of the costs were expected to be offset by a reduction of the health care costs already on the federal budget.

In any case, the complexity and many unanswered questions about the Health Security Act meant that it never came to a vote in a Congress controlled by Clinton's Democratic Party. The main lesson that Clinton drew from this experience was never again to propose a broad reform; his only later health proposals to be approved were limited expansion of coverage for children, the disabled, and long-term care.

All in all, the spending record during the Clinton Administration, importantly influenced by the Republican control of Congress, was remarkably restrained. Total nominal spending for defense and international affairs was roughly constant, and expenditures for domestic discretionary programs increased at an unusually low annual rate. The only budget elements with continued real expenditure growth were the formula payment programs for income security, medical care, and interest payments, programs that have yet to be brought under control.

Taxes

The major tax legislation supported by Clinton was incorporated in the budget act of 1993. This act changed the federal tax code in the following important ways:

- The top marginal tax rate on income was increased from 31 percent to 39 percent, and a new 36 percent rate was added.
- The tax base for the 3 percent Medicare tax was increased to include all earnings.
- The individual tax rate on the alternative minimum tax was increased from 24 percent to 28 percent.

- The amount of Social Security benefits subject to the income tax was increased from 50 percent to 85 percent.
- The earned income tax credit was increased again, primarily for larger families.
- One initially obscure provision of the 1993 tax legislation would have important later consequences: a limit of one million dollars on executive salaries that could be deducted as an expense contributed to the rapid increase in compensating executives via stock options.

Several minor tax bills that were approved through 2000 included many small measures, primarily supported by the Republican-controlled Congress. These measures included increasing the types of and allowed contributions to individual retirement accounts, introducing a child tax credit and an education tax credit, increasing the amount exempt from estate tax, and reducing the tax rates on short and long-term capital gains from 28 percent and 15 percent to 20 percent and 10 percent.

The combination of these tax measures had the following major effects on the tax code:

- The tax code became substantially more progressive, increasing the top marginal rates and exempting most of those with below-median income from income taxation.
- The tax bias against saving was substantially reduced.
- The tax code became substantially more complex.

The combination of the higher marginal rates and the independent increase in the inequality of income generated a substantial increase in federal tax revenues through 2000, but most of the tax measures approved during the Clinton Administration, other than those that reduced the tax bias against saving, were quite inconsistent with those that would promote economic growth.

The fiscal balance

The net fiscal balance of the federal government improved dramatically from a deficit of $297.4 billion in 1992 to a surplus of $189.5 billion in 2000. A good bit of this improvement, however, was not expected. In early 1987, the Administration expected deficits to continue and later increase, and Clinton submitted a budget proposing to balance the budget in 5 years. During the next three years, as it turned out, the federal budget surplus as a share of GDP was larger than at any time in the prior 50 years. This substantial improvement in the fiscal balance, however, seems more attributable to the spending discipline of divided government and the unexpected increase in federal revenues at the end of the decade than to any policy proposed by the Clinton Administration.

Monetary policy

Monetary policy during the Clinton Administration was unusually successful. There was no recession during this eight-year period, the average inflation rate was 1.8 percent with little variability, and the growth of nominal demand was maintained at a very steady 5.5 percent annual rate until early 1998. The best explanation for this record is the combination of Alan Greenspan's superior judgment about monetary policy and the President's superior judgment not to interfere with a process that was working very well. The major exception to this record is that the Federal Reserve allowed a demand bubble to develop in 1998 through early 2000, a bubble that was coincident with but much smaller than the bubble in the equity markets in this same period. My judgment is that the Federal Reserve allowed this bubble to develop through their response to a series of financial crises beginning in 1997 in Asia and later including Brazil, Russia, the collapse of Long-Term Capital Management, and the anticipated Y2K crisis at the end of 1999. The slow economic growth during the first two years of the second Bush Administration was largely attributable to the collapse of this bubble, a lesson from which Greenspan's successor should learn to avoid financing a future bubble.

Regulation and trade policy

Clinton did not initiate any major changes in regulation, although he created a problem for the incoming Bush Administration by approving several controversial regulations in the last hours of his Administration.

Clinton had a good record on trade, working to gain Congressional approval of NAFTA in 1993 and resisting most of the petitions for selective trade restraint. Some indiscreet remarks to a journalist on a flight to Seattle, however, contributed to the collapse of the Seattle meeting of the World Trade Organization.

Major reforms

Three major reforms proposed by the Republicans were approved by Congress and signed by Clinton in 1996, proving that neither divided government nor a presidential election year preclude major reforms:

- An agricultural reform phased out production subsidies and relieved farmers from much of the regulation to which they were previously subject; this reform was unfortunately reversed during the subsequent Bush Administration.
- A telecommunications reform increased competition in local telephone services but was unfortunately undermined by decisions by the Clinton-appointed chairman of the Federal Communications Commission.

- More important, over the strong opposition of his own party, Clinton approved a major welfare reform. This reform replaced a federal payment to low-income parents who do not work with a federal wage subsidy to low-wage workers, a reform that has reduced the number of welfare recipients by more than half. This reform is now perceived to be quite successful and will almost certainly be renewed by a Congress controlled by either party.
- Most important, Clinton came close to proposing a reform of Social Security that would allow younger workers to invest part of their payroll tax in an individual retirement account. In 1998, he sponsored and attended a number of town meetings on the subject and a White House conference in December, leading many of us to expect that he would make some proposal to reform Social Security in his state-of-the-union speech in January 1999. Unfortunately, this important potential reform was indefinitely deferred by Clinton's effort to avoid being convicted on the impeachment charge, and the prospect for bipartisan support for a reform of Social Security is now uncertain.

Conclusion

In summary, economic policy during the Clinton Administration was quite good, and economic conditions were very good. On the whole, however, the Clinton Administration is best described as one of missed opportunities. Richard Nixon and William Clinton were probably the two smartest men to be President since World War II, but both ultimately disgraced the presidency in different ways.

7

The Economic Policy of George W. Bush: a Continuation of Reaganomics?

Wojciech Bieńkowski

Introduction

The economic policy of the George W. Bush Administration, despite obvious relationships with or references to Reaganomics, cannot and should not be treated or portrayed as a simple continuation of the policies of the 1980s. Obviously, when one looks at George W. Bush's tax or international trade policies one could see George W. Bush as a true child of Ronald Reagan. The meat and potatoes of the tax cuts passed during the George W. Bush (from now on referred to as Bush II) Administration clearly echo if they do not fulfill what Reagan's economic policy initiated during the 1980s.

Tax cuts have been based on the same supply-side principles and aimed at stimulating growth through the long-term effects of permanently lower taxes, rather than having their basis in Keynesian policies of demand management. The Reagan approach can also be found in international trade. Bush II policy, with the shameful exception of pro-agriculture policies or the 20-month 'temporary' protection of the American steel industry, resembles that of Ronald Reagan's 'domesticism,' that is, the idea that the free market conditions existing in the US economy should be extended and promoted internationally (Nau, 1984/1985). Numerous recent US initiatives on free trade, both on regional and bilateral bases, as well as a push to implement the Doha Round agenda have offered still further proof of continuities from Reagan to Bush.

Another striking similarity between the two economic policies can be seen when looking at the almost perfect cooperation between the government and the Federal Reserve Board (the Fed). Although the Fed is an independent body, a proper coordination of the monetary and fiscal policies of the government is a very desirable combination because the correct policy mix helps to serve long-term growth as well as countering cyclical recessions. No doubt, both the Reagan and Bush II Administrations have had the understanding and support of the Fed when conducting their economic policies. Even when we take into account the facts that Reagan disliked the overly tight monetary policy of Paul Volker during his first term (Niskanen, 1988) and that George W. Bush cannot be happy with the too-long accommodative policy of Alan Greenspan. On balance, however, the cooperation between the Fed and both Administrations seem to have striking similarities, especially in regard to making the economy conducive to growth in a healthy, non-inflationary business environment.

Since both Reagan and Bush have been strong believers in what we could call neoclassical or classical economics, the similarities are likely to extend into the issues of property rights protection, deregulation, public choice related issues and the like.

On the other hand the social policy of Bush II is very different in substance from what we remember from Reaganomics or when thinking more generally about a conservative approach. Social policies in the past were seen as a means to buy off social forces that otherwise would be opposed to government policy. One of the biggest problems of the Reagan Administration was its inability to see social policy as anything more than a means to placate the various discontented forces within both Congress and the public interest sector. Because of this inability to see social policy differently, Ronald Reagan's economic policies were all too often criticized as cold-blooded and anti-poor.

In contrast, Bush II appears to understand that social policy can be an important and effective supplement to assist and support an economic policy. The Bush Administration seems to have discovered that liberal means can achieve conservative ends through a social policy that lowers the economic burdens of individual citizens and business. The other goal of this kind of policy is to have people more involved in using their own energy and initiative and money as part of the endeavor.

Another distinctive feature of Bush II policy, as opposed that of Reagan, is the longer horizon of some of the problems that the Bush II Administration has been willing to undertake. Among them are addressing the Social Security problem and some initiatives related to Medicare and Medicaid, although the latter seem not to be as well thought through or consistent with the framework that shapes the Administration's position on Social Security reform. But privatization of the Social Security problem, framed as 'the ownership society' is an ambitious goal with a long-term vision that definitely gives Bush II a positive mark even when it is only an attempt at this stage. But before we make a balance sheet or a final judgment on Bush II's similarities with Reagan, we must see in detail the record of Bush's first term.

George W. Bush as a true child of Reagan (or a continuator of Reaganomics): tax reforms

Let us look at taxes first. There have been three key tax cut reforms, and some complementary acts. The three most important were the Economic

Growth and Tax Reform Reconciliation Act of 2001, the Job Creation and Workers Assistance Act of 2002 and the Jobs and Growth Tax Relief and Reconciliation Act of 2003 (JGTRRA). These acts prove that George W. Bush is following Reagan in tax policy (Altman, 2004). Table 7.1 and Table 7.2 show us the effects of these cuts and the Reagan reforms from the early 1980s (Boskin, 1987; Bieńkowski, 1995).

An analysis of the tax cuts shows four clear relationships between tax cuts and national income, budget resources, defense costs, and deficits. First looking at tax cuts and national income we can see that contrasting the size of the tax cuts with national income shows that the Reagan tax cuts represented 1.4 percent of income while none of the Bush II tax cuts even breaks 1 percent of income. When we compare tax cuts and budget resources we see that, in 1981, Reagan's tax cuts represented 5.3 percent of the budget. Each of Bush's tax cuts is smaller than Reagan's – EGTRRA (3.8 percent), JCWA (2.5 percent) and the 2003 tax cut (1.8 percent). Although in combination the Bush tax cuts (at 8.1 percent) would be larger than Reagan's tax cut. Turning to tax cuts and defense costs it can be seen that when President

Table 7.1: Reagan and Bush tax cuts in historical perspective

Tax legislation	**Tax cut in billions of current dollars**[a]	**Tax cut in billions of constant 2003 dollars**	**Tax cut as a percent of national income**[b]	**Surplus or deficit as a percentage of national income**[b]
The Reagan tax cut: The Economic Recovery Tax Act of 1981	–38.3	–68.7	–1.4	–2.8
The Bush tax cuts:				
The Economic Growth and Tax Reform Reconciliation Act of 2001	–73.8	–75.8	–0.8	1.5
The Job Creation and Worker Assistance Act of 2002	–51.2	–52.0	–0.6	–1.7
JGTRRA – 2003 tax cut	–60.8	–60.8	–0.6	–3.2
The Bush tax cuts if combined in 2003	NA	–188.1	–2.0	–

Notes:
a. First year estimate.
b. National Income as measured by Net National Product.

Source: Center on Budget and Policy Priorities; www.cbpp.org.

Reagan pushed though his tax cuts during the height of the Cold War the Pentagon consumed 22 percent of the budget, whereas today defense spending consumes just 17.1 percent of the budget. And finally, when looking at tax cuts and deficits we can see that in 1981, Reagan cut taxes while running a deficit of 2.8 percent of national income. In contrast, Bush passed the largest of his three tax cuts, EGTRAA, in 2001 with a budget surplus of 1.5 percent of income.[1]

All three (2001–03) acts were designed to boost both aggregate demand and aggregate supply, but what was new in the third bill and what has been unprecedented in recent history of tax changes, was that a key provision of the Jobs and Growth Tax Relief Reconciliation Act of 2003 (JGTRRA) reduced the occurrence of double taxation by reducing the rate for both individual income tax (which included dividend earnings, which are treated as income) and the capital gains tax. This change should introduce both more fairness and more efficiency into the allocation of people's financial resources.[2]

Two acts signed by President Bush in 2001 and 2003 contained additional measures to regulate Internet taxation. Their goals were simple: to prevent multiple and discriminatory taxation by extending the application of traditional tax rules to electronic commerce and to promote the availability of the Internet to all by prohibiting taxes on access fees.

Table 7.2: Reagan and Bush tax cuts compared to other budget items (as a percentage of federal budget)[a]

Tax legislation	**Tax relief**	**Social Security**	**Defense**	**All other domestic spending**
The Reagan tax cut: The Economic Recovery Tax Act of 1981	5.3	19.5	22.0	53.2
The Bush tax cuts:				
The Economic Growth and Tax Reform Reconciliation Act of 2001	3.8	22.3	15.8	58.1
The Job Creation and Worker Assistance Act of 2002	2.5	22.1	16.9	58.5
The Bush tax cuts if combined in 2003	8.1	20.5	16.2	55.2

Notes:
a. Percentages created by treating tax relief 'as if' it were a budgetary item.

Source: Center on Budget and Policy Priorities; www.cbpp.org.

The Internet Tax Nondiscrimination Act extends for five years the moratorium on new and discriminatory taxes on the Internet, and makes permanent the ban on Internet access taxes. It does not allow for 'simplification' provisions that would allow the states to shift their tax collection burdens to merchants outside of their jurisdictions. It amends the ITFA (Internet Tax Freedom Act) to ensure that all current and future Internet access technologies are spared from taxes that would slow the growth of e-commerce and discourage use of the Internet.[3]

Straight tax-cutting policy, so typical for Republicans and Ronald Reagan, is also seen in the latest bill approved by the Senate and the House of Representatives, which is still awaiting signature by President Bush. The approved bill lowers tax rates for domestic manufacturers to 32 percent from the top corporate rate of 35 percent. It will surely help US manufacturing, which has lost millions of jobs in the last few years. Total tax cuts for companies resulting from this act will amount to $238 billion.

Tax cuts are combined with social policy, which is so important for George W. Bush. That these two policies go together is confirmed in the Working Families Tax Relief Act, signed by President Bush on 4 October 2004. Due to the President's actions, a family of four with an income of $40,000 will save more than $900 on their taxes. Overall, 94 million Americans will have a lower tax bill, including 70 million women and 38 million families with children. This legislation:

- Extends the full *marriage penalty relief* to couples who are unfairly taxed just because they are married.
- Lessens the tax burden of lower-income Americans by ensuring the full benefits of the *10 percent tax bracket.*
- Helps working parents by ensuring that the full *$1000 per child tax credit* is available through 2010.
- *Supports military men and women living in combat zones* by providing nearly $200 million of assistance in the form of higher child credit refunds and earned income tax credits.
- *Protects middle-class taxpayers from the Alternative Minimum Tax* by exempting from it the first $58,000 of a married couple's income. Without this AMT relief, taxpayers would be saddled with an extra $23 billion AMT levy through 2005.
- *Simplifies the tax code* for families who qualify for the child tax credit, the Earned Income Tax Credit, the dependent care credit, the dependent exemption for children, and those who file as the head-of-household.[4]

In social matters, the Bush II Administration's plan is not only to create more jobs, but also to help people gain the skills that will offer them not only greater employment security but also greater opportunity in a growing economy. The Administration's goal is to stimulate people and to boost their initiative by improving access to education so that they may acquire such skills.

International trade policy

George W. Bush's international trade policy follows that of Reagan closely, both with respect to its commitment to free trade generally and with respect to doubtful exceptions made for the steel industry.[5]

Due to the commitment to free trade the Bush Administration has advanced multilateral (via the World Trade Organization), regional and bilateral trade agreements in order to open global markets and to maintain free access to the American market for imports, even when facing a US current account deficit reaching over 5 percent of US GDP in 2004. The Administration believes that imports will not necessarily harm the American economy. There has been no evidence, over the past decades, of a negative correlation between deficits in trade and growth in unemployment or declines in GDP.

Of course, the Administration has been well aware of the fact that growing import penetration in certain sectors of the US economy causes problems and has tried to counter the negative effects by various initiatives such as the High Growth Job Training Initiative and the Community-based Job Training Grants.[6] Recent proposals include such ideas as Personal Re-employment Accounts, an innovative approach to worker retraining that will provide both support to unemployed workers and incentives to find new employment. In addition to these broadly or universally defined aims, which could apply to the unemployed in any situation across the US, the Administration has worked to enhance the longstanding Trade Adjustment Assistance program, which provides training and income support to workers directly hurt by import competition. The assistance, which will total $12 billion over 12 years, should ease the adjustment for displaced workers and help them into new jobs. The program is part of The Trade Act of 2002 which extended eligibility to workers directly affected by trade competition (CEA, 2005, p. 177).

The Administration does not fear the negative impact of FDI (foreign direct investment) either, and it seems to have rejected the strong criticism of those who see foreign investment as a danger. The Administration views subsidiaries of foreign firms in the US as good suppliers of new skills and technology, as well as sources of new employment opportunities. According to estimates accepted by the Bush II Administration, US subsidiaries of foreign companies employed 5.4 million US workers in 2002, around 5 percent of total private sector employment, up from 3.9 million workers in 1992.

The Bush Administration holds a similarly positive view about outward FDI. According to various studies, US firms investing or setting up enterprises abroad increase exporting opportunities for their goods; and increased employment at the foreign subsidiaries is associated with a corresponding increase in employment in US parent companies. Similarly, according to studies quoted by US government sources, one dollar of spending on capital investment abroad by US firms is associated with an additional 3.5 dollar capital investment at home (Department of Commerce, October 2004).

These positive attitudes towards free trade and free flow of capital benefits translate into various US government actions during George W. Bush's first term. The Administration pushed aggressively to open global markets to trade via WTO negotiation and through numerous trade agreements on regional and/or bilateral bases.

One of the most characteristic features of this Administration has been the strong push for protection of intellectual property rights. In 2004, the Administration launched a major initiative, STOP! (Strategy Targeting Organized Piracy), to protect these rights. STOP! aims at countering trade in pirated and counterfeited goods (ICE, 2004). Protecting intellectual property rights has become a major issue because America is a major producer of innovative goods and specialized services. These services, as well as recordings, films, books and software need strong property rights protection.

In addition to WTO negotiations aiming at the completion of Doha Round initiatives, which include elimination of agricultural export subsidies and reducing tariffs on manufactures to zero, the US Administration has pursued numerous bilateral trade agreements (free trade agreements) with various important trade partners or regional associations. This, as well as free trade arrangements made in the past, places the US as the second-best country of 145 in terms of ease in doing business by foreigners and with the easiest entry access for foreign exports. Increased security measures introduced since 9/11/2001 have only slightly altered the bright picture. The policy is, on almost all accounts, a continuation of that of Reagan.

Where and when George W. Bush went beyond Reagan

Bush II policies go well beyond those of Reagan in social issues related to re-employment, education, Medicare and so on. These undertakings differ both in scope and in time horizons. They have or may have a profound impact on US development in that social policy helps shape economic policy and this in turn translates into creating conditions that will influence economic performance (Peterson, 2004). Some of the re-employment and job restructuring issues have already been discussed under the effects of import competition on the US economy. Let us turn now to education and Social Security initiatives.

In education and training, Bush II, during his first week in office, submitted a plan to reform the nation's elementary and secondary schools. The reform proposal was passed by Congress in 2001 and signed into law by President Bush as the No Child Left Behind Act (NCLB) and represents the most important federal education reform in a generation. The NCLB aims to help to expand opportunities for American students and workers. The proposal helps more Americans to graduate from high school prepared for college or the workforce, or to access post-secondary education, and get the job training and skills to compete in a changing and dynamic economy and fill jobs in emerging industries. In addition the Bush Administration has proposed community-based job-training grants and significant reforms to federal worker-training programs under the Workforce Investment Act (WIA) in order to double the number of workers receiving job training in high-growth sectors. Two-thirds of America's economic growth in the 1990s resulted from the introduction of new technologies – and 60 percent of the new jobs of the twenty-first century require post-secondary education, presently held by only one-third of America's workforce. The US needs to close the skills gap and that is why the federal government provides state and local governments with over $4 billion to train workers through the Workforce Investment Act (WIA).[7]

Breaking from previous educational policy, the Bush Administration via the WIA insists that states, school districts and schools must be accountable for ensuring that all students, including disadvantaged students, meet high academic standards. States must develop a system of sanctions and rewards to hold districts and schools accountable for improving academic achievement. As a way to ensure accountability each state will be offered a one-time bonus if it meets accountability requirements, including establishing annual assessments in grades 3–8, within two years of enacting this plan.

The plan also insists upon consequences when schools fail to meet the goals or targets that it sets. The Secretary of Education will be authorized to reduce federal funds available to a state for administrative expenses if a state fails to meet its performance objectives or to demonstrate results in academic achievement. This plan also incorporates the key market concept of parental choice which allows for greater opportunity for children. Parents will be enabled to make informed choices about schools for their children by being given access to school-by-school report cards on student achievement for all groups of students. The following are ways in which choice will be permitted under the plan:

- *Charter schools.* Funding will be provided to assist charter schools with start-up costs, facilities, and other needs associated with creating high-quality schools.
- *Innovative school choice programs and research.* The Secretary of Education will award grants for innovative efforts to expand parental choice, as well as to conduct research on the effects of school choice.

The purpose of the plan is to promote parental choice and to increase the amount of flexible funds available to states and school districts for innovative education programs.

George W. Bush on 'ownership society', Social Security reform and a reform of government programs in general

When listening to the President's plans to restructure various government programs one has a feeling that the Bush II team has embarked on a '*Republican New Deal*' (Economic Report on the President, 2004), an ambitious program that embraces an attempt to privatize the pension system and ultimately part of the health care system too, to simplify the tax code and create what is called an 'ownership society.'

The term 'ownership society' includes various initiatives that aim at increasing ownership of homes and businesses and making it easier for Americans to save more of their money in retirement and health savings accounts. The main priority of the Bush II Administration at present is Social Security because it leads the way to other entitlement programs. The main argument of his team is that the Social Security system is unsustainable in the longer run if not changed dramatically (Kotlikoff and Burns, 2004). This program is difficult politically because the immediate cost of it is high and the true gain may not be seen for decades. In trying to solve this problem the Bush II Administration looks almost visionary, taking risks that ordinary politicians would not take.

The motivation of Bush's team for reforming the Social Security system and similar government entitlement programs has deep ideological roots. The shift to personal responsibility for retirement and health care through personal saving accounts leads to, in Bush's words, 'personal freedom to choose and bigger involvement in the future of the country.'

The renewed emphasis on 'ownership' and inculcating the message that citizens should be the owners of their opportunities and controllers of their own futures, not mere consumers of government services that others will pay for, is an attempt to shift the way in which ordinary Americans understand government entitlement programs. In changing people's understanding, there is the hope that it will create an friendly environment where reforming government entitlement programs becomes possible. In this George W. Bush sounds more like Margaret Thatcher when she shifted British society from welfare-state and community housing to the rules of the market and personal freedom through privatization and deregulation.

Conclusions

Whether Bush II is a true child of Reagan or whether he deserves a different label for what he has done and attempted to do, one might think of giving him two different grades. The President deserves a good grade for the continuation of Reagan's policies and a distinction for extending and updating his policies as well as for proposing completely new programs.

A good grade should be given for making the most of the best aspects of Reagan's economic policies such as tax cuts, decentralization and free trade. With respect to taxes, however, one should add that although the Bush tax cuts have been based on the same ideological foundation as Reagan's policies, one can distinguish Bush's approach from Reagan's for making tax cuts permanent, for simplifying the tax code, and for eliminating, at least in part, the system of double taxation by cutting taxes on returns to investment.

A distinction should be given for Bush's determination – not so much for limiting government by cutting government programs as Reagan did, or as in 1994 the Republican Congress tried to do – but for an attempt to reduce the demands on government in the long run. Policies advanced by George W. Bush embrace a long-term vision, a paradigm shift in thinking regarding the relationship between the people and their government that echoes, and is consistent with, the structural changes created by the decentralizing global information age in which we live. The way George W. Bush has addressed the pressing issues facing the US makes him more than just a simple continuator of Reagan policies.

Notes

1. http://www.taxpolicycenter.org/TaxModel/tmdb/TMTemplate.cfm?topic3id=57&topic2id=40.
2. http://www.whitehouse.gov/news/usbudget/budget-fy2004/work.html.
3. The US Department of Commerce reported that e-commerce was a $5.39 billion industry in 1999 – and doubled to $11.92 billion in 2003. This act relieved 143 million American Internet users from taxes on activities that have become a part of daily life: reading their email, catching up on the latest news, buying and selling products, instant messaging friends and loved ones, checking sports scores, doing research, listening to online radio stations and just surfing the net.
4. See Public Law (2004), 'Working Families Tax Relief Act of 2004', *Public Law*, No. 108–311, signed by President George W. Bush on 4 October 2004.
5. In December 2003 President Bush signed a proclamation ending the temporary steel safeguard measures he put in place in March 2002. Prior to that time, steel prices were at 20-year lows, and the US International Trade Commission found that a surge in imports to the US market was causing serious injury to our domestic steel industry. The President took action to give the industry a chance to adjust to the surge in foreign imports and to give relief to the workers and communities that depend on steel for their jobs and livelihoods. These safeguard measures may have now achieved their purpose, and as a result of changed economic circumstances it is time to lift them. There is some evidence however that the steel protection measures had been approved by George W. Bush on a qui pro quo basis for the support of some US Congressmen from Rust Belt States for the Trade Promotion Authority (TPA) that George W. Bush wanted to get from Congress. The signing of the steel protection measures secured for the President the needed support from Ohio representatives.

6. *The President's High Growth Training Initiative*, from: http://www.doleta.gov/BRG/JobTrainInitiative/.
7. See US Department of Labor; http://www.doleta.gov/usworkforce.

References

Altman, D. (2004), *Neoconomy: George Bush's Revolutionary Gamble with America's Future*, New York: Public Affairs.

Bieńkowski, W. (1995), *Reaganomika i jej wpływ na konkurencyjność gospodarki amerykańskiej*, Warszawa: PWN.

Boskin, M.J. (1987), *Reagan and the US Economy: the Successes, Failures and Unfinished Agenda*, Stockton: International Center for Economic Growth.

CEA (Council of Economic Advisers) (2005), *Economic Report of the President*, Washington: US Government Printing Office.

ICE (US Immigration and Customs Enforcement) (2004), *STOP!: Strategy Targeting Organized Piracy*, US Department of Homeland Security.

Kotlikoff, L.J. and S. Burns (2004), *The Coming Generational Storm: What You Need to Know about America's Economic Future*, Cambridge, MA: MIT Press.

Nau, H. (1984/85), 'Where Reaganomics Works', *Foreign Policy*, 57, 14–37.

Niskanen, W.A. (1988), *Reaganomics: an Insider's Account of the Policies and the People*, New York: Oxford University Press.

Peterson, P.G. (2004), *Running on Empty: How the Democratic and Republican Parties are Bankrupting our Future and What Americans Can Do about It*, New York: Farrar, Straus and Giroux.

Public Law (2004), 'Working Families Tax Relief Act of 2004', *Public Law*, No. 108–311, signed by President George W. Bush on 4 October 2004.

Part II

Applicability of the US Economic Model

Section 3

The US Economic Experience and Its Applicability to Countries in Transition

8

Successes and Failures in Catching Up: the Post-Communist Case[1]

Leszek Balcerowicz

I will start with a description of the initial conditions, that is, just before the collapse of communism, and then proceed to an analysis of the outcomes, both economic and non-economic. How to explain the emergence of huge differences in these outcomes among the post-communist economies is the topic of the next section. Then I would like to add some observations on fiscal developments, the evolution of the financial sector, privatization and so on, and conclude with a few personal recollections about the reforms in Poland.

Initial conditions

Initial conditions that mattered for the subsequent developments included, first of all, the communist institutional system. Its main feature was an exceptionally extensive set of state controls which limited individual liberties, both economic and non-economic:

- Private entrepreneurship was banned, which, together with the initial nationalizations, resulted in the monopoly of the state sector.
- State-owned enterprises were subject to central planning, which included output commands, rationing of inputs and foreign exchange, price controls and directed foreign trade.
- The range of financial assets available to enterprises and individuals was extremely limited, as a market-type financial system could not have coexisted with central planning.
- The setting up and functioning of non-economic organizations were also heavily controlled; that is, civil society was suppressed and political opposition was banned.
- Foreign travel was restricted.
- Media were subject to formal censorship, direct party controls and personnel policy – mass media were largely an instrument of communist propaganda.

These extensive controls banned both the market and democracy. In other words, communism was a special form of anti-market dictatorship. They also coexisted with a bloated communist welfare state that included:

- relatively large transfers in kind (education, health);
- social protection delivered via state-owned enterprises (SOEs);
- artificially low prices for foodstuffs, energy and housing rents;
- a social safety net, typical of some market economies, did not exist as the need for it was sharply limited through the curtailment of individuals' opportunities and risks.

Part of this welfare state was the reverse side of waste. For example, overemployment provided job security but contributed to low productivity.

Finally, the communist state was peculiar with respect to the provision of public goods.

- Defense expenditures were excessive and shaped by the imperial aspiration of the Soviet elites.
- Law and order were kept at a reasonable level, although at the cost of practices typical of a police state.
- The legal framework and the juridical system criminalized private economic activity and independent political activity, and were ill-suited to the market economy, rule of law and free society.

The inherent weaknesses in communist economies emerged and worsened over time relative to market economies. Whereas in 1950 Poland had about the same per capita income as Spain, in 1990 it had 40 per cent of Spain's per capita income (Maddison, 2001). A similar gap emerged between East and West Germany, Hungary and Austria, not to mention North Korea and South Korea. This was the price of a system that deprived individuals of economic liberties. This was – indirectly – the price of Marxism, which claimed that the market – or in other words, economic liberty – is the source of underdevelopment. Unfortunately, such thinking was quite influential in developmental economics for many years.

The inefficiency of the communist system was reflected, among other things, in very low industrial productivity relative to countries like Mexico, Chile or Thailand, as is evident from Figure 8.1.

Being wasteful economically, communist economies were also wasteful ecologically, because economic efficiency is necessary for ecological efficiency. An economically inefficient system uses a lot of energy per unit of output, which damages the environment. Communist economies produced much less GDP per unit of energy use than comparable market economies and generated more carbon dioxide emissions per unit of GDP. This is why

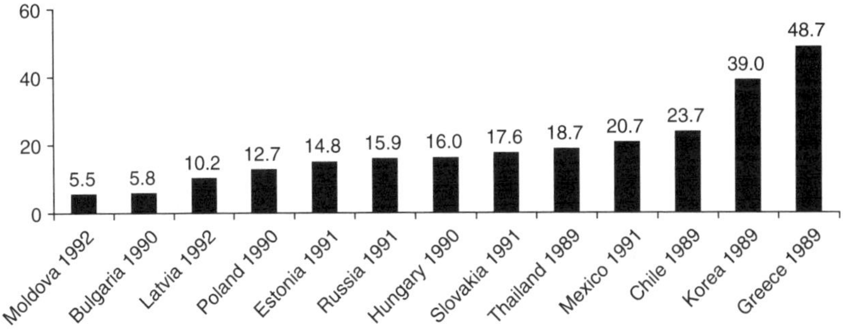

Figure 8.1: Value added in industry per worker, various dates (Eurozone = 100)
Source: World Bank (2004).

market-oriented reforms are necessary for environmental improvement, when starting from communism.

The nature of the communist system, pervasive state controls and the lack of market institutions, called for a vast two-track institutional reform. The first direction was wide liberalization, to reverse the constraints upon economic freedom and, thus, to release private entrepreneurship and market forces. The second was institutional restructuring, which consisted of building new institutions (for example, a stock exchange or banking supervision) or transforming the inherited ones (for example, privatizing the SOEs or reforming the court system). The institutional reforms had to be accompanied by macroeconomic stabilization, the urgency of which depended on the inherited macroeconomic imbalances (see later). Although all these efforts could be started at about the same time, it takes more time to create efficient market-friendly institutions than to liberalize and stabilize the economy. However, this was not a reason to delay liberalization and stabilization until institution building bears its fruit. Quite the contrary, under such a strategy economic disarray could only grow while the precious moment of 'extraordinary politics' would be wasted, seriously putting under risk each of these three operations (for more on this see Balcerowicz, 1995).

The communist institutional system interacted with the policies, themselves the product of personality factors and institutional constraints in producing other categories of initial conditions that mattered for subsequent developments. One of the most important of these was the economic structure. Although all communist countries depended on other communist countries for trade because they were isolated from the West, there were important differences in this trade dependence, reflecting differences in size, political status and other factors. For example, exports to Comecon countries accounted in 1989 for 41 per cent of GDP in Lithuania, 37 per cent in Latvia, 30 per cent in Estonia, 27 per cent in Armenia, 24 per cent in Ukraine, 14 per cent in

Hungary, 11 per cent in Russia, 8 per cent in Poland, 6 per cent in the former Czechoslovakia and 4 per cent in Romania (IMF, 2000). Obviously countries more dependent on the Comecon trading system were bound to suffer a larger decline in their GDP because of the disintegration of this system than less dependent countries.

Human capital is another important category of the initial conditions, involving health and education. The health indicators varied among the communist countries as shown in Figure 8.2; however, with the exception of Central Asia they tended to be comparable or better than in Chile, South Korea or Mexico.

The communist countries also displayed high enrollments in primary and secondary education (Figure 8.3). The quality of educational output is more

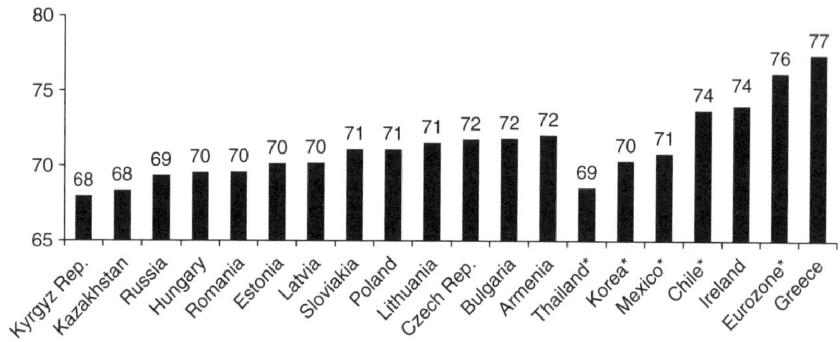

Figure 8.2: Life expectancy at birth, 1989
Note: * Data from 1990.
Source: World Bank (2004).

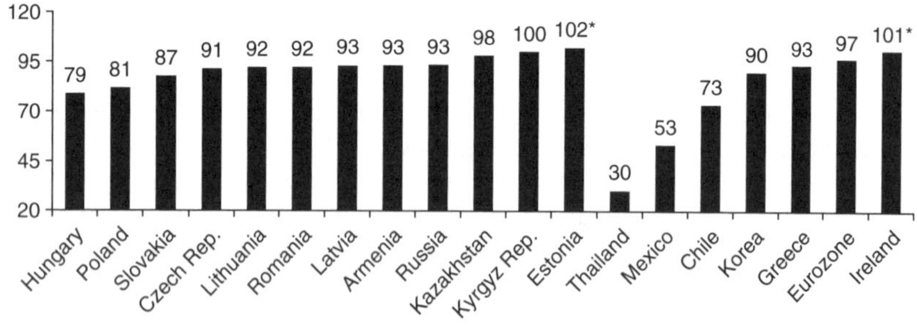

Figure 8.3: Secondary school enrollment, the ratio of total enrollment to the population of age that officially corresponds to the level of secondary education,* 1990 (%)
Note: * The value of this indicator exceeds 100 per cent when the number of secondary school pupils is higher than the total population of age that officially corresponds to the level of secondary education.
Source: World Bank (2004).

difficult to judge. It appears that it was relatively high in science and mathematics, that is, in fields immune to ideological distortions. In contrast, social sciences, especially economics, were not spared from official dogma. Also, certain skills, for example, in marketing, were not required in a shortage economy and correspondingly they were not taught and acquired. However, with the relatively high level of general education such gaps could quickly be eliminated. All in all, the educational system produced a better output than the communist economic system could use. This 'surplus' human capital was largely wasted during the professional lives of educated individuals, although the remaining stock of human capital represented one of the few assets at the start of the transition positively distinguishing the post-communist countries from most other emerging economies. However, human capital is mobile, and – with the newly introduced freedom of emigration – the challenge has been to retain it domestically. It is here that quality of policies turned out to be doubly important: by shaping the economic situation and its prospects policies not only determined current welfare but also influenced the propensity of educated people to continue working in their countries thus impacting upon longer-term developments.

Finally, there were huge differences in the inherited macroeconomic imbalances as measured by the indicator of repressed inflation and the black market premium (De Melo et al., 1997, table 2). Macroeconomic stabilization was for Poland, Romania, Bulgaria and countries of the former USSR a much more urgent and demanding task than for Hungary and former Czechoslovakia.

From the point of view of the subsequent developments it is less important how bad or good are the inherited conditions than how quickly they can be improved given proper policies. From this perspective one can distinguish treasures from burdens. The former are initial conditions that, under the right policies, generate rapid economic growth. The relevant examples include an economic structure characterized by a large share of repressed but easily privatized sectors, a large pool of educated people or a favorable location. The latter are inherited conditions that, at least in a short run, hamper economic growth. Trade dependence on collapsing markets, a large share of declining sectors or difficult access to large and dynamic markets are examples.

The communist economies differed in the relative weight of inherited treasures and burdens. The small former republics of the USSR were much more dependent on exports to Comecon than Poland, Hungary or Czechoslovakia. The Kyrgyz Republic and Armenia, both small and landlocked countries, have a much less favorable location than the Baltics or Moldova.

However, a far more important difference existed between the initial conditions prevailing in most countries of the former Soviet bloc, including Russia, and those in China at the start of its reforms in the late 1970s. The former, being much more developed had a much higher share of industry and much lower share of easily privatized agriculture than the latter. In

China, 69 percent of the labor force in 1980 was employed in agriculture relative to 14 percent in Russia in 1990. Also, China displayed significantly fewer macroeconomic imbalances than was typically the case in the Soviet bloc countries. These differences in initial conditions explain much of the Chinese superiority in transition performance. One should also note the important role of radical external opening (foreign trade, FDI inflows) in Chinese development.

Outcomes: a great divide

Perhaps the most striking feature of outcomes since the collapse of communism is their enormous variation. In other words, the living standards in communist countries some 15 years ago were much more uniform than they are today. This variation is evident from the variety of indicators in a wide range of areas.

Consider GDP, where there have been enormous differences relative to the initial level (Figure 8.4). In Poland in 2004 GDP was 42 per cent higher than in 1989, while in Ukraine it was 45 per cent lower. Bear in mind that these are official data, so if the informal sector were added the differences would be smaller although still very large. One should also remember that a number of factors overstated the decline of GDP in post-communist economies. For example, the levels of GDP under communism were largely inflated due to wasteful investment, excessive stocks, large military expenditures and value-diminishing activities, all of which were counted as positive contributions to GDP (Aslund, 2001). The correction for these inflated figures was recorded as a decline in GDP and often interpreted as a decline in welfare. However, these and other factors do not fundamentally change the relative picture.

All transition economies have made considerable progress in lowering inflation (Figure 8.5). Generally speaking, better long-run growth performance went hand in hand with lower inflation. This confirms a well-known fact

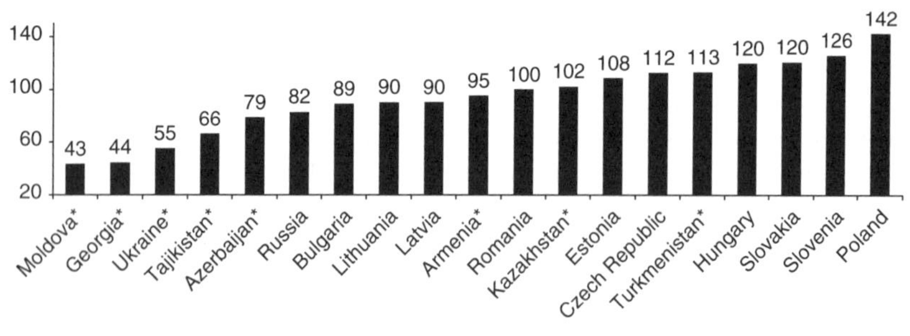

Figure 8.4: Real GDP, 2004 (1989 = 100)
Note: * 2004 estimates.
Source: EBRD (1995–2004).

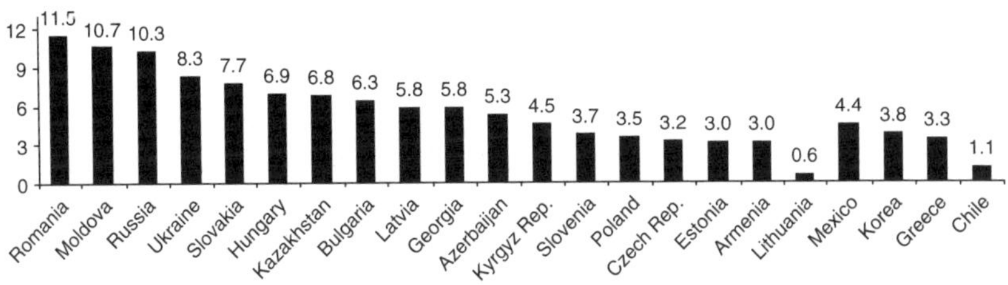

Figure 8.5: Inflation, 2004 (annual average, %)
Source: IMF, The World Economic Outlook Database; Polish Central Statistical Office.

that in countries that inherited high inflation, successful disinflation is conducive to long-term economic growth.

There emerged huge differences with respect to labor productivity growth in industry in the years 1992–2003 (Figure 8.6). The range is from 172 per cent in Hungary to 35 per cent in Ukraine. Part of these differences was due to a difference in the extent of enterprises' restructuring. Countries with a lower increase in labor productivity tended to preserve more labor hoarding and subsequently to display less statistical unemployment than countries with higher increases in labor productivity.

Massive differences are also apparent in per capita inflows of foreign direct investment (Figure 8.7). FDI usually follows economic success and strengthens economic growth, especially through technology transfer. This is why the displayed differences in the magnitude of FDI are very indicative. Note that the post-communist leader, the Czech Republic, has attracted substantially more FDI than Chile, the star performer in emerging economies. Poland received $1355 FDI per capita, about the same as Greece ($1308) and

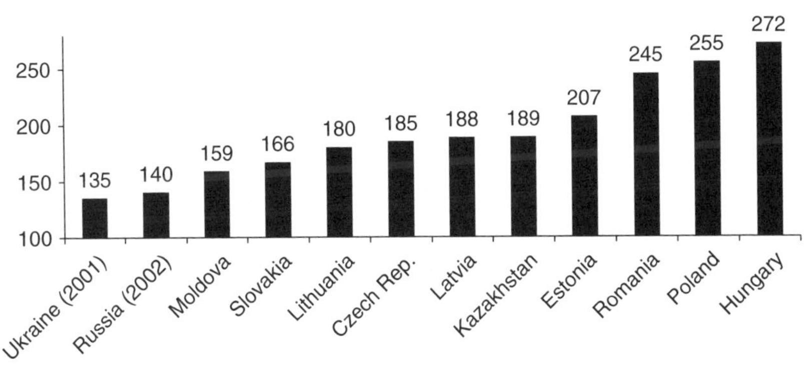

Figure 8.6: Change in labor productivity in industry, 1992–2003 (1992 = 100)
Source: EBRD (1995–2004).

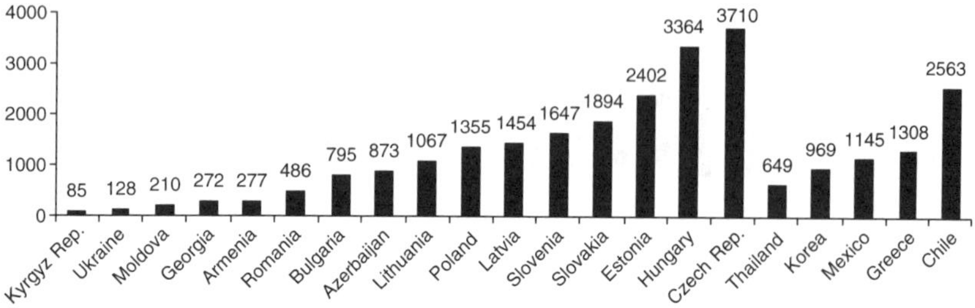

Figure 8.7: Cumulative per capita FDI inflows, 1989–2003 (US$)
Source: EBRD (1995–2004).

more than Mexico ($1145). By contrast, the Kyrgyz Republic attracted $85, Ukraine $128 and Moldova $210.

A great difference in outcomes occurred not only with respect to economic dimensions but also with regard to non-economic ones. Countries that performed better on the first scale tended to perform better on the second as well. Take the environment; being highly wasteful, the Soviet-type economy was also very damaging to the environment. One of the main reasons for this was a low ratio of GDP to energy consumption. The transition economies have differed in the evolution of this measure, that is, in the impact of the economy on the environment.

One can see the countries of Central and Eastern Europe (CEE) have increased the energy efficiency of their economies considerably (Figure 8.8). Great progress was also achieved in the Kyrgyz Republic and Kazakhstan. In contrast, the energy efficiency in Russia and Ukraine has remained at very low levels.

The post-communist countries have also displayed differing developments in public health. With respect to life expectancy at birth (Figure 8.9) the best

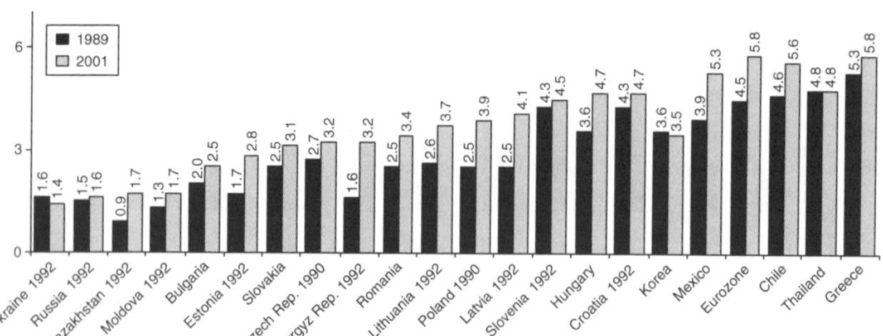

Figure 8.8: GDP/unit of energy use, 1989 and 2001 (PPP $ per kg of oil equivalent)
Source: World Bank (2004).

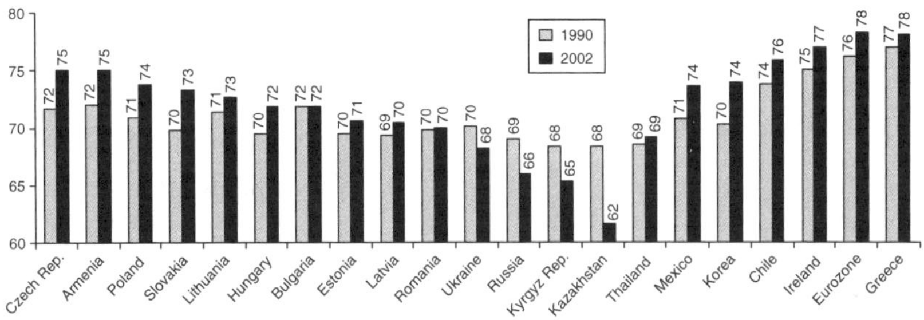

Figure 8.9: Life expectancy at birth (1990, 2002)
Sources: World Bank (2004); EBRD (1995–2004).

performers – the Czech Republic, Armenia, Poland, Slovakia and Lithuania – have achieved similar levels to those of Mexico and South Korea and better than those in Chile. Generally speaking life expectancy increased in the CEE countries while it declined in Russia and Ukraine (but also in Kazakhstan and the Kyrgyz Republic). A similar differentiation is also evident in infant mortality. CEE countries have recorded substantial declines in these levels in comparison to those in Mexico, Thailand and Chile while in Bulgaria and Uzbekistan infant mortality has registered no improvement.

While an optimal distribution of income cannot be established, sharply increased earning inequalities are often regarded as a negative phenomenon. A popular belief is that faster growth goes hand in hand with larger income inequality, as measured by the Gini coefficient, across transition economies (Figure 8.10).

As can be seen, the fastest increases and the highest levels of income inequality have been recorded by Russia and Azerbaijan, countries with a rather poor relative growth record over the investigated period of 1987–90 and 2000–01. Better growth performers during this period such as Poland

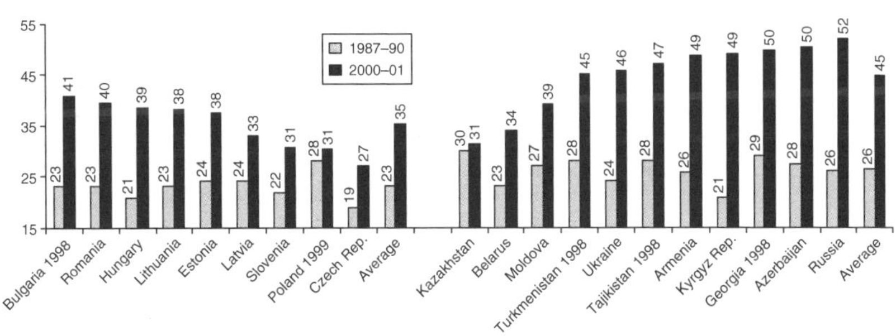

Figure 8.10: Gini coefficient of income per capita, 1987–90 and 2000–01 (%)
Sources: World Bank (2002); World Bank (2004); UNICEF TransMONEE (2003).

and the Czech Republic, have, on average, displayed a smaller increase and lower level in the Gini coefficient.

Explaining differences in outcomes

The enormous differences in outcomes after the collapse of communism obviously pose questions about their causes. There is already a large amount of empirical literature that focuses on relative growth performance and tries to disentangle the roles of initial conditions, external factors and policies.

The initial conditions in the post-Soviet economies were, on average, less conducive to quick economic improvement than those in China in the late 1970s but also highly varied. The small former Soviet republics, heavily dependent on exports to Russia were to suffer huge external shocks as a result of the collapse of the former Soviet Union and the Soviet trading system. Some of them were constrained in the reorientation of their foreign trade owing to their geographical distance from the West. Being less dependent on the Soviet trading system, the East European countries were exposed to less serious shocks to GDP. Russia was in the most favorable situation as its size meant that it was not very dependent on exports to other socialist economies. As a large exporter of oil and gas to its former satellites, it was to obtain large terms-of-trade gains thanks to changes in the world prices of these exports. Therefore Russia's profound decline in official GDP cannot be explained by unfavorable external shocks.[2]

However large the differences in the initial conditions, they can explain only a part of the relative growth performance and only in the early phase after the collapse of communism. The differences in long-run growth are mostly due to different policies, that is, the different extent of market-oriented reforms.

Figure 8.11 compares GDP developments in the Kyrgyz Republic and Moldova. It shows that a larger extent of reforms as measured by the share

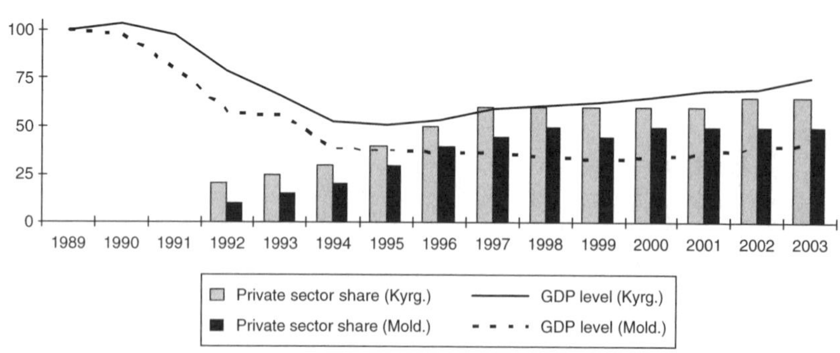

Figure 8.11: Kyrgyz Republic vs Moldova (private sector share in GDP and GDP level)
Note: GDP level 1989 = 100 – lines; private sector share in GDP – bars.
Source: EBRD (1995–2004).

of private sector in GDP can dominate the effects of an unfavorable location. As a result the Kyrgyz Republic has recorded a more favorable GDP dynamic than has Moldova.

Figure 8.12 shows that if one excludes three dictatorships, Belarus, Uzbekistan and Turkmenistan, on account of the questionable quality of their statistical data, then one gets a strong correlation between the EBRD index of liberalization and GDP growth.

The strong link between the extent of market-oriented reforms and growth has also been found in a number of empirical studies. Table 8.1 summarizes the main findings of such studies. At the same time, there is no single empirical study I know that shows that less reform was, under comparable conditions, better for economic growth than more reform.

It should be stressed that a picture of relative economic growth among the transition economies is not static. Some CIS countries during recent years started to grow considerably more rapidly than the average for the East European economies. A good case in point appears to be Armenia, where the improved growth performance cannot be linked to favorable external developments. Instead one must look at an improved economic system: a low tax/GDP ratio, fiscal discipline and a considerably greater economic freedom.

There has been a tendency for non-economic outcomes to improve in line with the economic outcomes. This issue has not been investigated as much as the relative growth performance. It can be shown, however, that some crucial factors conducive to economic outcomes are also conducive to

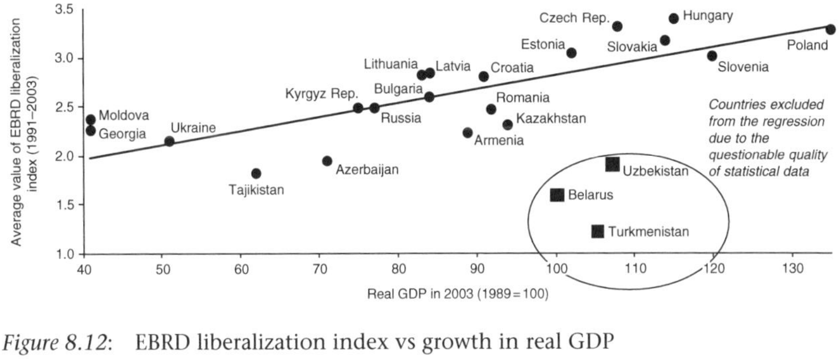

Figure 8.12: EBRD liberalization index vs growth in real GDP

Notes:

The index level is a composite index calculated as an arithmetic average of the 8 EBRD liberalization indices published in the EBRD *Transition Reports* (index of price liberalization, index of forex and trade liberalization, index of small-scale privatization, index of large-scale privatization, index of enterprise reform, index of competition policy, index of banking sector reform, index of reform of non-banking financial institutions).

EBRD Index ranges from value 1 (minimum) – very little (or no) progress since the fall of communism, to value 4 – standards and performance typical of advanced industrial economies.

Source: EBRD (1995–2004).

Table 8.1: Empirical studies reviewing experiences of transition countries

Havrylyshyn and Wolf (2001)	'Unfavourable initial conditions should not become an excuse for inaction... First, their negative effects decline over time. Second, the empirical studies clearly suggest that these effects can be compensated by modestly faster progress on reforms. Third, perhaps the main fact is indirect; that is, unfavourable initial conditions result in less political will and capacity for reform, and less reform means less growth.'
Mervar (2002)	'After the dominant influence of "transition" factors, such as structural reforms, macroeconomic stability and initial conditions in the early transition years, increasing importance in explaining economic activity during later years is attributed to the openness of an economy as well as indicators of institutional development.'
Polanec (2004)	'...we find that in later stages of transition, measures of economic reforms matter for productivity growth, although with a lag, which is in our exercise equal to four years. This result confirms importance of reform efforts in enhancing the potential for growth.'
Krueger (2004)	'...it is worth noting that those transition countries that experienced the most rapid structural reforms have, by and large, experienced more rapid growth. This is true, for example, of the Baltic States. In recent years, Russia has also seen higher rates of growth – a result, in large measure, of reforms that were implemented in the 1990s.'

non-economic ones. Market-oriented reforms increased economic efficiency, inter alia the production and consumption of energy and raw materials, and that has contributed to a reduction in environmental pollution. In addition, the separation of enterprises from the state via their privatization and the introduction of the rule of law helped the enforcement of ecological regulations. Both privatization and the rule of law are fundamentally important determinants of long-run growth.

Different health developments can also be largely linked to economic reforms. For example economic liberalization changed the availability and the relative prices of foodstuffs, and at the same time, this liberalization was crucial for economic growth (Balcerowicz, 1998).

Some additional observations

There is a number of more specific topics related to the developments after the collapse of communism. Let me only mention a few of them.

Fiscal developments

The post-communist countries started with a very high ratio of general government spending to GDP, much higher than was typical of the Asian Tigers, as exemplified by South Korea (Figure 8.13).

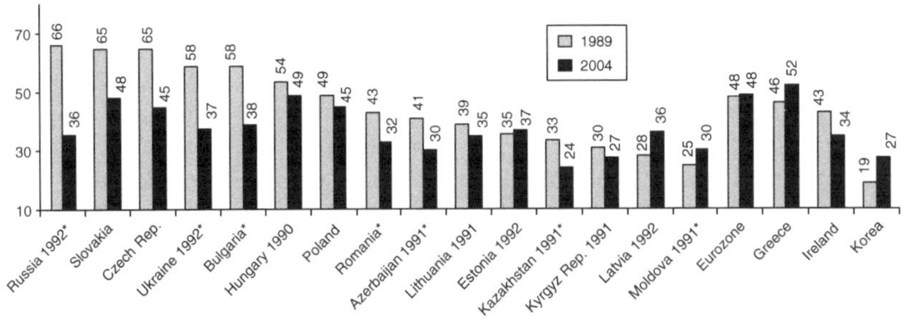

Figure 8.13: General government expenditure (% of GDP)
Note: * 2003 EBRD data.
Source: EBRD (1995–2004); Eurostat and EcoWin.

The subsequent fiscal developments differed enormously across transition economies. Most CEE countries lowered this ratio but to a level that was still much higher than what is typical of countries with their per capita income. This raises the question of whether such a fiscal stance is compatible with a rapid and sustained real convergence. Only a few countries have managed to bring down their spending-to-GDP ratio in an orderly manner and to levels typical for fast growers. These countries include Kazakhstan, the Kyrgyz Republic and Azerbaijan. The challenge for them would be to keep these levels in the interest of future growth.

Financial sector

The financial sector, as measured by the shares of domestic credit to private sector and market capitalization of listed companies to GDP (Figure 8.14), is clearly underdeveloped in the post-communist economies relative to Thailand, Chile, South Korea or Greece.

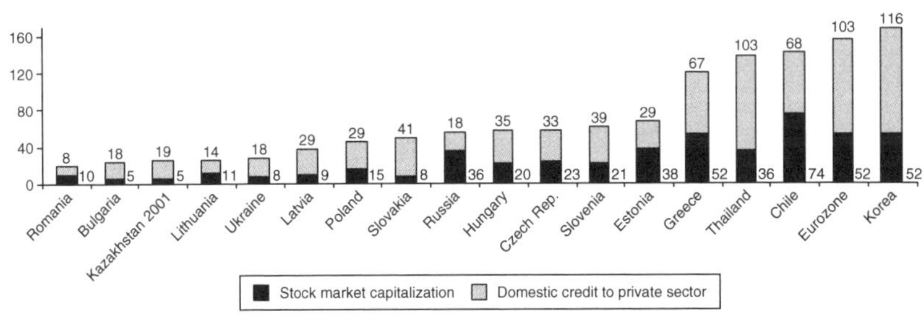

Figure 8.14: Domestic credit to private sector and market capitalization of listed companies, 2002 (% of GDP)
Source: World Bank (2004).

However, it is certainly much healthier, on average, than the huge financial sector in China, burdened with a high share of non-performing loans. Given the present position, the post-Soviet economies can expect a lot of financial deepening if they are able to grow over the long run.

It is striking that most of these economies achieved an extensive external and internal liberalization of their financial sectors in a relatively short period of time and, on the whole, without major disturbances. This casts doubts upon the claim that financial liberalization was a major reason for growth failures (in the post-socialist world). These reasons lie elsewhere; as has already been pointed out, the lack of or insufficient extent of market-oriented reforms blocked the growth of the former communist economies.

Privatization

Privatization of a state-dominated economy takes more time than its liberalization and stabilization. In the short run, a radical change in the SOE environment, thanks to a decisive liberalization and stabilization, can improve the behavior of these firms (see Pinto et al., 1993). However, in the long run, there is no substitute for their privatization, and, to my knowledge, there is no example of a successful SOE-dominated economy. As time passes, the 'normal' forces of politics tend to eliminate the effects of macro- and microeconomic shock upon the managers' behavior. The lack of prospects of official privatization and the inherently poor corporate governance of SOEs lead to asset stripping, that is, 'wild privatization'. This is why a delay in privatization typically does not lend value to a SOE, but, conversely, reduces it. In assessing actual privatization one should avoid a 'Nirvana approach', that is comparing it with an ideal but most likely unachievable yardstick. Instead, one should make comparisons with feasible options. Such an approach would make people think twice before condemning, say, privatization in Russia.

Non-market dictatorships and reforms

The post-communist countries also differed in their political evolution, and it is interesting to ask how differences in this respect relate to the extent of market-oriented reforms (Figure 8.15).

As one can see, among these countries, dictatorship goes hand in hand with a strongly anti-market stance, as countries that achieved the highest scores on economic liberalization also achieved the highest scores on democracy. As these are all new members of the European Union, it is likely that the prospect and requirements of EU entry have played an important role in inducing and maintaining both economic and political liberalization.

Some personal recollections

The basic questions that interested me as a student of economic reforms were, why had the economic reforms in the socialist countries been partially

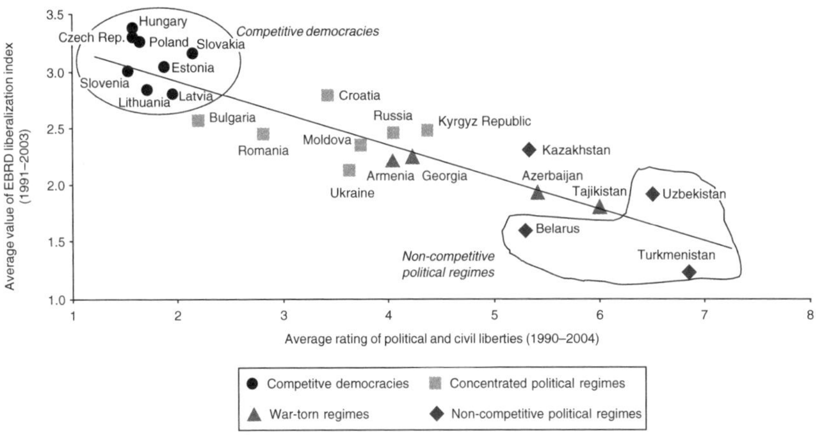

Figure 8.15: Average value of the EBRD liberalization index and average rating of political and civil liberties, 1991–2004

Note: The index level is a composite index calculated as an arithmetic average of the 8 EBRD liberalization indices published in the EBRD Transition Reports.

Source: Freedom House, EBRD (1995–2004) *Transition Reports*.

or wholly reversed, and why had they failed to bring about any significant increase in overall efficiency? My general response to these questions was that the economic reforms failed because they were not radical enough. They did not reach a certain threshold of necessary changes rapidly; in other words, a 'critical mass' of such changes was not achieved. So I entered the government with a strong 'anti-gradualist' attitude towards economic reform. This belief was based not only on experience of the previous reforms, but also on conclusions I drew from social psychology, especially from Leon Festinger's theory of cognitive dissonance. One of the findings of this theory is that people are more likely to change their attitudes and their behavior if they are faced with radical changes in their environment that they consider irreversible than if those changes are only gradual.

With respect to stabilization, I knew that, irrespective of the institutional differences, a radical approach was needed to put the brakes on the momentum of hyperinflation. The institutional differences had, I felt, two consequences. First, given the asymmetry of the labor market, because of the absence of private owners in what was still a socialist economy, there was a need for extraordinarily tough wage controls to rein in the tendency towards runaway inflation. Second, because the tough program of stabilization had to be introduced into a basically non-private economy, its supply response was more uncertain and could be even worse than that seen in Latin American economies. But the alternative strategies had, I believed, much less chance of success.

With respect to the elimination of shortages, I believed the problem was price controls and the rigidity of supply, and not the 'soft budget constraint' of enterprises. The latter, in my opinion, was one of the main factors responsible for their low efficiency, as it implied the absence of competition. Another important lesson was that the absence of competition, import substitution and the heavy regulation of the economy are sufficient to cause low efficiency and widespread rent-seeking; private property cannot remedy this situation. These were the negative conclusions I drew from the experiences of many Latin American countries and India, and from the economic literature, especially from the writings of Bella Balassa and Anne Krueger.

In the spring of 1989 I wrote a paper on which reforms should be introduced in Poland if it were free. I had no idea that a few months later I would be in charge of the Polish economic stabilization and transformation. The proposed steps included rapid liberalization of prices, tough macroeconomic policy, convertibility of the Polish zloty, the liberalization of the foreign trade regime and the quickest possible privatization. I had a clear perception from the very beginning that because of the inherited hyperinflation, we had to choose between an almost hopeless strategy and a risky strategy. There was no option without risk. An almost hopeless strategy would have consisted in neglecting the stabilization part of the program, and focusing instead on the transformation part. It was my view that the strategy of tolerating hyperinflation would make stabilization more and more difficult with the passage of time, and the related chaos of hyperinflation would make rapid transformation, including privatization, scarcely possible. So this strategy, 'privatization first, stabilization later,' would probably have resulted in neither privatization nor stabilization.

It was thus reasonable to choose a strategy that was merely risky but not hopeless: that of starting stabilization and transformation at about the same time. Stabilization measures and the liberalization part of the program of transformation could be implemented more rapidly than privatization and other institutional reforms. The radical strategy consisted, therefore, of the rapid introduction of a stabilization and liberalization package while at the same time undertaking more time-consuming institutional reform. This implied, given the differences in possible speed, that radical stabilization and liberalization had to be introduced in the economy before it was fundamentally transformed. The risk in this strategy was that the supply response of such an economy was weaker and more uncertain than that of a free-market economy. But I always compared these risks with those of delaying stabilization or liberalization, or implementing them gradually. It was obvious to me that the latter strategies were almost hopeless.

I viewed the economic reforms in the terms of a radical and comprehensive package, the elements of which complement one another. Within liberalization, the freeing of prices was a crucial measure, necessary for the rapid elimination of shortages and for obtaining better price information.

Radical price liberalization required, in my view, a decisive liberalization of foreign trade, which, in turn, included the unification of exchange rates and currency convertibility. They were also indispensable for obtaining better relative prices. In addition, the fixing of the newly unified exchange rate played an important role in the program of stabilization, and the introduction of convertibility signaled a decisive break with the past partial and unsuccessful reforms.

Liberalization also included the elimination of the remaining restrictions on the creation and growth of private firms. This was a very important part of a legal framework for economic activity, as it introduced the mechanism of free entry and enabled the spontaneous growth of the private sector. Privatization of enterprises was, for me, the key part of the institutional restructuring. I viewed privatization as the most important type of enterprise reform and as the most important condition for enterprise restructuring. The extension of private enterprise was, to my mind, crucial for solving the main structural problem: that of low and decreasing efficiency. I remembered that the potential inherent in the private sector can be fully released only if there is competition and an outward orientation of the economy. That is why a liberal foreign trade regime was for me an important complement to privatization and an important condition for increasing the overall efficiency of the economy. I also believed that an increase in efficiency might be achieved through foreign trade liberalization, preceding the full privatization of state enterprises. However, in order to obtain the maximum possible increase in efficiency, privatization and other changes must be combined.

While I was reasonably sure about the general features of the target model and the related broad lines of policies, there was a number of specific issues where I felt that economics supplied little advice and thus I perceived a substantial uncertainty, which I tried to reduce with additional analytical work, if possible.

Practically all the important economic variables were subject to great uncertainty. For example, there were conflicting hypotheses about how fast the initial large price increases would spread across the economy; in other words, what the inflation path would look like. I did not know how long we would be able to keep the exchange rate at its initial level. We were uncertain when and on what scale the bankruptcies of enterprises would occur. In fact, they started later than expected and on a smaller scale. We forecast a moderate growth of exports in 1990. In fact, they exploded, growing by 43 percent.

However, I was reasonably certain about the general directions of change, that is the general relationships between the policy measures and the changes in economic variables, the time lags between the two, and the magnitude of the reaction. Therefore, I was sure that the stabilization and liberalization package, if maintained, would stop hyperinflation and eliminate shortages. I was also sure that sooner or later, privatization of the economy, competition and export-oriented growth would bring about greatly enhanced efficiency and solve this perennial problem that plagued the former socialist economy.

There were many questions with respect to the methods of enterprises' privatization. Should we privatize using only the classical methods applied, say, in the United Kingdom, or should we adopt mass privatization schemes? As it turned out, although we were ready to pursue mass privatization, we encountered political obstacles. Therefore, it is not true that Poland opted for slower privatization than, for example, the Czech Republic: we were blocked. Our economic performance probably would have been better if we had privatized more quickly, including through mass privatization.

Concluding remarks

Countries that inherited a communist economy had to launch and implement two basic kinds of institutional reforms: a comprehensive liberalization and a vast program of building or restructuring of institutions conducive to or required by a free society and a stable and dynamic market economy. These post-communist reforms have provided a spectacular example of a broader tendency to reduce the excesses of statism and to move toward free markets present in Western countries and in many developing countries as well.

The experience of post-communist economies strongly suggests that the larger the extent of market-oriented reforms, the better were both the economic and non-economic outcomes. The post-communist transition has produced several policy innovations such as mass privatization, pension reform and a flat tax. It also confirmed, I believe, that a successful transition towards a limited state and its counterpart, the market, is the key to long-run development.

Notes

1. This article is an abridged and updated version of the World Bank publication: L. Balcerowicz (2005), 'Postcommunist Transition in Comparative Perspective', in T. Besley, and N.R. Zagha (eds), *Development Challenges in the 1990s: Leading Policy-makers Speak from Experience*, Washington DC: World Bank.
2. Russia's decline in its recorded GDP may be largely due to an especially large share of military expenditures that were previously counted as part of GDP. For more on this and other reasons for this decline see Aslund (2001) and Schleifer and Treisman (2003).

References

Aslund, A. (2001), *Building Capitalism. The Transformation of the Former Soviet Bloc*, Cambridge: Cambridge University Press.

Balcerowicz, L. (1995), *Socialism, Capitalism, Transformation*, Budapest: Central European University Press.

Balcerowicz, L. (1998), 'Economic Forces and Health', *Dialogue and Universalism*, 8, Warsaw University.

De Melo, M. et al. (1997), *Circumstance and Choice: the Role of Initial Conditions and Policies in Transition Economies*, Washington DC: World Bank.

EBRD (1995–2004), *Transition Reports*.

Havrylyshyn, O. and T. Wolf (2001), 'Growth in Transition Countries, 1990–1998: the Main Lessons', in O. Havrylyshyn and S. Nsouli (eds), *A Decade of Transition: Achievements and Challenges*, Washington DC: IMF.

IMF (2000), *World Economic Outlook*, October.

Krueger, A.O. (2004), 'A Work in Progress: Building on the Achievements of the Transition Economies', IMF Institute for the Study of the Economy in Transition: Moscow Conference on Transition in the CIS: Achievements and New Challenges, September 13.

Maddison, A. (2001), *The World Economy: a Millennial Perspective*, Paris: Organization for Economic Cooperation and Development.

Mervar, A. (2002) 'Economic Growth and Countries in Transition', *Privredna kretanja i ekonomska politika* [*Economic Trends and Economic Policy*], 92, 53–87, Institute of Economics, Zagreb.

Pinto, B., M. Belka and S. Krajewski (1993), 'Transforming State Enterprises in Poland: Microeconomic Evidence on Adjustment', Poland Resident Mission, Country Dept. II, Europe and Central Asia Region, Washington DC: World Bank.

Polanec, S. (2004), 'Convergence at Last? Evidence from Transition Countries', discussion paper 144/2004, LICOS Centre for Transition Economics, Katholieke Universiteit Leuven.

Schleifer, A. and D. Treisman (2003), 'A Normal Country', NBER Working Paper No. 10057, November, Cambridge, MA.

World Bank (2002), *Transition: the First Ten Years*, Washington DC: World Bank.

World Bank (2004), *World Development Report 2004*, Washington DC: World Bank.

9
The American Economic System: a Model for Poland?

William A. Niskanen

Introduction

Most of my professional career has been focused on the problems of the American economy and the changes in public policy that would reduce these problems. But in this chapter, I welcome the opportunity to reflect on the strengths of the American economic system as well as on some of our more important continuing problems. For we must have been doing something right. Average income in the United States is the highest among all major nations, even though we continue to have many immigrants whose initial income is far below this average. And the United States is tied for third among all nations in the most recent annual report on economic freedom. The American economic system, however, may or may not be the best model for Poland. That is for Poland to decide – based on its own values and the history, culture, and other conditions specific to Poland. Poland's decisions, however, would be better informed with a full understanding of both the strengths and the continuing problems of the American economic system.

In his book on *Power and Prosperity*, the late Mancur Olson concluded that only two general conditions are required for a successful market economy: 'secure and well-defined individual rights' and 'the absence of predation.' The historical and continuing political dilemma is that although some government role, what Adam Smith called 'the strong arm of the civil magistrate,' is usually necessary to secure property rights and enforce contracts, governments are often the major agents of predation. The economic future of any nation depends critically on how this dilemma is resolved.

The legal structure

Let me focus first on the American legal structure as it bears on the security of property rights, the enforcement of contracts, and the integrity of the courts.

As a nation that was first a collection of former British colonies, we were blessed from the beginning with the Common Law. As a rule, US property rights provide clear title, the authority to separate a specific use right from a package of rights, and the authority to exchange these rights. Our system of property rights is also quite extensive, the necessary condition to avoid the abuse of 'common pool' resources, that is, the characteristic origin of environmental problems. In effect, the political economy of a nation is defined by the nature and distribution of these rights, and the distinctive principle of a market economy is that any change in the distribution of rights must have the consent of all those who own the affected rights. And, finally, US courts are subject to very little corruption. Overall, the quality of the US legal structure is ranked second only to that of Switzerland.

For all the strengths of the US legal structure, it is now vulnerable to several threats:

- Local governments are increasingly prone to using eminent domain to assemble smaller private parcels for another private use, even though our Constitution authorizes the use of eminent domain only for public use.
- The Federal Government has increasingly taken partial use rights from private property, usually for environmental objectives, without any compensation.
- Our patents and copyrights are increasingly vulnerable to political pressure to permit some parties to acquire intellectual property at a lower price; this is now a special problem for pharmaceuticals, movies, and music.
- The costs of the tort system are now about 2 percent of GDP and are expected to double over the next 10 years.
- Our higher courts are too often tempted to make law, to act as a parallel legislature, rather than only to interpret the law.

Each of these threats is still at issue in our courts and legislatures, and how these issues are resolved will affect whether the US legal structure is a valuable model for other nations.

The labor market

Compared with most other nations, the US labor market is unusually flexible and adaptive. Most workers have relatively little security in their specific job but a great deal of employment security. For example, the US labor market has been relatively slack for several years, but the current unemployment rate is only 5.4 percent. And the median period of unemployment is only 9.5 weeks, even though unemployment insurance is available for up to 26 weeks. There are few restrictions on entry except in such professions as law and medicine, no general wage rate controls, and a relatively low minimum wage rate. American labor continues to be mobile between employers and regions, a condition now somewhat reduced by employer-provided health insurance. And higher management positions are increasingly open to qualified women and minorities. Overall, these conditions are probably better than at any time in the past 50 years. Compared with other nations, the variance of US wages is relatively high, but it is important to understand the several reasons for this condition. Low skilled employees, many of whom are immigrants, are more likely to be employed than unemployed. Fewer than 10 percent of private employees are members of unions. The rapid introduction of new technology has increased the relative wages of more skilled employees. The major problem that contributes to the low relative wages of those employees who have not attended college has been the poor performance of American public schools. Real spending per student in our public schools from kindergarten through high school has more than tripled over the past 40 years without any increase in average student test scores. Average spending per student is much higher than in other nations but American students are placed only fifteenth to twentieth on international tests of reading and mathematics. The poor performance of American public schools has created problems for the labor market, but the origin of this problem is the public schools, not the labor market.

The major continuing threat to the superior performance of the US labor market is political pressure to protect jobs in specific firms and locations by tariffs, subsidies, restrictions on competition, or restrictions on employment practices. As a rule, the American record in resisting such pressure, except from the agricultural sector, is better than that of most other democratic governments. In much of Europe, for example, the high cost of firing employees has turned labor into a capital good, substantially reducing the willingness to hire new employees.

Stable money

A third condition that has contributed to the superior performance of the American economy has been stable money. Over the past 25 years, with superior leadership of our central bank, the inflation rate was reduced from over 13 percent to about 2 percent. Over the past 20 years, the rate of increase of nominal domestic demand has been remarkably stable, and the US has had only two shallow recessions. You will notice that I define stable money as a stable path of nominal domestic demand that is consistent with a low inflation rate, not as a stable exchange rate with some other currency or gold, because any attempt to stabilize exchange rates would increase the variance of domestic output and employment. Poland has made a commitment to join the Eurozone at some future time, but might want to keep this in mind when taking that fateful step.

Freedom to trade

The freedom to trade is necessary for any person, firm, or nation to make full use of their comparative advantage. The United States, of course, has a large internal market with very few restrictions on trade between the states, making us less dependent on international trade. The US government, however, has led the effort to achieve multilateral reductions in trade barriers for 50 years. Our own tariffs and other trade barriers have been progressively reduced to a level among the lowest in the world, with the unfortunate exception of agricultural products. In contrast with other dimensions of economic freedom in the United States, however, we rank only twenty-ninth on the index of freedom from restrictions on international trade. My own judgment is that the necessary condition for the success of the Doha trade round is a joint prior commitment by the European Union, the United States, and Japan to a substantial reduction in trade barriers on agricultural products. Otherwise, I suggest, we have no basis for bargaining with other governments for the protection of intellectual property and a reduction of their trade barriers on our manufactured products, and the Doha Round will fail

Government services and taxes

Finally, the economic performance of a nation is strongly related to the size and characteristics of government expenditures, taxes, and state enterprises. On this basis, the US record is mixed. Over the last seventy years or so, Federal Government expenditures have increased from 2.6 percent of GDP, most of which was for the military and the deferred costs of prior wars, to 20 percent of GDP, most of which is now for programs for which there is *no* explicit constitutional authority. Despite that huge and mostly unconstitutional increase in the relative size of Federal Government expenditures, total US government expenditures as a share of GDP are among the lowest in the world! So the relative effect of government on US economic performance must be evaluated for each major component of spending and each type of tax.

Compared to other governments, US defense expenditures are relatively high with no obvious incremental benefit. US education expenditures are also relatively high, with the mixed record of a superior system of colleges and universities and a mediocre system of public elementary and high schools. On the other hand, US transfer payments for pensions, health insurance, welfare, unemployment, and so on are low relative to those in Europe, Canada, and Japan, a condition that probably increases our relative economic performance. And the United States has few remaining state firms other than our huge postal service.

The top marginal tax rate on individual income is about 40 percent, depending on one's state of residence, one of the lowest among the industrial nations. The marginal tax rate on corporate income, however, is also about 40 percent, second highest only to Japan among the industrial nations. My own estimate of the marginal economic burden of taxes in the United States is that the last dollar of tax revenue reduces after-tax income by about $2.75, an estimated cost that is both higher than the marginal benefit of most US government programs and lower than the marginal economic burden of taxes in most other nations.

Overall, the US ranks sixteenth lowest among the world's governments in terms of the burden of government. Our major near-term fiscal policy challenges are to reduce the deficit, reduce the least beneficial spending programs, and reduce the most burdensome taxes on personal saving and corporate income. In the next decade or so, our major fiscal policy challenge and an even larger challenge in most other industrial nations, will be to avoid the explosion of expenditures for government pension and health insurance programs. Our most important continuing political challenge will be to restore a shared commitment to limited constitutional government so that our children and grandchildren do not face burdens of an even larger magnitude.

Conclusion

Polish government has wisely rejected the Russian model for the Polish economy. As a consequence, the performance of the Polish economy has been much better than the Russian economy since 1991. I would suggest that the most important decision now faced by Poland is the choice between something like the German model or the American model for your economy. That is Poland's choice to make, but I hope that this brief chapter may have informed that choice.

10
What Has America to Offer?

David Lipton

The topic of this volume, the American economic way, is an enduring theme. Europeans have been curious about the American model since its inception. Frenchman Alexis de Tocqueville visited the United States in 1831, just 42 years after the birth of our country. He reported his observations and his critique of America's peculiar experiment back home in France. In Central Europe in recent decades, many people have grown suspicious of ignorant American interlopers making short visits and announcing long conclusions. But, de Tocqueville, a European interloper, was a keen observer who discovered deep truths in a short time. He came to America only once, stayed only nine months, and wrote a book, *Democracy in America*, that remains required reading in most US high schools and colleges.

That book captured much of the essence of the emerging American democracy and society, then only half shaped. He divined one of the most significant and enduring differences between the US and European economic models, in fact one that is sure to be a focus of this discussion almost 175 years later: the American willingness to take personal risks in the pursuit of productivity and profit. To paraphrase, de Tocqueville wrote that, in comparison with the aristocratic societies of Europe, Americans make immense progress in productive industry but, as a result, are exposed to unexpected and formidable embarrassments. The least shock to business and all private fortunes are put in jeopardy at the same time. These setbacks are an endemic disease and originate in the temperament of the nation.

Poland has had no shortage of American interlopers coming to make observations and offer advice. Jeff Sachs and I spent a couple of years doing so at the beginning of Poland's transition. Neither we, nor the international financial institutions (IFIs), which also began their support for Poland's transition in 1989, were ever promoting an American model per se. The theme of my chapter will be that there are both strengths and weaknesses in the American model. America does some things well, and others not at all well. It is arrogant but true to say that today, as in 1989, Poland and other central European countries should do as we say, not as we do, or to put it more politely, you should pick and choose, developing your own blend of economic institutions, laws, policies, and practices.

When Sachs and I first came to Warsaw, there was little need to be precise about the endpoint of Polish capitalism. The communist economic system had laid Poland low, and the remnants of that system had to be dismantled and the financial instability had to be ended. Sachs used to say to the Polish economists and politicians who argued over numerous conflicting visions for the Polish system, that if Poland were an airplane, whether you want to go to America, the United Kingdom, or West Germany, you should rev up the engines and take off heading westward.

Leszek Balcerowicz led Poland's transition with shock therapy combining stabilization, liberalization, and privatization. He did so with the financial and political backing of the US and with the major involvement of the international financial institutions, both in terms of financing and technical assistance. The goal of that economic program was to make Poland a normal, functioning market economy, rather than to emulate America. While some of his choices drew more from one economic tradition than another, none of these initial steps were predominantly American or European. They were intended to create stability and the legal and institutional infrastructure of a market economy. Although there were fits and starts, that effort not only paved the way for Poland's return to Europe, but served as an example for the transitions of so many countries liberated by the collapse of the Soviet Union.

Now, fifteen years later, Poland has a market economy, has joined Europe and is preparing for monetary union. The airship of state has attained cruising altitude and now must program its landing pattern into the onboard computer. Accession to the European Union has predestined many choices, both legal and institutional. But, many degrees of freedom remain. What kind of economy does Poland want to have? Given that Poland is joining Europe, should it just adopt a European model? Can it adopt important elements of the American model, like Ireland and others, and still be an integral part of Europe? Those are hard questions.

First, let me say a few words about what works and what does not in America. That is not a simple matter. Some things work better than others. Moreover, those that do not work still have some positive aspects, and those that do work have some negative aspects. So, it is important to be careful in the adoption process. Who, for example, reading about current events in the United States, would want to emulate our fiscal system, either the tax code or our expenditure appropriation process, which has produced chronic budget deficits, follows no multiyear framework, and is too open to influence from special interests? As I've suggested, even this problematic system has its plusses: we have maintained a more modest government share of GDP and lower marginal tax rates than Europe, and we have kept our

Treasury bonds the safest asset in the world, but surely we – and Poland – can do better. Similarly, who would want to emulate our social security system? Ours has protected retirees at a reasonable cost for two generations, but with demographic change and the great private opportunities in the capital markets, our system is in need of reform, while that of Poland is already undergoing reform.

On the positive side, there is a wide consensus among economists regarding the strengths of the US model. Those strengths include clear property rights, widespread private ownership, a liberal regulatory framework for entrepreneurs, well-developed capital markets, and the freedom of labor markets. Those are the features that anchor our culture of entrepreneurship and underlie the dynamism of our particular brand of capitalism. Those features are not all found in many European countries. Larry Summers used to praise US capital markets by saying that only in America could a budding entrepreneur raise $100 million before buying his first business suit. Of course, as de Tocqueville observed so long ago, dynamism carries its costs, or at least, its consequences. Not only are Americans more exposed to the risk of market swings, but also as we have seen in recent years, the relative lack of regulation opens up the possibility that corporate malfeasance will hurt stockholders and stakeholders alike. That said, the advantages of those particular features of the American model predominate and are well worth the attention of central European politicians and policy-makers deciding exactly what kind of European countries to become.

Next, let me turn to the role of the International Monetary Fund and the World Bank. Their role as financiers of Poland is for the most part finished. The capital markets can finance Poland's further development. But, the IFIs continue to advocate for good policy and good institutions, both here and across Central Europe. What they promote is neither an American nor a European model, but a hybrid set of recommendations, drawing upon common sense, decades of experience, and the distillation of best practices. Their advice today, as over the past 15 years, is valuable, though by no means without flaws or omissions.

A quick review of recent IMF policy advice serves to illustrate that point, and to highlight the important economic issues facing Poland. The IMF's most recent assessment of Poland warns that to sustain economic growth requires re-igniting investment and boosting employment demand. Their three key policy recommendations, aimed at achieving those objectives, are fiscal consolidation, tackling deep-seated structural weakness, and reducing the size of the public sector. Their structural agenda includes streamlining social transfers, restructuring state-owned enterprises, broadening the tax base, and reforming the labor market. They advocate a renewal of the privatization process. This agenda is not novel to informed observers. But it does cover much of what is needed. Does it promote elements of the American model? Surely fiscal consolidation is key to managing public debt and lessening the risk of financial market impairment to investment and growth. That is just macroeconomic reality, not any particular country's model. The structural and public sector agenda, when you look at the details, embraces positive elements of the American model, and Poland would be well advised to follow.

The IFIs do not always get it right, and sometimes miss, or pay lip service to policies of fundamental importance. Three that I would like to mention are, enterprise privatization, the fight against corruption, and public sector infrastructure. For fifteen years, Poland has neglected these three crucial policy areas. I believe Poland is already paying a price for that neglect, and that the price will only grow with time. America's economic success over the past two centuries has been based on widespread private ownership. In recent decades, Europe has accepted that lesson. In Poland, however, the job of privatization is only part done and has been stymied by management claims that restructuring should pre-date or can even substitute for privatization, by labor's fear of private owners, and by political inertia. Privatization, including bank privatization, must be reinvigorated and completed.

In America, the public sector has played a crucial role in supporting productivity and limiting the costs and risks of business. One public sector role is our strong judiciary process. Our system is not without malfeasance and corruption, and there is growing concern about the costs of litigation. But widespread faith that our judicial system will protect property rights and punish misdeeds helps moderate the riskiness of investment. Corruption in Poland is not what doomsayers predicted in 1989, but anti-corruption efforts are not what they ought to be. A second public sector role throughout US history has been to provide and foster a modern physical infrastructure. That history extends from the building of railroads, canals, and highways, to modern efforts such as public–private partnerships in research and development and the development of the internet. Communist Poland had a public investment program that largely comprised financial transfers to state-owned enterprise. For fifteen years, too little effort has been put into developing a long-term public investment program to bolster the productivity of the private sector. Budget consolidation should not delay or derail this priority, but rather make room for it.

To summarize this point, Poland's efforts in shedding the mantle of state ownership and updating the infrastructure inherited from the communist period has been intermittent and without conviction. The IFIs always put these items in their policy matrices, but have never pushed them hard enough. Poland's political and economic leadership should take up these tasks.

I believe there is a role in Poland and across Central Europe for dialogue with outsiders to compare economic approaches. The US government, European governments, and the IFIs can contribute to that dialogue. All of those participants should do better than to promote any one model, they can promote best practices, drawing upon the positive and relevant features of the American model, incorporating other approaches as well. The goal should be to craft a hybrid economy, taking the constraints of membership in the European Union as given, but adopting laws and institutions that will inspire a dynamic private sector. Let me end where I started with de Tocqueville. He concluded that the American democracy had its strengths and weaknesses and recommended Europeans cull the good from the bad. And he was optimistic about the prospects for European democracy. He ended his book proclaiming that he came away from his visit to America with 'a firmer hold to the belief, that, for democratic nations to be virtuous and prosperous, they require but to will it.'

11

American Economic Experience: Russian Perspective, Possibilities and Limits of Application

Ruslan Khasbulatov

Introduction

The role of the American economy as an engine of world development is intact. The impact of the US economy on the world economy as a whole and on separate countries has been significant during the post-war development, although it has differed among countries and regions. The US has drastically affected the formation of three regional centers of economic power of the capitalist system, that is, the US itself, Western Europe and Japan: the global triad.

The true scale of American economic impact on world development is so big that the whole world worries about the internal problems of the US, such as a huge budget deficit and unfavorable trade balance. Economists fear that these factors could have a serious negative effect on the global economy.

These and other factors need to be analyzed from the point of view of the interaction between American, world and national economies, and through an assessment of the US economy. At present, economists argue about the ability of maintaining this budget deficit without an adverse effect on the world economy. It may cause an increase in long-term interest rates and lower the growth rate of the world economy in the long run. Apart from that, the direct link between the budget deficit, the foreign trade deficit and the exchange rate of the dollar could intensify the direct risk to American and world economy stability.

Such facts could lead to the hasty conclusion that the US economy no longer plays the role of an engine for the world economy, as this engine is set in motion by borrowed resources. The situation is worsened by the growing current account deficit, which now exceeds 5 percent of GDP. Many analysts conclude that the duration of US economic expansion is directly connected with the readiness of other countries to lend to the US.

Many economists believe that such interdependence between the US and other countries cannot be viable in the longer term.

However this conclusion, in spite of its persuasiveness and appeal, is questionable. One of its key arguments, that is, other countries' willingness to lend to the US, is not convincing. These resources are going to the US following the logic and laws of world demand and supply, not because foreign governments and investors wish to improve or worsen the economic situation in America. Moreover, I am sure that the conclusion of many analysts in different countries that China is replacing the US as the world's economic engine is incorrect. This role is likely to pass over to the EU, as the euro is strengthening while the dollar is weakening. But neither China nor the European Union will be able to replace the US as the principal economic center of the world economy. In general, this trend is rather vague, it has no serious industrial, economic, scientific or technological basis and now is too early to discuss it.

The American economic experience has always attracted the attention of experts. It has been studied by many governments, including socialist governments throughout the period of world socialism. This research lay in two spheres: first, scientific and cognitive and, second, practical. Naturally, under socialism, when the principle of private property was denied, it was impossible to use the positive American experience, as well as the experience of other advanced Western countries, with the exception of certain aspects of enterprise management, innovations, systems of finance control in accounting and so on.

American economists influence economic thought worldwide. Textbooks written by them are used in all countries of the world. We should also mention the fact that former socialist countries, to be more precise, their governments, used European and American patterns and consultants when they passed from the socialist to the capitalist economic system. East European countries such as Poland, Hungary, the Czech Republic and Slovakia, headed in these dramatic times by competent leaders and governments, were influenced by American experience. American consultants exerted a positive effect which can be compared with the experience of Western Europe after World War II within the framework of the Marshall Plan. It should be pointed out that the governments of these countries did not use any shock therapy, although in Russia much was said and written about it. Perhaps, this was done to justify the foolish steps that were taken.

The theoretical experience of Western Europe is also valuable. I am sure that the American and Western European experiences complement each other and both can be useful to countries where market institutions are underdeveloped. It is often difficult to differentiate between the American and European theoretical schools, but we can illustrate it by Keynesian and neo-Keynesian or monetary concepts: both were developed in Western

European countries and the US and successfully applied. The difference is slight, but even this can be very important.

As a negative experience I can briefly describe the use of American experience and American consultants in Russia. To be more precise, I will describe some events in the Russian economic transformation in which I was involved as the second person in the official hierarchy of those days and as a professional economist who can analyze the economic policy tools of the transition period. I would like to emphasize the following important circumstances:

- Gorbachev was short of time and financial reserves to complete the declared economic reforms with due regard for the interests of people. His steps were restricted, on the one hand by orthodox communist bosses, who did not want to lose their influence and, on the other hand, by ultra-left radical democrats, neo-Trotskyists, as I called them, who insisted on 'immediate transition to full democracy and private property.'
- Communist bosses tried to stop Gorbachev's reforms by force through a *coup d'etat*. They formed a junta, the so-called State Committee for Emergency Situation (GKChP) headed by the vice-president, who obtained all power in the USSR.
- In the USSR nearly all central and regional authorities recognized GKChP, the Parliament of the USSR (Supreme Soviet of the USSR), Government, Ministry of Defence, Ministry of Home Affairs, State Committee for Security, all republics and their leaders: even the Baltic republics took a temporizing position.

In opposition to GKChP stood only one Russian institution of higher power, the Supreme Soviet of Russia, the parliament that was headed by me and the president of Russia, Boris Yeltsin, who had recently been elected. The principal political force that suppressed the GKChP was the Russian parliament, which demanded Gorbachev's release and, supported by Moscow dwellers, rebuffed the claims for dictatorship on the part of the GKChP.

The GKChP dealt a deadly blow to the framework of the USSR and accelerated its downfall or transformation into a confederation of independent states. It is quite possible that if Gorbachev and Yeltsin were not so incompatible, another confederative union of states, not the CIS would have come to life. I consider the following fact to be the most important: after the defeat of the GKChP, nearly 95 percent of Russian society supported the Supreme Soviet of Russia and President Yeltsin: they trusted us and were ready for any reforms that would not worsen people's material situation. An extremely favorable situation was created, Russian reforms were not hindered and there was no opposition, even a communist one, because the powerful party bureaucracy was demoralized and discredited, the population had abandoned it and supported President Yeltsin and the Supreme Soviet of Russia. This unique situation, which emerged after the defeat of the GKChP was stymied by Yeltsin: he appointed complete unknowns to the government; people who were incompetent in economics, knew little about either socialist or capitalist economies and were oriented toward the ideas of overseas economists, who turned out to be casual and dull-witted consultants. It was the government of radical democrats who focused not on creation but on revolutionary destruction. All their energy was directed to the demolition of a huge economic system but not to its reform. Fundamental economic reforms require intelligence, patience, thorough analysis of new realities, catering for the interests of millions of people. Members of Yeltsin's government, as true revolutionaries, strove for immediate results. For example, they announced that 'in six months markets will be saturated and key difficulties will be overcome.' When deputies of the parliament laughed at these ideas, the 'reformers,' as they used to call themselves, took offense and accused us of being incompetent in market reforms.

Their first shattering step was President Yeltsin's decree 'About Economic Reform,' which cancelled price regulation for goods and services, including the consumer sector. It took place in conditions of monopolistic state property and absence of private property. Do you know anything more stupid? As a result of this step, prices for goods rose a thousandfold, people's savings became worthless and the whole population of the country became poor. A month passed and people who had trusted us began to hate Yeltsin and his government and to a lesser extent the parliament, because people knew my views and especially the demand of the parliament to carry out privatization first and only after that to pass to free prices. Yeltsin and his government began to panic, but 'clever people,' including former party functionaries proposed a 'reliable way out,' searching for an internal enemy – and labeling the Supreme Soviet as this internal enemy because it resisted Yeltsin's reforms. Therefore, Yeltsin's followers changed their focus from economic reforms to political issues. They started to promote the idea of rapid adoption of a new constitution, which gave dictatorial authorities to Yeltsin. The West, as well as the US, began to see the conflict as between Yeltsin, a 'reformer,' and 'communist deputies' who wanted to return the country to Soviet times. They did not want to know that the parliament demanded from the executive only the power to conduct reforms in a professional manner and to observe laws that were signed by President Yeltsin.

Consequences

In this way, the support of Western public opinion and governments created the situation that led to a Kremlin putsch against the Russian parliament in autumn 1993. I think this was the first act of terrorism in the history of the new Russia. A year later the Chechen war was unleashed, initiated by Yeltsin's followers in order to strengthen their weakening positions in society and to distract people's attention from their extremely poor material circumstances. I am absolutely sure that this war would not have been feasible without the events of autumn 1993.

After the forcible overthrow of parliamentary democracy in Russia, similar events took place in the Central Asian republics. Russia and these new states quickly adopted new constitutions of an autocratic and, to be more precise, semi-dictatorial nature but the West did not pay attention to that. And only recently, in connection with some of Putin's steps, have several influential politicians voiced criticism. Where were they 11 years ago? They do not seem to understand that Yeltsin's constitution of December 1993 allows the President of Russia to carry out reforms without violation of the constitution. I think that we should criticize not only President Putin, but also the 'democratic constitution' that, since December 1993, 'has delighted' Western leaders.

I would not like to dwell upon acute political problems, I would rather draw the reader's attention to other specific features of Russia's capitalist economic system, which, in view of the situation around the oil company YUKOS, can be more informative. The first after-effect stems from the fact that the formation of Russian capitalism was, from the very beginning, illegal, often criminal, parasitic. Thus it is incapable of fostering market competition and requires the creation of monopolistic conditions that protect against competition and suppress small businessmen. The second after-effect is that the creation of such large firms gave rise to Russian monopolies that are incapable of competition and that replace Ricardo's formula of capital accumulation 'Money–Product–Money' with the exclusively Russian one 'Money–Power–Money.' Nowhere else in the world would you be able to watch the operation of this formula. The first two caused the third after-effect. There is an unprecedented level of corruption in all echelons of power and in all business. Since the initial moments of new Russian entrepreneurship, corruption has been its typical feature. Its elimination or decrease to a normal level is an enormous task for Putin. The fourth after-effect is the artificial creation of the so-called oligarchs. In the creation of capitalism, the state did not pay sufficient attention to creating conditions for the development of business on the basis of universal laws, but instituted directly-appointed oligarchs, that is, allocated factors of production, factories, capital, labour, land, privileges, to certain individuals.

In general these 'reforms' were not connected with Shumpeter's ideas about creative destruction of the system, where disruptive elements simultaneously exert creative effect on the existing material base. Reformers deliberately destroyed this base. They did not even try to restructure it on a rational basis. At the same time through the efforts of dull reformers and mediocre foreign consultants the ugliest features of nineteenth-century capitalism were introduced into the new system, including disrespect for workers and society, neglect of law and use of ideological methods against forces opposing the economic policy pursued by Yeltsin.

Russia's bureaucratic model of capitalism has created millionaires and billionaires, but has not developed their business abilities. A Russian Ford, Morgan or Gates unfortunately has not emerged. Our large corporations and their top management are not interested in the creation of full-scale competition or a real market economy guided by demand and supply. Market mechanisms were replaced by close contacts with the government and local bureaucracy. Thus, they were not interested even in setting up a standard capitalist economic system with small and medium-sized business as a foundation of this system. This model could be called private bureaucratic capitalism, in contrast to the state monopolistic economic system that existed before August 1991.

This type of development leads to social stratification through the process of concentrating wealth in the hands of a narrow group of well-known businessmen which is simultaneous with the impoverishment of the majority of the population. It should be noted that in Russia the Gini is the same as in Latin American countries. This means that Russian society is characterized by a high degree of social stratification: a narrow group of capitalists and bankers rule in finance and economic life; medium-sized business is underdeveloped; small business is struggling for survival, as it is under strong fiscal pressure from the government, police and criminals. A middle class is absent, as the incomes of those who would constitute a middle class are too low.

Lessons of Russian economic reforms for American economic theory and policy

The US has spent vast sums supporting economic reforms in Russia, without result. What caused this failure, which cost the people of Russia so much? I do not think that it can be a conspiracy against Russia aimed at its weakening and even disintegration, although this is suggested now and then. The cause is that leading circles in Russia and the US adhered to simplistic ideas about swift and effective transition from socialism to capitalism, although neither country had the slightest experience of this at the level and scale of Russia.

Bias on the part of certain Russian economists and politicians and serious efforts by the Russian parliament showed that the possible failures of Yeltsin's policy were viewed in Washington as attempts to restore communism. The IMF and foreign consultants were involved in ideological struggles in the country, and, instead of fostering national consensus in the field of national reforms, they began to impose them on society by force. The consequences of such reforms can be illustrated by the dramatic example of

YUKOS, which is based on the illegal denationalization of the economy. The foundation of this drama was laid when tanks shot at the parliament on 4 October 1993. Privatization was conducted by decrees of executive bodies, not by parliamentary laws and even contrary to some laws that had been adopted by the parliament earlier.

These lessons should be noted not only in Russia but in the US too. America will continue to play the role of the leader in world economic policy and international economic relations. The US will influence the policy of such important international organizations as the WTO and IMF. Thus it is necessary to assess the experience of economic reforms in Russia and other countries. Possessing huge financial power and opportunities, the IMF has not achieved stable positive results in any country. The policies of the Fund seem to rest upon vicious, outdated, inadequate concepts. In nearly all countries, its policy prescriptions include:

- Withdrawal of the state from the economy, even when there are inadequate private corporations, financial markets, competition, and so on;
- Cutting the deficit at extremely fast speed, irrespective of the drop in people's standard of living;
- Raising domestic prices to the level of world prices, which always leads to the destruction of agriculture and light industry;
- Opening markets, and so on.

All these requirements were reasonable, but they assumed the existence of the basic institutions of a market economy and ignored the fact that these did not exist in Russia and that they should have been formed prior to taking the above-mentioned steps.

These requirements were almost always disastrous – for other countries as well as for Russia – but their leaders usually agreed to them, for various reasons – some were in despair and were ready to accept any conditions, others believed that such a powerful organization as the IMF could give only good recommendations. The majority of these conditions have never been fulfilled and the reasons for this non-fulfillment have never been studied, which is strange. As a result, the IMF was not able to become a respectable international consultant, one whose recommendations could have serious stabilizing effects.

We should differentiate between spheres of private business, and try not to idealize business relations or introduce them into fields of social life where they are inappropriate. For instance, in Russia energetic steps are being taken to transfer the public health system and educational institutions to the private sector, justifying the transfer by the fact that in America it is the usual practice. Very often, the contrast is drawn between business and bureaucratic states, saying that business is always good and state is always bad. These arguments do not take into account that in the absence of serious regulatory mechanisms and insufficient protection of workers' rights, with low wages and weak democracy, business can become a greater exploiter of the poor than can the state. This policy has already had grave results. The quality of medical treatment is decreasing, it is unaffordable for the majority of the Russian population. The situation in secondary and higher education is worsening. I would like to ask a question: why are we not discussing the issue of transferring the functions of national defense, police and security to private companies? Why does society rely only on the state in this very important sphere? And why do we economists treat so thoughtlessly the education of the younger generation, the health of people and their culture and even try to engender a false idea, that private companies can cope with this task better than the state? Perhaps, in wealthy countries, which had already, in the seventeenth and eighteenth centuries, created effective systems of education and health care, which have established traditions of private medical services and education, it is acceptable, but why should this model be imposed on all countries as a progressive one, while it fosters, at least in Russia and other CIS countries, the degradation of institutions of public health, education and culture? These problems should be solved through differentiation, with due regard for the level of development, traditions, availability of social infrastructure and many other factors. The universal approach to economic reforms on the basis of similar requirements always leads to negative results, or to negligible positive result obtained at high costs. It is obvious that recommendations that could bring positive results in the Czech Republic and Poland would not be useful for Russia or the former republics of Central Asia. And it can be ridiculous to demand the execution of similar steps in the countries of Latin America, Africa or ASEAN.

In countries where there is no market environment or where market institutions are lacking and the market infrastructure is underdeveloped, policy recommendations which anticipate reaching the level of America are the same as asking countries to commit suicide. But the IMF advanced these requirements throughout the transformation era of the 1990s. I am absolutely sure that if IMF experts and top management of the Fund in general had had well-developed programs of economic reforms in respect of the USSR and Eastern Europe their results would have been different and today's social and economic standing of Russian citizens would have been much higher than it is.

Frankly speaking, today there are two key directions in economic thought and two models of economic policy: the American and European. There are no Asian, Japanese, Chinese or Russian, African, Latin American theories. I am not going to humiliate any countries, but this reflects the realities of capitalist economic history. Capitalism emerged in Western Europe and colonists brought its elements to the US from Western Europe. Therefore on these two continents it acquired its classical forms. In all other regions – Asia,

Africa, Latin America, Russia and Japan – capitalism had the nature of a transferred social and economic system.

This means, from my point of view, that the development of two types of capitalism, Western European and American, does not differ. We can speak of shades, and these shades are very important, and, together with geographic, geopolitical and other differences between America and the European Union, they become more and more significant. On this basis we can draw the following conclusions:

- Competition between American and Western European economic schools has a positive impact fostering the progress of theory;
- There are doubts that key provisions of economic policy pursued by the American government, in particular ideas of global monetarism have a constructive character for European countries;
- These doubts are growing, if we consider the consequences of their application in Russia and many developing countries;
- For countries like Russia it is necessary to develop an adequate economic policy on the basis of traditional Russian, American and European economic schools. It should be a combination of traditional Russian, Keynesian and neoclassical monetary approaches in order to influence economic growth and development.

The globalization of financial and trade markets has reached its peak, speeding up the linking of national economies and making the world economy vulnerable to shocks in any industry or region. By the beginning of the twenty-first century a new global system had been shaped, for which an adequate universal regulatory system is an imperative. The Bretton Woods institutions, established to regulate the post-war economic order, as it was conceived after World War II, cannot operate in modern conditions. The policy of universal liberalization and global monetarism as the key instrument of world regulation is no longer effective. In this connection I can reach the following conclusion: global monetarism having completed its historical role is no longer an adequate instrument for regulating financial and economic processes in the twenty-first century. Perhaps we should speak about the development of a new international economic policy on the basis of neo-Keynesianism and monetarism with clear supranational regulation. Our world is volatile and each era needs a new economic order. The economic order established in the 1990s was not the result of thorough preparation conducted by the best representatives of mankind. It emerged all of a sudden. I do not think it is correct to attribute the downfall of world socialism to the cunning ideas of certain leaders or the intrigues of secret services. Contradictions within socialism turned out to be unsolvable for its leaders. The combination of different objective and subjective circumstances, internal and international conditions and factors, all this has led to the absolute predominance of the capitalist economic system. Apart from the obvious positive results of this phenomenon, the disappearance of world socialism can also have negative consequences for triumphant capitalism. One of these consequences is the disappearance of competition in the world economic system. Earlier, when the global economic system consisted of two world economic subsystems, capitalist and socialist, keen competition existed between them in efficiency, social policy, help to developing countries, lifestyle, standard of living and so on. This struggle and competition between systems made world capitalism act in a more organized and effective way. Actually, it played the role of a powerful regulator in the most developed segment of world capitalism.

What can replace this global competition today? Not the WTO and IMF. Perhaps the economic interests of some countries? This is an important factor, but it is not sufficient to replace the former global competition. Moreover, the concept of interests of countries can be interpreted in a narrow way, representing the limited ideas of their leaders. It is not enough to attain world economic harmony. I think that other qualitative approaches are necessary, that is, another paradigm of policy. In this respect we should mention two points: first, actual understanding of the current world economic situation in all its complexity and second, realization of the fact that this world economic situation requires a complete revision of the existing mechanism and development of a new, adequate global mechanism of regulation. Stability of the world economy is to some extent deformed by global political instability. For example, local wars, from the twentieth to the twenty-first century, destabilize the system of political relations. This instability in turn affects the stability of the world economy, deforms the economic cycle and neutralizes measures aimed at stabilization.

Neither wars nor trade in arms, which often get to the wrong people, correspond to the logic of twenty-first century world policy, and we should give them up as instruments of solving any problems. For example, what is the difference between trade in arms and trade in drugs? But the existing system of the UN with its Security Council cannot solve the problems of war and peace. Without a powerful institution that will solve these problems, the modern world is doomed, we can hardly rely on the wisdom of national leaders. These issues have become so important that they cannot be ignored by the international economic community. Due to their universal significance they need an international mechanism of regulation through suprastate institutional mechanisms.

In the field of international relations, destruction of the two-pole military and political balance has led not to their expected improvement but to numerous local conflicts and more intense terrorist acts. In this respect I am sure that economists have to research more thoroughly the social roots of the growing alienation between West and East. The poverty of vast masses of people, growing inequality and injustice of the world order for the majority of poor peoples and countries, which are exacerbated by local corruption, are reasons for the above mentioned alienation. We should look for the cause of international terrorism in this alienation and forget the myths of Muslim, Christian or Jewish terrorism. This is a non-constructive approach, the same as ideas about clashes of civilizations, which in spite of their appeal have no serious foundation.

I am sure that the world economic community, with the active participation of scientists from all countries should discuss and work out reforms in the system of world cooperation that can promote a gradual elimination of the problems of alienation between East and West, West and South.

12

Why Russia Cannot Abide the American Economic Model: Round Peg/Square Hole

Steven Rosefielde

Introduction

The American economic experience is a useful guide for Eastern Europe, if properly understood. The United States has grown at appropriately 3.3 percent per annum since 1820. It is a mass consumption society that has successfully assimilated successive waves of polyglot immigration, with an entrepreneurial culture rooted in the rule of law and economic liberty offering high living standards, equal opportunity and social justice. The US experience demonstrates the virtues of democratic free enterprise, private property, and entrepreneurial vigor, combined with a business-friendly welfare state. It shows that Adam Smith can cohabit with government regulators without impoverishing the nation.

The American model as idealized by Vilfredo Pareto, Kenneth Arrow and Abram Bergson (PAB model) also provides a worthy paradigm (Bergson, 1938, 1948, 1954, 1966, 1967, 1976; Samuelson, 1977, 1981; Arrow, 1963, 1981). It can accommodate a spectrum of efficient models from libertarianism to social democracy. If economies abide strictly by its axioms, then outcomes are likely to be favorable. But the assumptions of PAB are seldom satisfied, and consequently performance depends critically on cultural factors such as attitudes, norms and rules, particularly those governing personal conduct and governance in the public domain, referred to hereafter as public culture. They cause the American system to deviate from its ideal, and therefore no one should be surprised that the same may be true in other cultures.

Foreign leaders considering borrowing aspects of the American experience, or the PAB model, consequently must finely calibrate costs and benefits, taking full account of their nation's cultural particularities. Post-Soviet Russia suggests that this may be a dismal exercise. PAB never stood a chance in Muscovy. Balloting, business, entrepreneurship, private property and markets were introduced, but swiftly subordinated to illiberal ends. Instead of serving as the foundation for Pareto-efficient social welfare enhancement, they were pressed into the unjust service of authoritarian rent-granting. Eastern Europe is doing better, but must pay careful attention to its own cultural vulnerabilities. Neither American economic arrangements nor PAB is a panacea.

The American model

America prides itself on its democratic free enterprise. The Founding Fathers, influenced by the *philosophes* and by Adam Smith, believed that all men were created equal, that they have an inalienable right to own property and to apply their talents in the pursuit of happiness under the rule of contract law, without unwarranted government intervention. They held that the best governments governed least, in accordance with the people's democratic will. These ideals are the pillars of contemporary Paretian welfare economics. Like the *philosophes*, Pareto assumed that people have well defined, orderly tastes and act rationally upon them (Pareto, 1906). They always choose the goods they prefer whether operating alone in a rude state of nature or engaging in honest exchange. Their preferences are transitive. They never acquire goods they do not prefer at prevailing prices, unless mistaken and then learn from the experience. They comprehensively search the opportunity space in education, training, employment, production, distribution, finance and transfers. And since each individual optimizes, and utility maximizes within his budget constraint, under the rule of contract law, everyone is best off, and social welfare maximized in this sense.

It is often alleged that Paretian transactions are selfish, but this need not be so. Adam Smith admonished liberals to be moral, compassionate and charitable in their private dealings and where appropriate through the actions of democratic government (Smith, 1759; Griswold, 1999).

Consumers in Pareto-optimal models are always sovereign in the market place, and determine the State's provision of public goods within the limits imposed by Arrow's paradox. Abram Bergson and Paul Samuelson, moreover, have shown that a voluntary contracting framework is also compatible with a larger class of Pareto optima where 'system directors' modify initial conditions for this or that purpose. For example, they might prefer an egalitarian outcome where the population is progressively taxed, with the proceeds redistributed as lump sum dividends. And Bergson and Samuelson have shown further that these adjustments can be 'scientifically' made and evaluated with well behaved social welfare functions, findings which informed James Meade's concept of a just society and undergird European Union social democracy (Meade, 1976). Clearly, a nation that does not abide by PAB norms of efficiency has something to learn from them, unless its leaders are paternalists or despots.

Public culture

But we should not conflate theory with practice. As Pareto himself understood, the rationalist assumptions of PAB are never satisfied (Pareto, 1896–97, 1916). Human behavior is partly governed by passions, addiction and psychopathologies. People are forced to operate with incomplete information, and to deal with imponderables. Deficiencies of this sort, however, are easily brushed aside. Instead of claiming that PAB is ideal, theorists merely assert that it is best given human foibles and bounded rationality. Nor are they disheartened by monopolistic and oligopolistic distortions or corruption, arguing that democratic free enterprise is its own best defense.

Both arguments have some merit in virtuous cultures. If people adhere to a Lockean social contract, acting scrupulously in accordance with the Christian and Confucian golden rules, and strive to be as rational as they can, then the shortcomings of PAB should not be severe. Outcomes in other less hospitable cultures, however, may be degenerate. Bounded rationality works because it assumes that individuals, businessmen, social activists, politicians and governments are moral, judicious and wise in accordance with the credo of democratic free enterprise or social democracy. But if the public culture guiding private action in the social domain and government policy-making is notably tolerant of participant misconduct, stressing ritual persuasion such as appeals to ideals, emotions, opportunistic self-interest, concepts and symbols, over science, reasoned discourse and balanced judgments, then all bets are off. The rationalistic structure of PAB crumbles. Rent-granting, market power, and corruption may displace fair competition, severing the link between value added and compensation. Business may produce shoddy goods, and people may be beguiled into purchasing things they do not really want. Government bureaucracies may be self-serving, and proclaimed state policies may mask hidden agendas. Even worse, decision-makers of all stripes may be so befuddled by their webs of deceit that they cannot discern the national interest even if they desire to do so.

The discrepancies between the lofty ideals proclaimed by leaders and saluted by the people on one hand, and unprincipled behavior originating in individuals but condoned by public culture on the other, are apparent in American factionalization, governance, and economic misconduct, although few fully appreciate the contradictions. Most see the faults in their rivals' attitudes, symbols and loyalties better than in their own.

The resulting biases are not easily dispelled in American public culture by enhanced information, science, and public discourse because the body politic is misinformed, addicted to partisan ritual and superficial thinking, and is misled. What passes for knowledge from private and government sources too often is a pale semblance of the truth: a virtual reality deadened to dangers and opportunities. It is a perverse case of the tail wagging the dog. Free enterprise and democratic theory, the touchstones of the

American credo teach that people are able to see through the snares of public culture, maximizing utility in private and public domains. But they cannot do either if they are wrongly-informed, mis-educated, and deluded.

The fact that America on balance is a success story despite its self-inflicted wounds should be encouraging to other nations with their own imperfect public cultures. Apparently PAB can withstand considerable abuse. The G-7 conviction that any kind of democracy and market is virtuous enough to generate prosperity and bring living standards in less developed countries to the high global frontier may partly reflect this experience. This is precisely the position recently taken by Andrei Shleifer and Daniel Treisman in their controversial *Foreign Affairs* article 'A Normal Country,' which hails Russia's post-Soviet 'democratic market transition' as a great triumph. If they are right, then Eastern Europe can throw caution to the wind in appropriating anything it likes from the American experience and PAB. But a close scrutiny of the facts shows the need for caution.

'Normal' Russia

Andrei Shleifer and Daniel Treisman have tried to rewrite history (Shleifer and Treisman, 2004; Shleifer, 2005; Rosefielde, 2005a).[1] At a time when serious scholars and analysts agree that Russia's feeble democratization has misfired (Tenet, 2004); when the state has reasserted control over the media, and the security services, especially the FSB, have become the dominant force in the government,[2] they tell us that Russia has 'changed from a dictatorship to a multiparty democracy in which officials are chosen in regular elections.'

When there is increasing awareness that Russia is ramping up for a major military modernization drive (Rosefielde, 2005b), they remind us that it has withdrawn its army from Eastern Europe and the former Soviet republics; when Russia is developing new ballistic missiles to outmaneuver America's national missile defense (NMD),[3] and maintains 40,000 retargetable nuclear weapons, more with the simple reinsertion of nuclear triggers, they discover a reliable partner for peace. When Russia still finds itself mired in hyper-depression (GDP officially acknowledged to be approximately 23 percent below 1989[4]), having sustained 3.4 million excess deaths 1990–98 (Rosefielde, 2001), and unemployment in the vicinity of 25 percent during the 1990s (Rosefielde, 2000),[5] with a vast 'virtual' economy serving a tiny coterie of oligarchs and kleptocrats, they enthuse that Russia's 'centrally planned economy has been reshaped into a capitalist order based on markets and private property,' claiming that 'although economic output fell initially after the Soviet Union collapsed, plausible estimates suggest that the decline had been reversed by 2003.' No data show this; neither Goskomstat's nor any international organization's. Plausibility, it seems is whatever Shleifer and Treisman assert.[6]

Russia's re-invention, they contend, is a cause for celebration, because it has become a normal country, [7]just as Shleifer, the World Bank, the IMF and the EBRD have persistently maintained since 1995,[8] the year that Anders Aslund, in the spirit of the Washington consensus,[9] first revealed to the world that Russia had become a capitalist market economy (Aslund, 1995).

Shleifer and Treisman then proceed to substantiate their hypothesis with official economic statistics, much the way the CIA did during the Cold War when it failed to foresee the Soviet Union's impending demise (Rosefielde, 2003, 2004a, 2005b).[10] They adjust statistics to taste, and then make improper comparisons to show that the behavior implied proves 'normalcy.' Their assertion that Russian GDP has recovered to the 1991 level illustrates the first technique, and comparisons with Argentina (1991) and Mexico (1999) exemplify the latter. We are expected to accept that 'normal' Argentina and Mexico provide sound benchmarks for gauging the 'normalcy' of Russia because both are 'middle-income countries' with GDP per capita around $8000 at purchasing power parity, neglecting to mention that former Goskomstat expert Aleksei Ponomarenko's estimate is closer to $5000, and the CIA's figure in current prices exceeds $20,000.[11] Purchasing power parity estimates are sensitive to assumptions. When the Soviet Union or Russia is made to look good, this is opaquely accomplished by assuming that rust belt goods and inferior services are world class.

Soviet-era goods and services produced in the 'virtual economy,' as Clifford Gaddy and Barry Ickes portray it (Gaddy and Ickes, 2002),[12] were anything but world class, to say nothing of the 23 percent of Russian GDP for which Ponomarenko and academician Valery Makarov acknowledge Goskomstat has no data. They are non-comparable precisely because the Russian system is abnormal.

Shleifer and Treisman concede that Soviet-era goods were shoddy. They could not deny it and still support their claim for a capitalist miracle. But in sharp contrast to Gaddy and Ickes, they contend that yesterday's worst goods have already been transmuted into today's best, even though investment in these sectors has been negligible. This enables them to argue, as they did in the early 1990s, that Goskomstat exaggerated Russia's hyper-depression because the guns and shoddy goods lost were worthless, despite the Kremlin's status as the world's second largest arms exporter. Indeed, some contended that the value added of Soviet goods was actually value subtracted,[13] so the steeper the decline the better the outcome.

It is also claimed that Russia's hyper-depression has been exaggerated by over-reporting during the communist period and under-reporting thereafter, without any serious effort at quantification. Are Shleifer and Treisman really contending that the Genshtab (Soviet General Staff) tolerated these abuses in the military industrial complex? They make no effort to prove it. Since Vitaly Shlykov, former deputy chairman of the Russian Security

Council, and academician Yuri Yaremenko, who audited the numbers for the Politburo, put defense spending at 30 percent of GDP in the late 1980s, fraud in the military sector matters. Nor do they acknowledge that Roskomstat made allowances for some of these alleged biases. They neglect to factor in the 'second economy' production omitted from Soviet production, showcase electricity consumption as a reliable proxy for economic activity, even though they should know it is not because industrial users paid virtually nothing for electricity during much of the 1990s.[14] The other rules of thumb cited suffer from the same deficiencies, and Shleifer and Treisman fail to seriously consider substitution and index number relativity issues associated with absence of price control. They do not adduce a shred of evidence that has not been previously discredited. Also, it should be noted that Soviet statistics were never consistent or reliable and always exaggerated the performance of the consumption sector. With Russia suffering from mass involuntary unemployment throughout the 1990s, with only token official acknowledgment, it seems reasonable to infer that reports of the good life are drastically overdrawn.

And they save the best for last. The opinion of the majority of experts and Russian human rights activists notwithstanding,[15] Shleifer and Treisman assert that Russia has been wrongly accused of authoritarianism.

Where Grigory Yavlinsky finds...

> There are six major features of Russia which must be taken into account today. First, Russia has no independent judicial system. Second, since December, Russia has no elements of independent parliament. Third, Russia has no parliamentary control or oversight of the secret services and law enforcement agencies. Fourth, Russia has no politically important independent media. Fifth, elections in Russia are manipulated by the government. Sixth, the Russian economy is an instrument of the state.[16]

...they insist: 'Russia's politics have been among the most democratic in the region.'

Muscovite 'democratic free enterprise'

This disregard for counter-evidence stems from the unstated premise that Russian public culture is either similar to America's or is otherwise supportive of democratic free enterprise. Since as they correctly assert, post-communist Russia has borrowed many elements from the PAB model, it is reasonable to expect positive results, even if Muscovite culture is a bit rough around the edges.

What they fail to consider sufficiently is the possibility that the Muscovite autocratic rent-granting traditions, traceable at least as far back as Ivan the

Great (1462–1505), that undergird Russian public culture are fundamentally incompatible with the axioms of PAB. Russian authoritarianism, unlike its Western counterparts is predicated on '*pomestie*' rent-granting, the obverse of rent-seeking, rather than inalienable property and the rule of contract law. Muscovy from the mid-fifteenth century onward has been a patrimonial society where the ruler owned all he surveyed and granted his supporters '*kormlenie*,' feeding troughs, in return for state service (Hedlund, 2005; Pipes, 1999; Gerschenkron, 1961). Czars could and did make gifts of private property, but they were revokable, without the right of judicial appeal. Property and the rule of contract law, accordingly, were always tenuous, raising serious problems of deception, moral hazard and adverse selection. No one in Russia was secure. No one was protected by the rule of contract law, and therefore everyone had erratically and fragmentally to optimize as best he or she could in an imponderable world. Investment, innovation and entrepreneurship were seriously hampered, encouraging the state to compensate for its backwardness with oversized land armies, secret police, and foreign technology transfers.

The dead hand of this tradition is readily apparent in the breakdown of the communist control mechanism under Mikhail Gorbachev and the rapid re-emergence of authoritarian market Muscovy in the late 1990s, both driven by the contradictions of Russian public culture. For a variety of good and bad reasons, Gorbachev introduced a new law on enterprise management in 1987 authorizing red directors to maximize profits by producing optimal assortments at state fixed prices and selling them without limit to the government wholesale network. According to the Langean market socialist version of PAB, this reform should have enhanced efficiency (Lange and Taylor, 1938; Bergson, 1966, 1967; Rosefielde, 1986), and it would have in a regime governed by American public culture servicing Douglass North's role of 'credible enforcer' (North and Thomas, 1972). However, Russian managers attuned to the coded signals of Muscovite culture sensed that they could now operate as 'roving bandits' (Olson, 2000), acquiring inputs and producing outputs for the managers' own consumption at the expense of profits. And when this misappropriation went unchastized, they began 'spontaneously' privatizing assets, liquidating them where they could, and hotwiring the proceeds abroad.

The threat of roving bandits had always been the other side of the coin of the Muscovite model and in this instance swiftly lead to the Soviet Union's collapse, creating an opportunity for a post-communist transition to PAB. Boris Yeltsin, Russia's first president proclaimed this to be his goal. He would decriminalize business, entrepreneurship and private ownership, free prices, promote market competition, install the rule of contract law, float the ruble, and establish an open economy for goods, services and financial flows. Had he been sincere, and if Russia's public culture were American, the federation would have become the 'normal country' of Shliefer's and

Treisman's desiring. But there is no place in Muscovite culture for the rule of contract law, free and fair competition, equal opportunity, democratic sovereignty over public programs, or inalienable private property rights, and Russia's post-Soviet economic system cannot be PAB. Russia can have markets and asymmetrically negotiated prices, but Muscovy and PAB cannot coexist. It could and did borrow from the American experience, but harnessed Western institutions to Muscovite ends.

The *catastroika* that ensued chastened some, but most disciples of PAB steadfastly insisted that the era of roving banditry would pass, replaced by democratic free enterprise or social democracy (Fischer and Sahay, 2004). But once again cultural blinkers led them astray. Vladimir Putin, who headed the secret police, engineered a palace *coup d'etat* that culminated in the suppression of democracy, a controlled media, the destruction of Yeltsin's roving bandits replaced by his own coterie of subservient rent-seekers, and the restoration of a veiled martial police state by 2004 (Blank, 2004; Rosefielde, 2004b). Thus while Muscovy borrowed the rhetoric of PAB and successfully used this to its advantage with the West, it also lashed itself to a model that fabulously enriches privileged insiders to society's detriment.

Why Russia cannot abide the American model

Russian leaders cannot abide the American economic way because they are unwilling to relinquish their privileged control over men, resources, assets, and enterprise. Consumer sovereignty in the private sector, and popular sovereignty over public goods mutually exclude authoritarian Moscovite sovereignty. Russia's rulers have always desired to achieve the technical efficiencies of the West through markets, plans and mixed arrangements, but they have never seriously considered abandoning their ultimate power and control. They have been willing to embrace the rhetoric of democratic free enterprise, but not its substance, making concessions to the market only insofar as they advanced aspects of the authoritarian agenda. Power under the Muscovite scheme does not emanate from monopolistic machinations, but from the discretely camouflaged barrel of the gun. Muscovy is inseparable from the martial police state because it cannot maintain its authority through its superior economic and political merit. Its leaders could have a change of heart, but until they join the Enlightenment in earnest, they will never abide the American way.

Similar problems could beset other transition societies with aberrant public cultures. The Russian example proves conclusively that borrowing from the American experience and aspects of PAB does not assure happy endings for the majorities in many systems, obligating responsible East European leaders to delve beneath the façade of their own national credos to a dry-eyed assessment of costs and benefits (Ellman, 2004).

Conclusions

Many advocates of PAB know that human behavior is more complex than its axioms postulate, but nonetheless contend that their approach yields better results than do alternatives and should be emulated. The same reasoning based on past American performance and concepts such as bounded rationality makes it seem that transitioning countries should emulate democratic free enterprise or European Union social democracy without concern for the particularities of their public cultures.

A thorough review of Russia's warped post-Soviet marketization process however proves that there are ample grounds for caution. Contrary to Sheifer's and Treisman's characterization, Russia remains an abnormal country, in many ways as abhorrent as its Soviet and Czarist predecessors because the aspects of PAB Yeltsin and Putin adopted were hijacked by Muscovite culture. The majority of the Russian people are far worse off than they would have been if American public culture were somehow substituted for the Muscovite alternative. Despite all its conspicuous shortcomings, American public culture is not authoritarian, and does not have the extremely inegalitarian and unjust features of Russia's veiled martial police state. It offers superior opportunity, entrepreneurship, property rights protection, and fairer outcomes under the rule of law. Its micro and macroeconomic regulators are less corrupt and more concerned with social welfare. There is more effective social activism and personal freedom. Despite Putin's rhetoric about Russia's unbounded economic prospects, living standards in Muscovy for the vast majority are more likely to fall farther behind America's than to converge with them.

Eastern Europe, particularly Poland, Hungary and the Czech Republic are doing better than Russia and perhaps are destined to succeed where Moscow has failed, but still the Russian experience shows that PAB is not always path-dependent.

Notes

1. Lawrence Summers and Stanley Fisher expressed views similar to Shleifer and Treisman at the American Economics Association meetings, 4 January 2003. John Odling-Smee, former Director of the IMF's European II Department 1992–2003 shares the same outlook. Also see Fischer and Sahay (2004).
2. Compare Arkady Ostrovsky (2004), 'Is Russian Democracy becoming an Illusion', *Financial Times*, reprinted in *Johnson's Russia List*, No. 8042, Article 13, February 2004.
3. 'New Russian Missiles to Outwit US Defenses', *Krasnaya Zvezda*, 25 February 2004, reprinted in *Johnson's Russia List*, No. 8093, 1 March 2004. Russian forces will have the new missile, which will act like a swarm of bees against America's umbrella defense system by 2010.

4. United Nations (2005), *Economic Survey of Europe*, United Nations, No. 1, 2005, Appendix Table B. 1, p. 128.
5. S. Rosefielde (2000). At the end of 2003, 8.6 percent of Russia's economically active population (6.2 million people) were unemployed. The labor force was 65.2 million. But adjustment for discouraged workers puts the figure in the teens.
6. Shleifer and Treisman use 1991 as their benchmark, disregarding the 7.8 percent decline from 1989–91, when Russia's hyper-depression began. GDP 1991–2003 fell 19 percent on this measure. For comparison, American GDP plummeted 27.5 during the Great Depression 1929–33.
7. A. Aslund (1997), 'Russia Gets on Track to Be a Normal Country', *International Herald Tribune*, 19 March 1997, 8.
8. Shleifer was found guilty of violating the US False Claims Act in his dealings with the Russian government. See 'Harvard Professor, Employee Liable in Fraud Case', *Boston Globe*, 29 June 2004. From 1992 to 1997 Shleifer headed the (now defunct) Harvard Institute for International Development project to reform the Russian economy.
9. The Washington consensus refers narrowly to macroeconomic policies which stress financial discipline, and broadly to the advocacy of democratic free enterprise. J. Williamson (1989, 1993, 2002).
10. The CIA and many Sovietologists are still in denial. See Berkowitz et al. (1993) as well as Firth and Noren (1998).
11. S. Rosefielde (1998), Table 1, pp. xxii-xxiii. CIA (1992), Tables 7 and 21, pp. 25 and 39. The CIA's estimate for 1989 Russian per capita GDP in 1991 dollars was 15,631. Ponomarenko's figure for 1995 when production was 22 percent below 2003 was $3750.
12. The term 'virtual' refers to old Soviet physical production relations underlying the visible market economy, and applies to most of the industrial, agricultural, and public service sectors. It has another important resonance, suggesting that official statistics provide an unrealistically rosy impression of Russian economic performance.
13. Value added is the contribution primary factors of production make to raw materials. The claim that value has been subtracted means that processing diminishes the worth of raw materials. During Soviet rule this sometimes happened, but the incidence was small. For a brief time in the 1990s it became fashionable to conflate true value subtracted with differences in tastes. Soviet systems directors wanted and got goods with characteristics westerners did not esteem, but this didn't mean that processing reduced the Kremlin's utility.
14. Academician Valery Makarov, Director of the Central Economics and Mathematics Institute noted a decade ago that electricity is a small input into industrial production, and cannot serve as a reliable proxy for economic activity.
15. Sergei Kovalyov, a human rights legend, who spent 10 years in the Gulag, recently wrote, 'It turned out that 13 years after the fall of the Soviet Union, the society does not require democracy.' See Anna Badkhen, 'Democracy on the Brink: Russia Back on Track of Absolute Rule', *Johnson's Russia List*, No. 8109, Article 1, 10 March 2004. Compare Stephen Blank, 'Is Russia a Democracy and Does It Matter?' unpublished manuscript April 2004.
16. Grigory Yavlinsky, Chairman of the Russian Democratic Party Yabloko, 'Russia: Before and After the Elections', Carnegie Endowment for International Peace, 26 February 2004, reprinted in *Johnson's Russia List*, No. 8107, Article 11, 10 March 2004. The citation in the text is paraphrased.

References

Arrow, K. (1963), *Social Choice and Individual Values*, 2nd edn, New York: Wiley.

Arrow, K. (1981), 'Optimal and Voluntary Income Distribution', in Steven Rosefielde (ed.), *Economic Welfare and the Economics of Soviet Socialism*, Cambridge: Cambridge University Press, pp. 267–88.

Aslund, A. (1995), *How Russia Became a Market Economy*, Washington, DC: Brookings Institution.

Bergson, A. (1938), 'A Reformulation of Certain Aspects of Welfare Economics', *Quarterly Journal of Economics*, 52(1), February, 310–34.

Bergson, A. (1948), 'Socialist Economics', in H. Ellis (ed.), *A Survey of Contemporary Economics*, Homewood, Illinois: Richard D. Irwin, pp. 412–48.

Bergson, A. (1954), 'The Concept of Social Welfare', *Quarterly Journal of Economics*, 68(2), May, 233–52.

Bergson, A. (1966), *Essays in Normative Economics*, Cambridge, MA: Harvard University Press.

Bergson, A. (1967), 'Market Socialism Revisited', *Journal of Political Economy*, 75(4), October, 655–73.

Bergson, A. (1976), 'Social Choice and Welfare Economics under Representative Government', *Journal of Public Economics*, 6(3), October, 171–90.

Berkowitz, D., J. Berliner, P. Gregory, S. Linz and J. Millar (1993), 'An Evaluation of the CIA's Analysis of Soviet Economic Performance, 1970–1990', *Comparative Economic Studies*, 35(2), Summer, 33–48.

Blank, S. (2004), 'The 18th Brumaire of Vladimir Putin', paper presented at the conference on Succession Crises in Russia, Boston University, Institute for the Study of Conflict, Ideology, and Policy, Boston, April 20.

CIA (1992), *Handbook of International Economic Statistics*, CPAS92-0005, September.

Ellman, M. (2004), 'Russian Economic Boom, Post-1998: Illusion, Miracle or Recovery?' *Economic and Political Weekly*, XXXIX(29), 17–23 July, 3234–7.

Firth, N. and J. Noren (1998), *Soviet Defense Spending: a History of CIA Estimates, 1950–1990*, College Station: Texas A&M University.

Fischer, S. and R. Sahay (2004), 'Transition Economies: the Role of Institutional and Initial Conditions', Festschrift in Honor of Guillermo A. Calvo, April 15–16.

Gaddy, C. and B. Ickes (2002), *Russia's Virtual Economy*, Washington, DC: Brookings Institution.

Gerschenkron, Alexander (1961), *Economic Backwardness in Historical Perspective*, Cambridge, MA: Harvard University Press.

Griswold, Ch. L. Jr (1999), *Adam Smith and the Virtues of Enlightenment*, London: Cambridge University Press.

Hedlund, S. (2005), *Russian Path Dependency*, London: Routledge.

Lange, O. and F.M. Taylor (1938), *On the Economic Theory of Socialism*, Minneapolis: University of Minnesota Press.

Meade, M. (1976), *The Just Economy*, London: George Allen and Unwin.

North, D. and R. Thomas (1972), *The Rise of the Western World*, London: Cambridge University Press.

Olson, M. (2000), *Power and Prosperity: Outgrowing Capitalist and Communist Dictatorships*, New York: Basic Books.

Pareto, V. (1896–7), *Cours d'economie politique professe a l'universite de Lausanne.*

Pareto, V. (1906), *Manual of Political Economy.*

Pareto, V. (1916), *Trattato di Sociologia Generale.*

Pipes, R. (1999), *Property and Freedom*, New York: Alfred Knopf.
Rosefielde, S. (1998), *Efficiency and Russia's Economic Recovery Potential to the Year 2000 and Beyond*, Aldershot: Ashgate.
Rosefielde, S. (2000), 'The Civilian Labour Force and Unemployment in the Russian Federation', *Europe-Asia Studies*, 52(8), 1433–47.
Rosefielde, S. (2001), 'Premature Deaths: Russia's Radical Economic Transition in Soviet Perspective', *Europe-Asia Studies*, 53(8), 1159–76.
Rosefielde, S. (2003), 'The Riddle of Postwar Russian Economic Growth: Statistics Lied and Were Misconstrued', *Europe-Asia Studies*, 53(3), 469–81.
Rosefielde, S. (2004a), 'Postwar Russian Economic Growth: Not a Riddle – a Reply', *Europe-Asia Studies*, May 2004, 56(3), 463–6.
Rosefielde, S. (2004b), 'Russia 2084: the Treadmill of Muscovite Radical Reform', paper presented at the FOI Conference 'Whither Russia?' Stockholm, Sweden, May 6–7.
Rosefielde, S. (2005a), 'Russia: an Abnormal Country', *European Journal of Comparative Economics*, 2(1), 3–16.
Rosefielde, S. (2005b), *Russia in the 21st Century: Prodigal Superpower*, Cambridge: Cambridge University Press.
Samuelson, P. (1977), 'Reaffirming the Existence of a "Reasonable" Bergson-Samuelson Social Welfare Function', *Economica*, 44, 81–8.
Samuelson, P. (1981), 'Bergsonian Welfare Economics', in Steven Rosefielde (ed.), *Economic Welfare and the Economics of Soviet Socialism*, Cambridge: Cambridge University Press, pp. 223–66.
Shleifer, A. (2005), *A Normal Country: Russia after Communism*, Cambridge, MA: Harvard University Press.
Shleifer, A. and D. Treisman (2004), 'A Normal Country', *Foreign Affairs*, March/April, 84(2), 20–38.
Smith, A. (1759), *The Theory of Moral Sentiment*, London: A. Millar.
Tenet, G. (2004), 'The Worldwide Threat 2004: Challenges in a Changing Global Context', testimony before the Senate Select Committee on Intelligence, 24 February 2004, Washington DC.
UN (2005), *Economic Survey of Europe*, United Nations, No. 1.
Williamson, J. (1993), 'Democracy and the "Washington Consensus"', *World Development*, 21(8), 1329–36.
Williamson, J. (2002), 'Did the Washington Consensus Fail,' outline of remarks at the Center for Strategic and International Studies, 6 November: http://www.iie.com/publications/papers/williamson1102.htm.
Williamson, J. (1989), 'What Washington Means by Policy Reform', in J. Williamson (ed.), *Latin American Adjustment: How Much Has Happened?* Washington, DC: Institute for International Economics, pp. 5–38.

13

China versus the Orthodoxy: State and Ownership Reforms in Transition Economies

Jeffrey B. Miller and Stoyan Tenev[1]

Introduction

Why has economic transition led to rapid economic growth in China and a sharp initial contraction in Eastern Europe and the former Soviet Union? We argue that the answer, in part, is stronger state control of state enterprises and the privatization process in China where the government had a strong interest in economic growth. Furthermore, in pursuing growth the Chinese government recognized that it had to establish institutional arrangements that constrained its own power, an important requisite for successful governance.

Under central planning, the objectives for enterprise managers were laid out in the central plan. As the transformation process unfolded, the goals for enterprises and the incentives directing managers changed. In an important sense the transformation of enterprises was a two-stage process. First, since it was not possible to apply 'shock therapy' to turn over property rights to private citizens overnight, there had to be a stage where state enterprises operated in an environment where they were released, at least to some degree, from the constraints of the central plan. During this period, state enterprises were subjected to external pressures different from those they had faced under central planning as the environment became more market oriented. This first stage period varied considerably across transition countries and even within countries across sectors. The second stage was the establishment of private property rights. A variety of methods was used to release state assets into private hands. All had implications as to how the wealth represented by state ownership was distributed among citizens.

Privatization, as one of the defining characteristics of the transition process, entails both the emergence of new owners and a fundamental transformation of the role of the state (Brada, 1996). While both issues – the importance of ownership and the role of the state – have each generated an extensive literature, the interactions between the two have received relatively less attention. Is the reform of the state a precondition for successful privatization or is privatization the most effective mechanism to start the process of state reform? How does the political process influence both state reform and ownership changes?

In these, as in other aspects of the transition process, China and Eastern Europe offer contrasting experiences. It has always been a problem incorporating China's experience of ownership and state reform within a common framework including other transition economies. As an outlier, however, China is, perhaps, the most influential observation in the transition data set. As such it is potentially a very valuable observation and a better understanding of China's experience will lead to improvement in our implicit 'model specification' of the reform process.

We argue that there are sharp contrasts between the perceived role of government in Eastern Europe and China and that these contrasts led to very different economic outcomes. Eastern Europe followed an 'orthodox' weak government approach while the Chinese adopted a strong government approach. These differences are apparent in both the first stage of transition when state enterprises were still controlled by the state and in the second stage during the privatization process itself. Under the orthodox approach, state ownership is an obstacle to the introduction of market forces because it is seen as a channel through which the state will use its power to coerce enterprises to pursue non-economic objectives. Privatization is seen as a solution to the problem of state power. Under the strong government approach in China, the government envisioned an important role for itself in managing state enterprises and their reform. Private ownership, at least initially, was seen as a by-product of enterprise restructuring, not as a separate goal in and of itself.

In the next section we discuss why private ownership is not a panacea for weak government. Then we compare the role of government in China and in countries following the orthodox model. This is followed by an analysis of what happened with state assets in the two sets of countries. Then we discuss the issue of Chinese enterprise reform. Since enterprise reform in China is still incomplete, many analysts questions whether the reform will succeed. The last section illustrates the process of building regulatory capacity with examples from capital market reforms in China.

The problem with state ownership and government intervention

The problem of state ownership is typically viewed as emanating from the use of the coercive and redistributive powers of the state to make state-owned enterprises (SOEs) pursue non-economic objectives and to isolate them from the disciplining effects of contractual and regulatory constraints. It is believed that under state ownership the autonomy of the firm will inevitably be undermined (Dahl, 1985). Establishing property rights is therefore to a large extent equivalent to reducing political control (Shleifer, 1994). The problem is perceived as an intrinsic property of state ownership.

In this formulation, however, the problem is a manifestation of the so-called 'paradox of power.'[2] Its roots can be traced ultimately to the inability of the government cum owner to commit itself not to abuse its monopoly over coercion. In the orthodox approach to transition, privatization is seen as a pre-commitment device. The government, like Ulysses realizing his weakness, enters into a Ulysses-type contract with the electorate and binds itself to the mast by privatizing the state-owned companies, establishing in the process a boundary to its control. Privatization, it is believed, thus solves several problems simultaneously. It creates efficient ownership rights, a real government and real markets all in one go. Who exactly the initial new owner is does not matter as long as it is not the state because Coaseian bargains will quickly reallocate property rights to the individuals who value them most. Liberalize and privatize and all the problems will be solved. This was the promise sold to governments and electorates in transition economies in much the same way as nationalization and control were sold as a recipe for prosperity in the socialist experiments of the last century.

Expectations were for the most part disappointed. Private ownership, it was found, was not sufficient and some would argue not even necessary to establish an effective boundary of government control.[3] Under new property arrangements, enterprises continued to be common pool resources and their values dissipated. Markets as a result were largely dysfunctional, especially in the early years of reforms.

The disappointing results suggest that the problems of the state that were supposed to be solved by privatization are not orthogonal to the process and outcomes of privatization. Lack of ability to credible pre-commitment itself reflects serious issues with the internal incentive structure of the government. These issues are likely to have a major impact on the process and outcome of privatization. A government that cannot commit itself not to abuse its coercive and redistributive powers will find it difficult to attract serious investors.[4] The adverse selection problem of a weak government – 'weak' government defined as a government that cannot make a credible pre-commitment – reduced the options for privatization: only economic actors that have de facto physical control over state assets, as was the case with SOE managers in Russia and other transition economies, or were in a position to eliminate downward risks by 'investing' other people's money, as was the case with the investment funds in the Czech Republic, were willing to become owners. Or state assets had to be given away. This is largely what happened in a number of transition economies that followed the orthodox approach.

The problem of state ownership is not, therefore, so much an intrinsic problem of state ownership as such but a problem with the incentive structure of the government. The orthodox approach assumes an inherent conflict between state and society. However as Olson (2000) and others have shown, there are no intrinsic conflicts between the collective interest of the government as an organization and of the society overall. The government as a collective entity also suffers from the deadweight loss that its excessive interventions impose on society in the form of a shrinking tax and regulatory base. Excessive interventions arise in the first place because various government agencies responsible for designing and administering various interventions typically bear only a small fraction of the costs that these interventions impose on the economy. McGuire and Olson (1996, p. 73, italics in the original) have shown that, if the government has a sufficiently encompassing interest, it will be led as if by an invisible hand 'to act in ways that are, to a surprising degree, *consistent with the interests of society*.' Such a government will be able to exercise restraint over the degree of its interventions, including the scope and scale of state ownership, and will also provide, from a social point of view, an optimal amount of public goods.

Thus the causes of abuses and inefficiency associated with state ownership are not fundamentally different from the causes of excessive government intervention. If a rational and pragmatic government internalizes the negative externalities that its interventions impose on the economy, then this government should find it in its interest to refrain from excessive intervention and to stimulate the growth of the economy by the provision of productivity enhancing public goods. Such a government is likely also to recognize its limitations in ensuring an effective use of state assets under its control and is likely, as a result, to try to reduce the extent of state ownership to a level that is more compatible with economic efficiency. With a government whose interests are aligned with the interests of the public, the paradox of power disappears and the differences between the predictions and the outcomes of the helping and grabbing hand models of the government vanish.[5] Thus an alternative to the orthodox approach is to give a high priority to improving the incentive structure of the government. In other words, to make the government a real 'owner,' not only of the enterprise assets under its control, but in general with respect to the impact of its actions on the government's domain.

The state in transition: contrasting outcomes of the political process in China and orthodox transition

To paraphrase Schumpeter, reforms are accidental to the struggle for political leadership in the same way that production is accidental to the pursuit of profit. In post-Mao China, the state was 'valuable' in the light of the chaos that reigned during the Cultural Revolution. After Mao's death, reform initiatives to please the provinces became the main currency in the competition for political leadership.[6] In this political struggle, the Chinese discovered the winning properties of marginalism and residual claims in the form of the dual track approach to reforms.[7] The dual track approach to reform was first introduced in rural areas in 1979 along with the household responsibility system. It was later applied to the industry contract responsibility system; to fiscal relationships through the fiscal responsibility system, through external trade and payments, through the sharing of foreign exchange between central and local governments, trade contracting, and foreign exchange trading centers; and to labor markets through the contract system for new hires in the state sector. Creating residual in fiscal relationships had an important impact on the incentives of local governments. It transformed local governments into owners motivated to promote the economic development of their domains.[8] The reform initiatives leading to congruence of interests among various levels of the governments and the enterprise sector infused reform commitments with credibility.

Orthodox transition presents a contrasting picture. In many communist countries, a weakening of the implementation capacity of the state marked the years preceding the onset of transition. Litwack (1991) observes that the most common critique of Soviet reform is the reluctance of the leadership to decree large-scale non-government property rights. He argues that the inability of the Soviet leadership to infuse reform proposals with credible commitments is the main problem: 'The history of reform in the USSR has featured continual broken promises by the government' (Litwack, 1991, p. 84). The political revolutions of the late 1980s and early 1990s further weakened the state. This created an environment where privatization and liberalization were used as weapons in an antagonistic political struggle against the old elite. Bureaucracy was viewed as an inhibitor of market developments. There was a general and strong distrust of the state and its potential positive, constructive contribution (Klaus, 1999). The state apparatus was associated with the old regime; it was something that had to be destroyed and replaced by markets. In such an environment, strengthening the implementation capacity of the state received a low priority. Destruction dominated creation in the early transformation of the state in orthodox transition. A number of post-communist societies, such as Russia, designed and undertook mass privatization programs while in a crisis of statehood.

State assets in transition: contrasting policies in China and orthodox transition

In all transition economies irrespective of the speed of transition there was a relatively long period of coexistence between a large state sector and a newly emerging private sector in an environment of expanding economic freedoms. Citizens were allowed to engage in private commercial activities. Managers of state enterprises were given autonomy to undertake key economic decisions including investment, pricing, hiring and other decisions. Economic freedom engendered spontaneous processes in the economy.

A *de novo* private sector emerged. After certain prohibitions on private activity were lifted, the private sector began to grow quite spontaneously with 'individual enterprises sprouting up like mushrooms in a forest after rainfall' (Kornai, 1990). The emergence of a private sector does not put significant demands on the regulatory and implementation capacity of the government in the initial phase of its development. A nascent private sector needs very little in terms of legal, financial and regulatory infrastructure to sustain its development. Private entrepreneurs finance their undertakings primarily through personal savings and other informal ways including through family and friends. They rely on informal means to enforce their agreements; they use existing premises to start a business and so on (Rapaczynski, 1996). As the private sector evolves, grows and becomes more sophisticated, it typically runs against constraints, and its institutional demands increase. Entrepreneurs need to access external financing to finance their expansions and further growth, they need to purchase or rent land to build factories, as they expand their operations geographically. They begin to engage in less personalized transaction and need the assurance of legal enforcement to engage in contractual relations with unknown parties.[9]

The type of spontaneity that accompanies private sector development forms an interesting contrast with the spontaneous processes that accompany liberalization in the state sector. State-owned enterprise managers who have been given significant control but no ownership rights face a large discrepancy between control and cash flow rights. The discrepancy leads to perverse incentives, which if not checked by the state (the owner) can cause asset stripping and destruction of value. Given the prolonged coexistence of a relatively large state enterprise sector and *de novo* private firms, private enterprises may become an important vehicle for asset stripping and spontaneous privatization of state assets if the control over state assets is lax. This may lead to a private sector that is parasitic in nature, focused on redistribution rather than wealth creation because asset stripping and stealing of state assets typically offer much higher returns than the alternatives. Therefore an interesting contrast with the spontaneous emergence of the private sector is that the new economic freedoms given to state enterprise managers pose considerable demands on the government to develop new regulatory capacity to enforce its ownership rights and protect state assets in an environment of significant state enterprise autonomy. Thus a critical task of the state in an economy on the path to reform is to protect state assets. State property is the weaker property in the initial period of transition.

In orthodox transition countries, the ideological climate and the political process, as described in the previous section, were not favorable to the task of protecting state property rights. State ownership rights were equated with the absence of clearly defined property rights. Establishing property rights was 'to a large extent equivalent to reducing political control' (Shleifer, 1994). And reducing political control was, to a large extent, equivalent to privatization. The implication: state assets were viewed as an open domain, as a new territory waiting for the private pioneers to appropriate. This was reinforced by 'assessments' that state enterprises had little value; the dominant view was that the majority were actually subtracting value.[10] The implication was that the faster you destroy them the better off everybody will be. These ideological beliefs created a favorable environment for asset stripping. Stealing of state assets occurred in many transition economies on a massive scale, and, in the process, a significant part of the new private sector became rent-seeking and redistributive in its formative period.

There is an obvious parallel between what happened with the state and what happened with state assets in orthodox transition. The process is perhaps best summarized by George Soros who stated at a 1998 conference on Russia (Hedlund, 2001, p. 49) that first 'the assets of the state were stolen, and then when the state itself became valuable as a source of legitimacy, it too was stolen.' The macroeconomic consequences of this development were negative or low economic growth accompanied by significant growth in inequality (Ivaschenko, 2002; Milanovic, 1997).[11]

China again presents a contrasting picture. Asset stripping occurs in China and on a significant scale. The new private sector has also been a vehicle for this asset stripping through the so-called hybridization process. Through joint ventures with domestic private or foreign companies, state assets have been separated from the ultimate owner. This has often resulted in loss of control and dissipation of state assets. Still, although the evidence is anecdotal, one can argue that China was able to avoid the massive destruction of value in its state enterprise sector that has been evident elsewhere in transition economies.[12]

Various institutional characteristics of the Chinese reform process have limited the extent of asset stripping. Ideological bias against the private sector acted as a deterrent for asset stripping.[13] In orthodox transition, trade between state enterprises and parallel firms was an important channel for asset stripping. In China, for a long time private firms were not allowed to engage in trade activities and entry barriers continue to be high for private firms to enter trade activities even today.

On the state enterprise side, party control over managerial appointments has been an important factor in controlling asset stripping.[14] For a long time, state enterprise managers were not given the right to decide on investments and other activities without approval from the state. An elaborate system of approvals related to various aspects of foreign direct investment and joint ventures between foreign companies and SOEs had, among other things, the purpose of ensuring that the value of state assets is preserved. Areas of conflicts of interest between state enterprise managers and government officials with respect to state property rights were given special attention. The State Council has issued numerous circulars trying to define the legitimate business scope of officials. According to Article 166 of the Criminal Law, any employees who take advantage of their positions, turn management of their units over to their relatives or friends, purchase commodities from units managed by their relatives or friends at prices higher than the market price, sell commodities to such units at prices lower than the market price, or purchase commodities that are not up to standard from units managed by their relatives or friends face up to seven years in prison.

In China however, the main principal–agent conflict has not been between the state and the state enterprise managers, but between local governments and the central government.[15] Historically, the preferred channel of loss socialization used by local governments has been the financial system. Local governments looking for ways to socialize liabilities related to SOEs under their control have targeted the national banking system and the national stock markets. Reforms initiated by Zhu Rongji in the 1990s have made this more difficult.

China's enterprise reform

It has been a common belief that enterprise reform, and in particular the reform of large state-owned enterprises, has proved a failure in China's otherwise very successful experience with market reforms. Qian, an influential observer of China's reforms, notes: 'In one notable area reform has not worked in China. This is the reform of large-scale state-owned enterprises' (Qian, 2002, p. 43).[16] The reform of the Chinese state sector has been going on for more than two decades. However, over the last four to five years there have been some significant changes. The process has accelerated and has acquired some qualitatively new features. First, the scale of change is remarkable: every kind of SOE – small, medium, and large, under both central and local control – has been affected. Second, the extent of ownership transformation has been dramatic. One can argue that the wholly state-owned non-financial company in China has become an endangered species. Third, every known method of restructuring has been or is being used: bankruptcy, listings and de-listings, debt-for-equity swaps, sales to private parties both domestic and foreign, and standard corporate governance techniques. Finally, mass lay-offs, something unheard of just four or five years ago, have become a widespread phenomenon. Thus, the scale and scope of the transformation is impressive.

There are several relatively distinct restructuring initiatives that illustrate the scale and scope of the change. At the grassroots level, local governments have been particularly active in implementing corporatization and ownership diversification in SOEs, the most decisive actions in grappling with the financial burdens and unemployment pressures resulting from loss-making

SOEs. Close to 90 percent of the small and medium-sized SOEs under local governments' control have been restructured. Reforms have been most dramatic in the industrial sector where the number of SOEs has declined from 114,000 in 1996 to 34,000 in 2003. About half of the decline is due to privatizations. Privatization in China has not been limited to small enterprises only: the average privatized SOE has about 600 employees.

Local governments are trying to reduce their liabilities related to these enterprises, realizing that their capacity to monitor and control is declining with the continuing marketization of the economy. For local governments, the main concern as state assets are divested is to minimize social dislocation that could lead to social unrest. China is unique in that local governments are responsible for all social welfare expenditures. This leads to significant variation at the local level in terms of the pace, speed, and form of the changes. In poorer provinces the pace of privatization has been slower, as such provinces lack the financial resources to absorb the social costs of restructuring.

Another important aspect of enterprise reform in China is the public listing of large state companies. About 1400 large state-owned companies have been listed on the two domestic exchanges and on exchanges offshore. Their market capitalization is about 50 percent of GDP and they have about 65 million individual shareholders.[17] The majority of Chinese listed companies have been carved out of SOEs in a process known as 'packaging for listing.' They have strong linkages to local governments and are integrated with their SOE parents. For example, listed companies typically make regular payments to their parents to cover social obligations to existing and retired workers. Expropriation of minority shareholders through related party transactions has been pervasive in China and the Chinese Securities Regulatory Commission (CSRC) has stepped up efforts to curb such activities.

This process of transformation of China's state sector has been, and will be, socially painful. About 30 million SOE workers have been laid off since 1998, and, according to official government statistics, 8.7 million of these have not found a new job. Almost every SOE has laid off employees. This has quite understandably led to social unrest, but for the most part labor seems to be accepting these changes. State employees, perhaps the most powerful interest group in China, refused to accept lay-offs for a long time, but now accept the severance packages. Two economic factors account for labor's quiescence. (1) In recent years the government has shored up the social security system and increased unemployment benefits with a significant increase in central budget expenditures for social security from 1 percent in 1997 to 6.3 percent in 2002. (2) A dynamic *de novo* private sector has been creating jobs and alleviating the social costs of restructuring.

Privatization and the growth of the *de novo* private sector have transformed the structure of the Chinese economy. Over the past decade or so, the economy has made the transition from complete reliance on state-owned and collective enterprises to a mixed economy where private enterprise plays the leading role. The private sector, narrowly defined, has become the largest sector of the Chinese economy.

Enterprise reforms have led to a major transformation of the state sector as well. The state enterprise sector has shown consistent profitability in the last four to five years. Analysis of the financial performance of listed companies does not reveal significant differences between state and non-state companies. Return on capital of listed companies has been on the decline in the last few years, but this reflects more truthful accounting rather than a real deterioration in profitability. Overall, economic value added has remained positive, indicating that there is no wealth destruction by listed SOEs (Chan, 2002).

In the strategically important infrastructure and energy sectors, where the regulatory framework is still evolving, state monopolies have been broken up and competition has been introduced between large state companies. Chinese SOEs have shown that they are capable of competing not only in domestic markets, but internationally. China has nurtured over 20 giant corporations and conglomerates that have proven competitive in the international market. Some of these companies are laying off tens, indeed hundreds, of thousands of employees – really staggering numbers. They are doing this not because they are in financial distress, in fact some are hugely profitable, but because they want to impress their shareholders and become really first-rate international players.

SOEs have surprised observers who believed that they could not be reformed unless they were privatized. In this aspect, China is not unique. In other transition economies, especially the Czech Republic, Hungary and Poland, after some initial hesitation, many SOEs have responded quite flexibly, more or less along the lines expected of firms whose managers are fulfilling the objective of wealth-maximizing owners. Creation of a hard budget constraint and restrictions on credit for the enterprise sector, along with functioning markets, competition and bankruptcy laws, introduced an indirect, yet effective, form of corporate governance that had been lacking in the centrally-planned economies (Brada, 1996).

Thus significant ownership change has taken place in China. The ownership change was not, however, an end in itself, but the by-product of restructuring. Institutions, including the corporate form itself, were introduced as solutions to real problems. These new institutions were imperfect, but were generally sensible responses to existing problems. Because China adopted new institutions in response to actual, narrowly defined problems, these institutions were being put to use as soon as they emerged and over time they have evolved, gaining strength, and assuming new functions. This contrasts with the experience in many orthodox transition countries, where new capitalist institutions were introduced in a more or less ritualistic fashion, often as an end in themselves. As a result, many of these institutions were formalistic, and were not capable of performing a useful role (Stiglitz, 2002). In China the emergence of the corporate form, the stock market, and the private wealth accumulated by households and private firms coalesced over time to produce a significant degree of ownership diversification. At this stage, it has become hard in China to tell what is state-owned, a collective or a private enterprise. As a result, it has become equally difficult for the government to discriminate on the basis of ownership.

Building regulatory capacity: the example of corporate governance reforms in China

Is corporate governance reform a meaningful exercise under dominant state ownership among listed companies in China? Skeptics consider state ownership as the root cause of current problems with corporate governance of Chinese listed companies (Zhang, 2002), arguing that government departments and industry regulators cannot appreciate the importance of protecting minority interests. Both theoretical considerations and the actual Chinese experience, however, give cause for optimism.

Enterprise reforms in China have produced the absentee owner – millions of minority investors who are well diversified and are rationally ignorant about the companies they have invested in. With the dominance of passive and absentee owners, the identity of the owner becomes less important, that is, it does not matter who an absentee owner is. To address the problem of the absentee owner, the global trend has been to shift the costs of monitoring from shareholders to regulators and the courts. Regulation has substituted for 'investors beware.' In this context, the identity of the owners is important only to the extent to which it affects the regulator's capacity to regulate. Is it possible to have a powerful and committed regulator in the presence of dominant state ownership? China's experience so far gives reasons for optimism. Reforms have produced a variety of interests. Different coalitions are possible on various issues affecting the political feasibility of reform measures. It is often hard to establish a strong correspondence between these coalitions and ownership structures. Much also depends on the ability of the regulator to affect the formation of political coalitions on various issues.

A major focus of the CSRC's work has been the problem of related-party transactions. Here the CSRC has recorded some success. The CSRC has the support of company managers because these regulations made it more difficult for controlling parents to transfer or remove the senior management of listed companies. Shareholders were also supportive of these measures as they were intended to protect their interests. Banks and securities companies with direct or indirect exposure to the stock market are also supportive. Negatively affected by these measures are parent companies and ultimately local governments that own these companies. For local governments, concerned about social liabilities of companies under their control, cracking down on related-party transactions prevents them from using the listed companies as a conduit for funds to ailing companies under their control. However, the dramatic increase in social expenditures from the center to the provinces has helped to placate local governments.

The CSRC has shown a capacity to base regulations on incentives to enforce compliance. For example, the government as owner expects cash dividends from its investments in listed companies. As a result, Chinese companies pay dividends. In some cases, this has led to de-capitalization, but on the positive side, companies now need to go to the capital market more often. Companies therefore need their independent shareholders and this is perhaps the best foundation for minority protection. This dependence on the capital markets has been used by the CSRC to enforce regulations by including various corporate governance provisions in the conditions for listing and secondary issuance.[18]

This example highlights the importance of functioning institutions. Chinese capital markets may be fraught with problems, but they perform the basic functions of capital markets: raising capital and, to a lesser extent, providing liquidity. If firms do not need the market, either because there are no investment opportunities or because they have soft budget constraints, there is little a regulator can do to improve the markets and protect minority shareholders. Contrast this with the experience in Eastern Europe where stock markets evolved out of mass privatization programs. Forced onto the market by the mass privatization programs, many firms had little incentive to stay public, since the markets were not a realistic mechanism for raising capital. This eventually led to wholesale delisting of firms.

Concluding remarks

The Chinese transition experience and the European transition experience have been starkly different. Rapid growth in China can be contrasted with sharp output declines in the European transition economies during the early transition period. It is unlikely that these differences can be explained by a single attribute, but this should not stop us from looking at important policy differences in these experiences. We have argued that there have been important differences in government approaches to the transition process in these countries. In the orthodox approach government has been more hands-off and has had greater difficulty in committing to a policy course. The laissez-faire attitude towards SOEs in orthodox transition countries has also damaged enterprises that have been thrust into a new environment that required new governance arrangements. To argue that these firms should be privatized ignored the facts that appropriate legal and regulatory structures are needed once large enterprises are privatized and that these legal and regulatory structures cannot be created overnight (Murrell, 1992).

Liberalization and privatization may help to reduce the scope of the state, but they do not automatically create the state capacity needed to manage a market economy. This highlights the importance of administrative and government reforms in the transition, and indeed, in the development process in general.

In the early stages of transition in China, the governance of state enterprises changed as the environment moved towards greater openness and greater dependence on the market. These changes were not driven by ideological convictions about the intrinsic merits or demerits of various ownership forms, but rather by the pressures of competition, restructuring, social obligations, and hard budget constraints. The gradual build-up of regulatory capacity is enhancing the government's confidence that it can exercise control without the tools of direct ownership. Regulatory attenuation of ownership, in line with global trends, in the case of publicly listed companies is reducing the benefits of control associated with large controlling stakes. As a result there is a diminishing share of state ownership in the economy.

As the transition moves forward, some of the issues that led to such varied economic performance will also influence future economic performance. For example, while state enterprises will play a smaller role in the future of all these economies, corporate governance issues will be a continuing challenge, as indeed they are in developed countries like the United States. The role of the state will also continue to evolve as the Chinese economy becomes more open, and many of the orthodox transition economies adapt to their new positions in the EU and others adapt to the new growing EU sphere.

Notes

1. The authors would like to thank seminar participants at Columbia University and the University of Delaware for helpful comments.
2. The 'paradox of power' says that as the power of the government grows, the government can act more easily upon its own will, which renders its promises less credible. If economic agents do not believe in the government's policies, they will not have incentives to invest. On the paradox of power in connection with establishing a rule of law see Qian (2000).
3. See Nedelsky (1988), for a discussion on the disintegration of private property as an effective boundary of political control in the United States.
4. See for example, Mikhail Gorbachev's advice to US firms: 'Those companies who are with us now have good prospects of participating in our great country [whereas those who wait] will remain observers for years to come – we will see to it' (*International Herald Tribune*, 5 June 1990, p. 5).
5. For a discussion on the helping hand and grabbing hand models of government see Shleifer and Vishny (1998).
6. For an excellent account of how political competition shaped China's economic reforms see Shirk (1994).

7. Contrast this with Klaus's remark: 'We should be aware of the fact that the country in the moment of transition does not make marginal changes (as a non-transition country), that it makes substantial changes. This is a crucial difference' (Klaus, 1999, p. 4).
8. See Li (1998) for other initiatives to change incentives in the bureaucracy.
9. See Koford and Miller (1994) for an analysis of this process during the earlier phase of transition. As firms began to expand their market reach, the lack of legal support became a serious problem. For a similar analyisis of markets in Vietnam, see McMillan and Woodruff (1999).
10. The Treuhand experience in Germany may be of relevance in assessing how valuable state assets were since East Germany's privatization was comprehensive, fast, market-based and done without prior restructuring. Out of some 17,000 enterprises under Treuhand's authority only about 3000 were liquidated (Dyck, 1997).
11. 'The ability to enforce the law and to protect property rights seems to be a key reason why central Europe recovered from their fall in output, while Russia and other countries not facing the prospect of entry to the European Union experienced a much more prolonged decline of output' (Roland, 2002).
12. Only recently has the Chinese media begun to discuss the problem of the declining value of state assets as the government keeps holding them. Recently the Official Economic Daily reported that the net worth of local SOEs in Heilongjiang province is probably negative, as the book value of owners' equity of RMB36bn is offset by accumulated losses of RMB38bn.
13. While private ownership was allowed and encouraged for a long time in China, the private sector achieved a formal parity with state ownership only with the constitutional amendment of 2004.
14. See various articles in Naughton and Yang (2004) for a more detailed analysis of the appointment system. They argue that the system has become even more centralized since the Tiananmen Square incident in 1989.
15. Blanchard and Shleifer (2000) analyze the sharp contrasts between federalism in China and Russian federalism. They argue that, without a stronger central government in Russia, federalism cannot succeed.
16. Qian attributes the failure to the Party's control over the appointment of SOE managers.
17. These are actually accounts and individuals can hold several accounts. The active individual accounts in China are about 5 million.
18. The Asset Management Companies have also used the attractiveness of listing and secondary issuance to enhance cooperation from their debtors.

References

Blanchard, O. and A. Shleifer (2000), 'Federalism with and without Political Centralization: China versus Russia', MIT Dept. of Economics Working Paper, No. 00–15.

Brada, J. (1996), 'Privatization is Transition – Or Is It?', *Journal of Economic Perspectives*, 10 (2), 67–86.

Chan, V. (2002), 'EVA of China A Shares. UBS Warburg', *Global Equity Research*, 8 November.

Dahl, R. (1985), *A Preface to Economic Democracy*, Berkeley: University of California Press.

Dyck, A. (1997), 'Privatization in Eastern Germany: Management Selection and Economic Transition', *American Economic Review*, 87 (4), 565–97.

Hedlund, S. (2001), 'Can Property Rights be Protected by Law?', *East European Constitutional Review*, 10 (1), 48–52.

Ivaschenko, O. (2002), 'Growth and Inequality: Evidence from Transitional Economies', CESifo Working Paper Series, WP 746.

Klaus, V. (1999), 'Transition from Communism: a Decade After', Lovett C. Peters lecture at the Pioneer Institute for Public Policy Research, Boston, 21 April.

Koford, K. and J. Miller (1994), 'Contract Enforcement in the Early Transition to a Market Economy', University of Delaware Working Paper, 1994.

Kornai, J. (1990), 'The Affinity between Ownership Forms and Coordination Mechanisms: the Common Experience of Reforms in Socialist Countries', *Journal of Economic Perspectives*, 4 (3), 131–47.

Li, D. (1998), 'Changing Incentives of the Chinese Bureaucracy', *American Economic Review, Papers and Proceedings*, 88 (May), 393–7.

Litwack, J. (1991), 'Legality and Market Reform in Soviet-Type Economies', *Journal of Economic Perspectives*, 5 (4), 77–89.

McGuire, M. and M. Olson (1996), 'The Economics of Autocracy and Majority Rule: the Invisible Hand and the Use of Force', *Journal of Economic Literature*, 34 (1), 72–96.

McMillan, J. and C. Woodruff (1999), 'Trust and Search in Vietnam's Emerging Private Sector', *Quarterly Journal of Economics*, 114, 1285–1320.

Milanovic, B. (1997), *Income, Inequality and Poverty During the Transition from Planned to Market Economy*, Washington DC: The World Bank.

Murrell, Peter (1992), 'Evolution in Economics and in the Economic Reform of the Centrally Planned Economies', in Christopher C. Clague and Gordon Rausser (eds), *The Emergence of Market Economies in Eastern Europe*, Cambridge, MA: Blackwell.

Naughton, B.J. and D.L. Yang (eds) (2004), *Holding China Together: Diversity and National Integration in the Post-Deng Era*, Cambridge: Cambridge University Press.

Nedelsky, J. (1988), 'American Constitutionalism and the Paradox of Private Property', in J. Elster and R. Slagstad (eds), *Constitutionalism and Democracy*, Cambridge: Cambridge University Press, pp. 241–73.

Olson, Mancur (2000), *Power and Prosperity: Outgrowing Communist and Capitalist Dictatorships*, New York: Basic Books.

Qian, Y. (2000), 'The Modern Market Economy and the Rule of Law', *Perspectives*, 1 (5), April 30: http://www.oycf.org/perspectives.

Qian, Y. (2002), 'How Reform Worked in China', mimeo, University of California, Berkeley.

Rapaczynski, Andrzej (1996), 'The Role of the State and the Market in Establishing Property Rights', *Journal of Economic Perspectives*, 10 (spring), 87–103.

Roland, G. (2002), 'The Political Economy of Transition', mimeo, University of California Berkeley: http://emlab.berkeley.edu/users/groland/pubs/polectrans_ jpe.pdf.

Shleifer, A. (1994), 'Establishing Property Rights', in *Proceedings of the World Bank Annual Conference on Development Economics, 1994*, Washington DC: The World Bank.

Shleifer, A. and R.W. Vishny (1998), *The Grabbing Hand*, Cambridge, MA: Harvard University Press.

Shirk, S. (1994), *The Political Logic of Economic Reform in China*, Berkeley, CA: University of California Press.

Stiglitz, J. (2002), *Globalization and its Discontents*, New York and London: W.W. Norton.

Zhang, J. (2002), *China's Corporate Governance: Update*, mimeo, UBS Warburg.

Section 4

The US Economic Experience and EU Economic Policies

14
Economic Reform in the European Union: Will the 'Lisbon' EU Catch Up with the US?

Mariusz-Jan Radło

Introduction

In March 2000, the political leaders of the European Union decided that the Union must become 'the most competitive and dynamic knowledge-based economy in the world, capable of sustainable economic growth with more and better jobs and greater social cohesion' by 2010. They adopted a program of economic reforms, named the Lisbon Strategy, aimed at achieving this goal. It was probably the most comprehensive growth-supporting economic program in the history of the EU, covering reforms in several areas, including product and labor markets, research and development, investment in human capital, improving the business environment and social security systems and the like. The US economic performance of the 1990s was a crucial reference point for Europeans when accepting the Lisbon Strategy. What is more, an unofficial goal of the strategy was to catch up with the US.

Nonetheless, five years after its adoption, the Lisbon Strategy does not seem to have been a success. There were many weaknesses in the strategy that were identified by economists and policy-makers early on. Among the most commonly indicated were too wide a range of inconsistent priorities resulting in lack of clear priorities, and soft methods of implementation resulting in lack of implementation as well as omissions about how desirable reforms were to be implemented. The strategy's shortcomings caused the EU leaders to launch a mid-term review. The process started after March 2004 and was finalized in 2005 when the strategy was renewed.

In this chapter we analyze the GDP per capita gap between the EU and the US and from this perspective we examine the Lisbon Strategy, in both its editions, before and after the mid-term review. The problem we especially concentrate on is linked to structural inadequacies of the strategy related to mismatches between the EU's economic problems and the reforms stipulated in the strategy. We argue that there are several omissions in the strategy, making this program potentially ineffective and therefore inhibiting the EU's catching up with the US. Finally we try to assess the future effectiveness of the Lisbon Strategy and the factors conditioning it.

The gap

A crucial reason underlying the European Union decision to implement the Lisbon Strategy was the fact that in 2000 the GDP per capita gap between the EU and the US economies was larger than it had been since the beginning of the 1970s. The real GDP gap was even larger than that suggested by per capita indicators, because of the differences in population growth. From 1970 to 2000 the total population of the EU-15 rose by 19 percent, while the US population grew by 34 percent. Therefore the GDP[1] of the EU-15 decreased by almost 20 percentage points in relation to the US, from more than 113 percent of the US total GDP in 1970 to about 93 percent in 2000 (OECD, 2002h). Especially interesting observations can be drawn from the analysis of this gap. The GDP per capita of the EU-15 in 2000 represented about 70 percent of the US GDP per capita. But labor productivity per hours worked in the EU-15 was very close to the US level, about 93 percent. Furthermore, labor productivity per person employed in the EU-15 was also much closer than GDP per capita, representing about 85 percent (Eurostat, 2004). These differences were due to a shorter average working time in the EU in comparison to the US, lower employment rates and differences in demographic structures. It is worth noting that in 1970, in the 11 EU member states[2] average working time was very similar to that of the US, representing about 1915 hours per year. Until 2000, working time decreased both in the EU-11 and in the US, but the scope of the reduction in the EU was much larger. As a result, the average working time in the EU-11 was 1606 hours per year while in the US it was 1835 (OECD, 2002b). There were also substantial differences in employment rates between the EU and the US. The employment rate in the EU was only about 64 percent while in the US it was over 73 percent (OECD, 2002a). Moreover, the working age population's share in total population in the US was much higher than in the EU and represented three-quarters of the total population while in the EU it was only 66 percent (OECD, 2004).

Therefore lower labor utilization in the EU in comparison to the US can be seen as a crucial source of the GDP gap between these two economies. Lower employment rates and lower working time in the EU may of course reflect cultural differences and a preference for leisure time, as some authors think. Nevertheless, high unemployment rates in the European Union suggest that labor markets within the EU do not function effectively and are not able to generate more jobs.

Sources of the gap

The lower employment rate in the EU, to some extent, may result from a relatively low level of human capital. Only 21 percent of the people of working age in the EU-15 have a tertiary education, while in the US the figure is almost 37 per cent. These figures are very important when you take into account the fact that the employment rates of people with tertiary education in the EU are similar to the US rates, and only the rates of employment of people with less education are lower. These data show that the lower level of human capital is a source of lower utilization of human resources in the EU economies. But these data also indirectly show that it is likely that institutional solutions present in the EU do not support job creation for employees with low qualifications. Institutional problems are also indirectly confirmed by the fact that the Union faces much more serious employment problems than does the US, including also long-term and structural unemployment, although these problems are also connected with a lower level of human capital.

As was mentioned above, among the reasons for lower productivity per person employed in the EU are the lower average working time and low employment rates. According to some economists (for example, Turner, 2003), the systematic shortening of working time and falling employment rates in Europe can be seen to reflect a preference for leisure. Another explanation is proposed by Freeman and Schettkat (2005), who hypothesize that the greater time worked and the higher employment rates in the US are due to the greater marketization of traditional household production in the US. These explanations are interesting, but there are important reasons why the bulk of the blame should fall on labor and product market regulations as well as on welfare state benefits for the relatively short working time and low employment rates in many European countries.

As Figure 14.1 shows, the shorter average working time in many European countries can be explained by the fact that more sources of income other than salary are available for EU employees. Countries in which, in 2000, spending on income transfers represented a larger part of GDP had, at that time, a much shorter working time than the countries that spent less on these transfers. The correlation coefficient between these two variables amounts to –0.58, calculated on the basis of the data for EU member states, the US, Japan, Norway, Iceland, Australia and New Zealand. This means that there is an inverse relationship between the availability of income other than salary and the tendency to lengthen working time. Like income transfers, the level of income taxes also influences the reduction of working time. EU member states, in comparison to the US, have a relatively high level of taxes imposed on labor. The correlation coefficient, –0.55, between the level of taxes imposed on labor and the average working time also confirms a negative relationship between taxes and average working time.

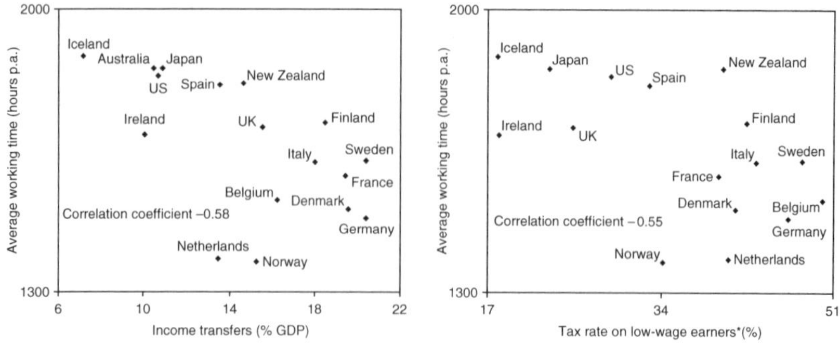

Figure 14.1: Average working time vs income transfers and tax rates on low-wage earners

Note: * The tax rate on low-wage earners calculates the income tax on gross earnings + the employee's and employer's social security contributions and then expresses this sum as a percentage of the total labor cost for the low-wage earner. Tax rates are calculated for a single person without children. When at work, this person earns 67 percent of the average wages of full-time production workers in manufacturing.

Source: Author's calculation using OECD (2002c) and Eurostat (2004).

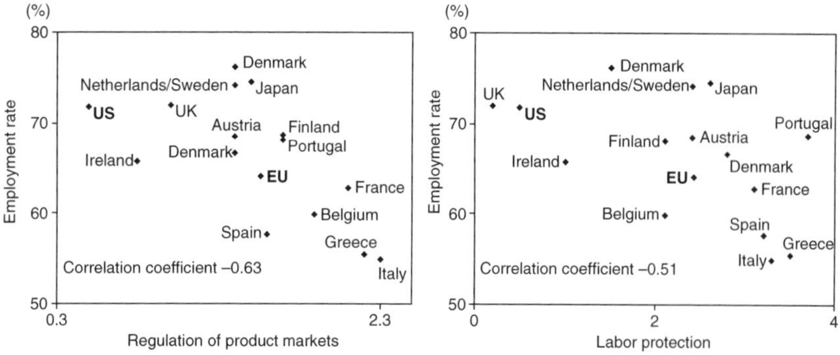

Figure 14.2: Employment rate vs regulation of product markets and labor protection

Source: Author's calculation using Nicoletti et al. (2000) and Eurostat (2004).

Institutional conditions influence not only average working time in the EU, but also employment. In Figure 14.2 we show the relation between the levels of product market regulation and the degree of protection of the labor markets on the one side, and employment rates on the other. The data show that the higher the level of employment protection and the more severe the product market regulation, the lower the employment rates in the economy. EU member states with the highest levels of product market regulation and the highest employment protection rates, such as Italy, Greece, Belgium, Spain and France, have at the same time the lowest employment rates. And vice versa, countries with lower product market regulation levels such as Great Britain, the US or Denmark, have the highest employment rates.

This is reflected in a substantial positive relationship between the level of product market regulation and employment protection and unemployment. A similar analysis prepared using the same data for regulation and rates of unemployment shows that the level of unemployment in the analyzed EU member states, the US and Japan is positively correlated with both the level of product market regulation and the employment protection level. The highest unemployment in 2000 could be observed in EU countries with the highest levels of regulation: Spain, Greece, Italy and France. Countries with the lowest regulation and protection levels – Ireland, Great Britain, Denmark and the US – had low unemployment rates.

These relationships have already been demonstrated in analyses carried out by Nickell (1999) and Blanchard (2000). Their findings are generally consistent with the earlier observations made by Siebert (1997), who analyzed institutional and regulatory change in labor markets in EU member states over the last four decades.

The difference between the EU and the US economies concerns not only regulations and institutions but also the role of government in the economy. In the most general way, government's role in the economy is described by indices showing public spending values in relation to GDP, and by the structure of this spending. The data presented in Table 14.1 show that the difference in the levels of public spending in the EU and the US amounted to almost 13 percent of GDP. Over 12.2 percent of this was due to much higher spending by the EU on income transfers, 6.87 percentage points, and higher spending on public consumption, 5.33 percentage points. An additional percentage point, which practically closes the entire public spending gap, comes from subsidies, which were higher in the EU

Table 14.1: Structure of public spending in 2000 in the EU and the US (% GDP)

	Government consumption	**Government investment**	**Subsidies**	**Income transfers**	**Total government disbursements**
EU-15	19.90	2.54	1.42	20.67	47.16
US	14.57	3.26	0.35	13.80	33.62
Difference: EU–US	5.33	–0.72	1.07	6.87	13.54

Source: Author's calculation using OECD (2003).

Table 14.2: Changes in the structure of public spending in the EU-15, 1963–2000 (% GDP)

	1963	1975	1985	1989	1993	2000	Change 1963–2000 (% GDP)
Government consumption	15.09	18.36	20.23	19.46	21.08	19.90	+4.81
Government investment	3.80	3.83	3.12	3.10	3.06	2.54	−1.26
Subsidies	1.44	1.97	2.24	1.96	1.84	1.42	−0.02
Income transfers*	11.58	17.45	19.29	18.68	21.39	20.67	+9.09
Total government disbursements	33.01	43.51	49.45	47.80	53.09	47.16	+14.15

Note: * Social benefits paid by government and other current transfers paid by government.
Source: Author's calculation using OECD (2003).

than in the US. What is more, a specific feature of the difference in the structure of public expenditure in the EU and the US was that the only item on which in 2000 the EU spent less than the US in relation to its GDP was public investment outlays. In addition, the structure of spending in EU countries in 1963[3] was very similar to that of the United States in 2000 (see Table 14.2). In this context, what is worthy of note is that, in the 1960s, the EU countries developed faster than the United States.

A continuous increase in income transfers and public consumption spending, which can be observed in European countries since the 1960s, was connected to the creation of the welfare state. It was based on extensive social aid and a far-reaching public redistribution of income. These processes had, however, a very severe impact on labor markets. Growing access to income other than wages, measured by the value of income transfers, resulted in growing unemployment underpinned by a lack of incentives for looking for a job. Therefore, the unemployment rate since the beginning of 1970s grew at the same pace as income transfers, as shown at Figure 14.3. The correlation between unemployment and income transfer levels in time series from 1970 to 2000 shows that there is almost a linear relationship between these two variables, and the correlation coefficient is 0.92.

In this context, Engen and Skinner (1992) investigated the impact of the growth of budget spending and tax revenue on the pace of GDP changes in 107 countries in the period from 1970–85. These authors showed that there is an inverse relationship between changes in the levels of the states' intervention in their economies and the pace of growth of their economies. They found that an increase in public spending and tax revenue of 10 percent of GDP with a stable budget results in an average decrease in the pace of long-term economic growth by 1.5 percentage points. This relationship is

generalizations about the role of 'the European social model' and evaded the question of its responsibility for providing ineffective solutions to labor market issues and making labor inflexible. Finally the strategy entirely omitted the issue of the negative influence of the level of employment protection on the level of unemployment, including structural unemployment, in the EU member states.

The same pattern reappeared in the schedule for actions planned by the strategy. The actions concerning support for ICT diffusion and reinforcement of inventiveness were well planned, while the reform aiming at improving the business environment was less satisfactory. Deregulation of network industries and financial market integration were successfully designed. Unfortunately, the issues of reforming labor markets and social security systems were only mentioned in the strategy, but reform was not planned. Although they were included in the document, the actually formulated recommendations were very general and involved more consulting than reforming. Such a state of affairs was supported by political declarations cherishing the idea of a welfare state with an extensively developed social security system. These declarations precisely defined the limits of the reforms postulated in this field.

These weaknesses, together with too many priorities and soft methods of implementation, made the Lisbon strategy ineffective. Without deep reforms, including reforms of labor markets and social security systems, it will be impossible to raise labor utilization in the EU. But a socioeconomic doctrine, according to which the EU has its own 'social model', which is a part of its identity and should be preserved, clearly defines the limits of the reforms postulated in several critical fields. Therefore, the whole economic element of the Lisbon Strategy represents a daring plan of reforms, embracing as it does deregulation of product markets, redirection of public expenses towards investments in human capital, research and development, and the integration of financial markets. Nevertheless, when getting to more sensitive areas from the perspective of the 'European social model' – labor markets and social security systems – the strategy almost entirely omits the need for thorough and complex reform.

This view is confirmed by the empirical analysis of changes in product and labor market regulation conducted by Conway et al. (2005) who argue that from 1998 to 2003, product market regulations have declined in all EU member states. In all EU economies, product market regulation has moved towards the regulatory environment of the more liberalized countries. Nonetheless, changes in labor protection legislation were less visible if not entirely absent. In consequence, in 2003, all EU member states had less regulated product markets, but most of them were still characterized by over-regulated labor markets. Such a situation was in part a consequence of the incomplete package of Lisbon reforms, with well-planned reforms of product markets and almost no reforms of labor markets.

What should Europe do?

There are only five years left if the Lisbon reform is to be completed in 2010. In this period the EU will not catch up with the US. But it can widen the scope of reforms planned, so as to address all its economic weaknesses. The most important problems are those of the diminishing labor force utilization which underlies the growing GDP gap between the EU and the US.

But in order to make the Lisbon reform work, the EU has to deal with all the factors that deter Europeans from looking for jobs and deter European companies from creating them. These are inflexible labor markets and high labor protection, relatively high indirect wage costs, excessive income transfers and last but not least the relatively weak educational structure of the working-age population. Therefore, in our view, in its second phase the Lisbon strategy should aim at:

1. Deep reform of labor market regulations and promoting a concept of job security that is based on fostering the ability to create new jobs and not on the protection of current job contracts. Such regulations should improve the ability of companies to create new jobs as well as facilitating labor flows between workplaces and thus accelerating structural changes in the economy as well as technological progress.
2. Reduction of non-wage labor costs to expand job creation in the economy and reduce the negative impact of high marginal tax rates.
3. Reduction of income transfers. It will be difficult to achieve a positive change in labor markets because of the incentives not to work created by overdeveloped social security systems. Therefore, in addition to regulatory changes in labor markets, a deep reform and reduction of social security should be performed.
4. Investment in human capital. Employment rates of those with tertiary education in the EU are similar to US rates, and only the rates of employment of people with lower education are lower. Therefore changes in the working-age population's education structure could improve the situation in the EU.

Not only labor market regulations influence economic growth and employment. Regulation of product markets is also important. Regulation of these markets has a negative impact on labor force utilization in the EU. Moreover these regulations often impose costly obligations on companies, making them less efficient. Therefore deregulation and promoting entrepreneurship should be implemented. The most important actions include:

1. Making the Single Market work in all EU member states and across all areas, including services and financial markets. The Single Market fostered the reduction of many barriers in European markets and

promoted competition. Nevertheless, there are still many countries that have not implemented all the required legislation. Moreover some markets, especially services, are not part of the Single Market. It is especially important when taking into account that in 1995–2000 almost 90 percent of new jobs in the EU were created in services.
2. Reduction of barriers for companies and promotion of entrepreneurship. A large part of all regulations that worsen the business environment are enacted at the national level and do not depend on the *acquis communautaire*. A lot of these regulations diminish the economic potential of the EU. Therefore, actions aimed at cutting red tape for companies and improving the regulatory business environment should be intensified.

All institutional and regulatory changes should be mirrored by changes in public finance, especially in the structure and the level of public spending. Therefore the third key area of the Lisbon Strategy in 2005–10 should include deep changes in the level and the structure of public spending. Reduction of income transfers and public consumption will create room for further reductions of taxes and facilitate increased spending on investment in human and physical capital, including infrastructure and research and technological development. Such changes in public spending will complement the positive outcomes of regulatory changes described earlier.

These priorities do not cover all the changes and reforms that should be implemented in the EU member states. Each member state has its own specific situation and problems. Moreover, almost all the new EU member states are much less developed than the EU-15 average. From this perspective catching up with the US is important, but internal economic convergence within the EU must also be considered as a key goal. Internal convergence is a goal of the EU Cohesion Policy with all funds supporting investments in physical and human capital. These investments seem to be more important, at the current stage of economic development of the new members, than other investments prioritized in the Lisbon Strategy. But, in fact, there are no real contradictions between the Lisbon priorities, especially those concerning regulatory reforms, and Cohesion Policy priorities. Indeed, regulatory reforms are of crucial importance for the effectiveness of the Cohesion Policy. Boldrin and Canova (2000), Ederveen and Gorter (2002) and Ederveen et al. (2002) argue that deregulation, competition and open markets are the precondition for faster growth through Cohesion Funds. Therefore Lisbon strategies aimed at such changes in new member states should go hand in hand with their national development planning, based on the EU funds.

In order to make the Lisbon Strategy a reality, the Union should improve economic policy coordination so as to monitor, evaluate and facilitate economic reforms in its member countries. But what is most important, and is also the weakest point of the strategy, is the fact that implementation of all the above reforms relies not only on good planning but is also a function of political will at the national level. Lack of such will today makes many reforms impossible.

Mid-term renewal?

The review of the strategy took place during the European Council's Brussels summit on 22–23 March 2005 (European Council, 2005). While this was not a turning point in the EU's socioeconomic policy-making, it produced some positive effects. During the summit, support for growth and employment was defined as a crucial priority for the next five years of economic reform in the EU. While not questioning the three dimensions of the strategy the economic dimension was prioritized. The renewed strategy covered three areas entitled as follows: (1) 'Knowledge and Innovation – Engines of Sustainable Growth'; (2) 'An Attractive Area in Which to Invest and Work'; (3) 'Growth and Employment Making for Social Cohesion.' In each area, a set of actions was planned or at least declared.

In 'Knowledge and Innovation,' while repeating the priorities of the former strategy, including 3 percent GDP spending on research and development, the role of framework programs for research and a new initiative for supporting dissemination of ICT, the document has some new, potentially risky, features. The most important is the role of an active industrial policy as a way to reinforce the competitive advantages of the EU's industrial base. This can strengthen the tendency to subsidize selected industries in better-developed EU member countries. As a consequence choosing winners can replace a policy based on creating a winning environment. Another feature, probably not so risky, is an intention to establish a European Technology Institute, which seems to be just another EU supranational agency.

The next area, 'An Attractive Area in Which to Invest and Work,' focuses on the regulatory environment of product and service markets, especially those making the internal market complete. The most important aspect here is the willingness to make internal service markets fully operational. Unfortunately, there is a catch: internal service markets need to preserve the European social model. This means that the 'Bolkenstein Directive' will most probably be watered down as a part of the Lisbon strategy. Other actions described in this area are similar to the previous version of the strategy and concern a reduction of state aid, improving the regulatory environment, cutting red tape, especially for SMEs, and supporting transport infrastructure. All of these seem to be in line with the EU's economic needs.

The third priority area, devoted to 'Growth and Employment,' was little changed. It starts with a declaration that 'raising employment rates and extending work life, coupled with reform of social protection systems, provide the best way of maintaining the present level of social protection.' This means that there is no political will in the EU to implement deep reforms, especially with regard to social protection. These parts of the renewed strategy contain no new instruments, nor are there any real instruments to support labor market reforms.

These minor improvements cannot qualify as a relaunch of the Lisbon Strategy. The corrections to the agenda by the European Council do not address either the crucial weaknesses of the former document or the EU economy's weak points. What is more, the sources of the new Lisbon weaknesses seem to be of political nature, linked to the socioeconomic doctrine dominant in the EU, which is now being imposed on all the member states of the enlarged European Union.

Despite these reservations, there are some positive features of the renewed Lisbon Strategy. One of the most important is the fact that all EU member countries can write down their own Lisbon strategies – as national reform programs – taking into account their specific economic problems. Moreover, the European Commission seems to be more aware of the economic problems faced by the EU than most political leaders at the national level. Therefore 'Integrated Guidelines for Growth and Employment' (European Commission, 2005) for the period 2005–08 presented by the Commission in April 2005 are much more realistic and consistent than the Presidency Conclusions agreed in March 2005 (European Council, 2005). Reforms presented in the guidelines are divided into three dimensions: macroeconomic, microeconomic and employment guidelines. Macroeconomic guidelines focus on growth – supporting reforms of public spending supported by structural reforms. Microeconomic guidelines include product market reforms and some actions based on facilitating ICT diffusion and investments in research and development. Employment guidelines focus not only on investments in human capital and active labor policy, but also on promoting flexibility of labor markets and reform of social security so as to support job creation. These three areas are to provide a framework for the establishment of national reform programs to be prepared by autumn 2005.

All this demonstrates that the EU as a whole is not politically ready to implement deep reforms especially in sensitive areas. Nevertheless the European Commission, while trying to make compromises between those for and against deeper economic reforms in the EU, supports the former.

Conclusions

Despite its many weaknesses, the Lisbon Strategy is at present the only EU-wide economic program supporting changes that can make the EU economy more competitive. It seems obvious that the strategy will not make the EU more competitive than the US by 2010, as was hoped in 2000, nor make the EU catch up with the US by this date. Nevertheless the Lisbon Strategy of 2005 is more realistic than the strategy of 2000. Regrettably, due to political reasons, there are still many omissions, especially in sensitive areas, such as labor and social protection.

Implementation of the strategy at national level, via the national reform programs, means that a crucial battle for more effective European economies will take place at the level at which most of the EU economic weaknesses have their source. Fortunately, the renewed Lisbon Strategy, while giving inadequate support to reforms at the EU level, provides national governments with enough room to maneuver so as to prepare more efficient national reform packages.

The Lisbon Strategy is not an economic program to be implemented, it is rather a temporary compromise between those for and against deep reforms. It however supports reforms above the status quo. The Lisbon Strategy is a catalyst for reform in the EU and gives support to the EU's reformers. It is, however, still weak.

Notes

1. Per head at the price levels and PPPs of 1995 (USD).
2. Unweighted average for the Netherlands, Germany, Denmark, France, Belgium, Italy, Sweden, Ireland, Great Britain and Spain.
3. As reconstructed thanks to OECD databases for the EU-15 member countries.

References

Blanchard, O. (2000), 'Rents, Product and Labor Market Regulation, and Unemployment', Lecture 2 of the Economics of Unemployment: Shocks, Institutions, and Interactions, Lionel Robbins Lectures, London School of Economics.

Boldrin, M. and F. Canova (2000), 'Inequality and Convergence: Reconsidering European Regional Policies', Paper presented at the 31st Panel Meeting of Economic Policy, Lisbon.

Conway, P., V. Janod and G. Nicoletti (2005), 'Product Market Regulation in OECD Countries: 1998 to 2003', Economics Department Working Paper, No. 419, OECD, Paris.

Ederveen S., H.L.F. de Groot and R. Nahuis (2002), 'Fertile Soil for Structural Funds? A Panel Data Analysis of the Conditional Effectiveness of European Cohesion Policy', CPB Discussion Paper, No. 10, August, The Hague.

Ederveen, S. and J. Gorter (2002), 'Does European Cohesion Policy Reduce Regional Disparities? An Empirical Analysis', CPB Discussion Paper, No. 15, November, The Hague.

Engen, E.M. and J. Skinner (1992), 'Fiscal Policy and Economic Growth', NBER Working Paper, No. 4223, December.

European Council (2005), *Brussels European Council – 22 and 23 March 2005 – Presidency Conclusions*, Brussels.

European Commission (2005) 'Integrated Guidelines for Growth and Jobs (2005–2008)', COM(2005) 141 final, Brussels.

Eurostat (2004), Structural Indicators Database.

Freeman, R.B. and R. Schettkat (2005), 'Marketization of Household Production and the EU–US Gap in Work', *Economic Policy*, 41, January, 7–50.

Nickell, S. (1999), 'Product Markets and Labour Markets', *Labour Economics*, 6, 1–20.

Nicoletti G., S. Scarpetta and O. Boylaud (2000), 'Summary Indicators of Product Market Regulation with Extension to Employment Protection Legislation', Economic Department Working Paper, No. 226, ECO/WKP(99)18, OECD, Paris.
OECD (2002a), LFS – Labour Force Statiscs Database, Paris
OECD (2002b), *OECD Employment Outlook*, Paris.
OECD (2002c), *Economic Outlook*, No. 71, Paris.
OECD (2002d), *OECD Employment Outlook*, Paris
OECD (2002e), Quarterly Labour Force Statistics Database, Paris
OECD (2002f), Main Science and Technology Indicators Database, Paris
OECD (2002g), Revenue Statistics 1965–2001 Database, Paris.
OECD (2002h), OECD Economic Outlook No. 72 Database, Paris
OECD (2003), OECD Economic Outlook No. 73 Database, Paris.
OECD (2004), Economic Outlook Database No. 75, Paris.
Siebert, H. (1997), 'Labor Market Rigidities: at the Root of Unemployment in Europe', *Journal of Economic Perspectives*, 11(3), summer, 37–54.
Turner, A. (2003), 'What's Wrong with Europe's Economy?' Queen's Prize Lecture, London School of Economics, Centre for Economic Performance, London, 5 February.

15

The EU Concept of Cohesion: Is It Compatible with the Anglo-Saxon Model?

John Bradley

Introduction

I would guess that most people will come to a book with Reaganomics in the title more in quest of affirmation of their own deeply held convictions – for or against the American model – than in any spirit of openness to new ideas. Hopefully, I am wrong. But since the term 'Reaganomics' is delightfully imprecise, we are all probably entitled to interpret it after our own fashion. Being a European, and feeling strongly that our American friends should have no monopoly on the terminology of successful economic policies, I have decided to call it 'the Anglo-Saxon' model.

Within the European Union, debate at an ideological level tends to have the Anglo-Saxon model in the blue corner, and what one might call the European model in the red corner. In a crude formulation, the Anglo-Saxon model shares many of the characteristics of the so-called 'Washington consensus' (henceforth WC): namely, stabilization, liberalization, and privatization. Although used mainly in terms of transition and developing economies, these three broad WC policy recommendations are also very relevant to developed economies who wish to stay developed.

It is more difficult to define the European model. The European way of doing economic policy can be subtle and nuanced. Certainly it is not the converse of the Washington consensus: destabilization, autocracy, and nationalization. In trying to pin down the European model, I am attracted to Gerard Roland's concept of the 'evolutionary-institutionalist perspective' (EIP), developed within his study of the economics of transition, but sharing many characteristics of the elusive European model. Let me mention two issues where the WC and the EIP differ dramatically (Roland, 2000, p. 331).

The first issue concerns attitudes toward markets and liberalization. The proponents of the WC assert that markets will develop spontaneously provided government does not intervene. Supply and demand will be the focus of analysis. The proponents of the EIP insist on the importance of the institutional underpinnings needed to enhance market growth: a minimum legal and contracting environment, law enforcement, political stability, building of business networks and long-term partnerships. In the EIP, the contracting agents and their institutional environment will be the focus of analysis.

The second issue concerns the main emphasis of government reform. The proponents of the WC advocate shrinking the size of government. The proponents of the EIP see reform in the organization of government in terms of the improved alignment of the interests of politicians and government bureaucrats with the development of markets.

Roland also makes a very interesting association between 'transition,' the passage from central planning to successful capitalism, and development, the process by which underdeveloped countries catch up with industrialized countries. Nobody who has read Bill Easterly's iconoclastic book *The Elusive Quest for Growth* can believe any longer in the existence of any single 'way' or 'model' that works for all times and in all places (Easterly, 2002).

I want to focus on a specific policy initiative of the European Union that has generated a strong debate, and that nicely illustrates some aspects of the differences between the Anglo-Saxon approach to EU policy-making, and the European approach. I single out the issue of National Development Planning with its associated Structural Funds because this is an area that will be of great importance to the future well-being of the new EU member states, but is also an area where the debate for and against is not always well grounded in research. It is also a policy area in which I have worked since the late 1980s, initially in Ireland, subsequently in the southern periphery of the 'old' EU, and more recently in the 'new' member states.

I will suggest that the policy activism involved in National Development Planning does not require the rejection of the Anglo-Saxon model; rather, it may be a precondition for the successful operation of that model in lagging economies.

The revival of National Development Planning

The term 'cohesion' first came into widespread use in the European Union in the late 1980s, at a time when major reforms and expansions of EU regional aid were being carried out. As set out in Article 130a of the Treaty on European Union, there is an explicit aim to promote 'harmonious development' with a specific geographical dimension: 'reducing disparities between the levels of development of the various regions and the backwardness of the least favoured regions.' Thus, there is an explicit recognition that wide disparities are intolerable in any community, if that term is to have any real meaning.

National development planning and industrial strategy had been features of the post-war revival of Western Europe, which had been kick-started by Marshall Aid. But it had largely gone out of fashion in the West by the

1970s. On the other hand, in the CEE region, which had suffered the trauma and dislocation of almost 50 years of central planning in one form or another, liberalization in the early 1990s was seen perhaps as a period when the state would take a back-stage role, and purely private sector initiatives would be the engine of economic reform and development.

Conventional or neoclassical economics – particularly in its New Classical revival in the 1970s – had asserted that market-based capitalism was a universal path towards development that was potentially available to all countries. Within the universally dominant paradigm of liberal market economics, it was widely believed that no underdeveloped country was likely to remain disadvantaged permanently simply because it was late coming to the growth process. Nor could the established industrial powers block the development of a latecomer, provided that country played by the rules of economic liberalism. Any remaining failure by a state to grow and prosper was deemed to be self-inflicted (Fukayama, 1992, p. 103).

This crude version of the Anglo-Saxon policy model took the view that all one had to do to promote real convergence (or 'cohesion') between groups of states was to put in place policies that facilitated the free movement of goods and the factors of production.[1] If this was done, then orthodox theory asserted that factor incomes would tend to converge to a common level across all nations in the group. So, if all markets were competitive, any initial national disparities would eventually vanish and there would be no need for specific structural regional policies.

By the late 1980s, when the EU began to get serious about trans-European regional development policies, the intellectual ground had begun to shift under the Anglo-Saxon model. Over the past two decades, three fields of economic research have undergone radical transformation: trade theory (Helpman and Krugman, 1985), growth theory (Grossman and Helpman, 1991), and economic geography (Fujita et al., 1999). The nature of the progress made has been summarized as follows:

> In each of these areas, we have gone through a progression that starts with models based on perfect competition, moves to price-taking with external increasing returns, and finishes with explicit models of imperfect competition. (Romer, 1994, p. 19)

Advances in the study of spatial economic processes suggested that the conditions required for automatic convergence to take place tend not to hold in practice (Krugman, 1995, p. 82). Rather, research attention began to be focused on the importance of such factors as the initial level of regional physical infrastructure, local levels of human capital, or on the fact that regions that start off at a structural disadvantage may never converge in any reasonable time period. Research even suggested that the removal of barriers to trade and factor movements might – in certain circumstances – actually lead to a relative deterioration rather than an improvement of some countries (Williamson, 1965; Krugman, 1987).

This was the intellectual background against which the EU reformed and expanded its regional policies in the late 1980s, into the so-called National Development Plans and their associated Structural Funds. The political rationale behind this reform came from the program of market liberalization, or Single Market initiative of the then EC President, Jacques Delors, which dismantled all remaining non-tariff barriers within the Union (Cecchini, 1988). In doing so, there was a fear that not all EU member states were likely to benefit equally from the Single Market. In particular, the less advanced, geographically peripheral economies of Southern and Western Europe, mainly Greece, Portugal, Spain and Ireland, but including the Italian Mezzogiorno and, after unification, East Germany were felt to be particularly vulnerable. Today, it is the new member states of Central and Eastern Europe, almost all of which have levels of income per head less than half of the EU average, that may be at risk.

What was special about the Structural Fund policies was their ambitious goals, that is, the provision of financial aid, in the context of a domestic co-finance requirement, to implement policies whose explicit aim was to transform the underlying structure of the beneficiary economies. Policies moved far beyond a conventional demand-side, cyclical stabilization role of public expenditure, and were directed at the promotion of structural change, the acceleration of medium-term growth, and the eventual achievement of real convergence mainly through efficiency improvements in supply-side processes. The main policies used were the improvement of basic physical infrastructure, the enhancement of human capital, and certain targeted aids to private productive sectors

The long-term nature of the EU investment aid, up to seven years, permitted domestic public investment policies to shift from a purely domestic process, buffeted by the short-term exigencies of maintaining balance in the public finances, to a more stable longer-term process that was carried out in cooperation with the European Commission. Of course, there continued to be a very natural desire to maximize national control over design, monitoring and evaluation of development policy. However, the ceding of some national policy autonomy to the Commission in Brussels seems to have generated minimal friction since the whole Structural Fund process was perceived to be a genuine partnership that allowed successive political administrations to break with the previous process of annual capital budgeting and put in place development plans of much longer duration, to finance them with far less difficulty in terms of increased public sector borrowing or taxation, and to benefit from trans-EU shared experiences in policy design, monitoring and evaluation.

Strict monitoring systems were mandatory for the Structural Funds, as well as the need to carry out ex ante, mid-term and ex post policy evaluations

(Bradley, 2001). Previous evaluation of public investment programs had at best been secretive, and at worst of very mediocre quality. The monitoring and evaluation aspects of Structural Funds served to promote and guide applied economic research agendas in Ireland and in Southern Europe since 1989, and they are now doing so in the new member states. Research at the most aggregate level of monitoring became something of an Irish area of specialization during the past fifteen years, and some of the approaches developed came to be widely used in other recipient countries as well as by the Commission itself.

Critiques of National Development Planning

There may well be convinced believers in the Anglo-Saxon model who assert that Structural Funds are a distortion of market forces and that the provision of physical infrastructure and human capital should be left to market forces. But this type of ideological critique tends to be rare in Europe, at least among economists. The critiques that are advanced tend to be more subtle. Basically, they assert that Structural Funds produce no significant beneficial effects.

Such a critique has been advanced recently in two papers published by the Dutch CPB (Ederveen et al., 2002a, b). They make the perfectly valid point that when macro-models are used to evaluate Structural Fund impacts on cohesion, they tend not to seek to establish if there is a positive impact on the cohesion objective due to the policies. Rather, they characterize model-based research on Structural Fund policy impacts as 'imposing' the results.[2]

One approach to testing the impact of Structural Funds suggested by Ederveen et al. (2002a, b) is to set up Barro-type growth regressions (Barro and Sala-i-Martin, 1995) and augment them with Structural Fund variables. Thus, the basic Barro-type regression will have growth of GDP as the dependent variable and the initial level of GDP per head, the domestic savings rate, population growth, and so on, as independent variables. They insert the Structural Fund expenditures into such a model and seek to estimate statistically significant and positive coefficients.[3] In general they fail to find any significant Structural Fund effect. But since they examine a wide range of countries, some of which received very little aid, and deal with a time period that stretches from the mid-1960s to the early 1990s, their findings are not surprising.[4] However, when they add a 'conditioning' variable such as openness, institutional quality, corruption index, and so on, their analysis suggests that a few countries like Ireland did benefit from an increased growth rate that was associated with the Structural Funds.

We suggest that this approach suffers from the fact that it posits a model where the only Structural Fund impact looked for is one on the growth rate. In most of the sample of thirteen EU countries and for most of the sample period 1960–95, the regional aid was trivially small, and was very unlikely to affect the growth rate, even temporarily. The macro-model-based impact evaluations usually posit a less stringent 'levels' effect, and draw on the international literature to support it. Such evaluations usually pick up long-term levels effects (see Bradley et al., 2004b for references). If the CPB approach were to be restricted to the poorer EU member states, and excluded such high income countries as Denmark, Sweden, the Netherlands and France, then significant effects on growth might reasonably be sought. However, the panel regression technique requires a wide range of countries, which frustrates application of the technique to lagging countries in isolation.

Within the literature of policy impact evaluation using structural macro-models, there are also differences of emphasis. For example, the EC's own model is called QUEST, and is a sophisticated neo-Keynsian model with forward-looking, or model consistent expectation mechanisms. In such models one tends to get policy crowding-out caused by the anticipation of tax increases in the future to pay for public investment in the present. Any impact analysis based on QUEST tends to show very small effects of Structural Funds on GDP, just as they show negligible effects of any tax-financed public expenditure.

But it is arguable whether crowding-out is a reasonable assumption in the lagging economies that are the main beneficiaries of EU investment aid. First, such economies tend to be operating well below full capacity. Second, the public expenditure involved is on public goods that provide direct inputs into private production processes, where the returns to the investments are almost all private, and where there are externalities involved. Third, the direct EU aid element of the Structural Funds lessens the tax burden, and revenue buoyancy offsets some of the deterioration in the public sector borrowing requirement.

But, in a sense, these debates may be missing the point. They focus exclusively on an economic perspective and the debate is essentially about the rate of return on investment. With carefully designed macro-models, one can examine the difference between performance 'with' Structural Funds, and performance 'without.'[5] Such evaluations tend to give rise to relatively modest boosts to cohesion (Bradley et al., 2004c). The more Anglo-Saxon your model, the smaller the impact. But the policy instruments of Structural Funds, mainly physical infrastructure and human capital, provide inputs into a cohesion process, but do not guarantee it. Only if individual businesses exploit the improved economic environment will cohesion happen.

Reaganomics is about business as well as economics!

At the risk of oversimplification, one might stylize economic theories as being useful for the study of how a representative firm is likely to behave when subjected to changes in the wider external policy environment.

Business research frameworks, on the other hand, tend to be focused on the analysis of the consequences of management actions that are intended to improve the prospects of a specific firm within a given external policy environment. It is interesting to note that while economic theories tend to be international, the main business frameworks tend to be of American origin.

Business researchers see the world broadly in terms of a diagram made up of three concentric circles, labelled broadly as follows:

- The outer business environment
- The middle ground of business strategy
- The inner ground of business/marketing tactics

From a business strategy perspective, the outer circle contains all the factors that serve to make up the strategic environment over which any individual firm has little or no control, and from which emerge the strategic opportunities and threats that face the firm as it operates in the marketplace. It contains all the economic and competitive forces that are the domain of the economic policy researcher.[6] Business researchers dip into these matters only when they need to, mainly as sources of opportunities and threats, but it is not their main domain of research activity. We economic researchers talk of little else.

The middle circle of business strategy is the domain where much business-oriented research is focused. Key issues include the determination of a company's competitive edge and differential advantage within the given outer business environment. It also includes the selection of target markets and the positioning of products and brands within the selected markets. Here, it is common for knowledge and research insights to be systematized into explanatory frameworks. Such frameworks usually stop well short of being testable paradigms in any scientific sense, but often take the form of taxonomies of useful and revealing facts and insights. Influential examples include Raymond Vernon's product life cycle (PLC) framework explaining the sequential nature of the different stages of industrialization, trade and foreign direct investment (Vernon, 1966); Michael Porter's diamond of competitive advantage, which shows how policy can be used to create national advantage even in situations where initial factor and other endowments are unfavorable (Porter, 1990); and Michael Best's capability and innovation perspective, the 'capability triad', which points to the need for synchronized advances on many fronts if dynamic growth is to occur (Best, 2001).

Finally, the inner circle is the environment of business tactics, encompassing all aspects of the so-called marketing mix. Here one has moved away from the wider role of public environmental policy and long-term business strategy, and emphasis is placed on the immediate actions of managers within individual firms. There may be a public policy regulatory oversight of this inner business environment to ensure fair play and open competition, as well as some targeted aid directed at improving the marketing skills of small or newly formed firms. But actions within the inner environment are normally left to the discretion of firms.

Thus, one might characterize the key challenge of successful policy-making in any underdeveloped nation as that of blending the techniques and insights of the economic analysis of the outer business environment with those of the business analysis of the middle ground of strategy.

At the level of the individual firm or corporation, strategy is usually formulated in a context where government policies are given, and firms address the challenges of assessing the business portfolio and identifying strategic goals. The crucial role of management is to formulate a corporate strategy that aligns with the nation's or region's wealth-building strategy. So, this issue is usually examined largely from the point of view of domestic or of regional companies adjusting to national strategy.

But in the poorer EU member states, causality as often as not must run in the opposite direction. For example, the Irish industrial development agency, the IDA, constantly scans the world for inward investment in high-technology sectors, even when the domestic environment is not initially attractive enough to persuade leading-edge firms to locate in Ireland. But information on firms' expressed needs is fed back to the Irish government by the IDA, and major policy changes can be executed quite rapidly.[7] Structural Funds played a big part in this process during the 1990s, and were one of the factors underlying Ireland's rapid convergence (Bradley, 2003).

The national wealth-creation strategy in poorer countries often needs to adapt to the requirements of firms in the global and local corporate environment, and not the other way around. The strategic challenges facing poorer economies are very different from those facing large developed nations such as America, Japan, Germany, France and the UK. Policy-making needs to be in tune with the best thinking on economics as well as on international industrial policy frameworks. To dismiss industrial strategy as 'picking winners' is to misunderstand its fundamental thrust. Perhaps 'picking winning environments' might be closer to the mark. A winning environment is essentially a public good, and is a legitimate target of public policy. EU Structural Funds are directed at improving the wider business environment.

Thus, transition economies like Poland are not faced with an either/or choice between the Anglo-Saxon model and the European model. The most successful economies, as demonstrated by the Scandinavian and Irish examples, appear to be those that get the blend right.

Notes

1. Real convergence or cohesion requires convergence in living standards. Nominal convergence requires convergence of inflation rates, interest rates, and public sector balances.

2. One line of research being critiqued by the CPB team is that of the HERMIN-based evaluations (see Bradley et al., 2004a, b). But in this literature, any imposition of impacts is not arbitrary. It draws on a large and authoritative research literature and uses impact elasticity values that are consistent with this literature.
3. A pooled cross-section regression is used, with thirteen EU countries in the data set and using seven five-year periods from 1960–65 through 1990–95.
4. It should be noted that the level of Structural Fund investment aid was very low prior to 1989, and was only expanded massively after that.
5. By 'carefully designed' we mean structural models where policy-induced changes in structure are explicitly modelled. Such models are less susceptible to the so-called Lucas critique of reduced form time-series models (Lucas, 1976).
6. The outer circle also includes the forces of technical progress, social forces, legal issues, environmental protection rules, and political forces (such as ideology).
7. A case of information feed-back was the transformation of the Irish university system in the mid-1970s, where massive resources were put into the enhancement of electronic engineering and chemistry to create a skilled labor force to attract potential inward investors (MacSharry and White, 2000).

References

Barro, R. and X. Sala-i-Martin (1995), *Economic Growth*, New York: McGraw-Hill.

Best, M. (2001), *The New Competitive Advantage*, Oxford: Oxford University Press.

Bradley, J. (2001), 'Experiences with Building Systems of Monitoring and Evaluation of EU Funds: the Irish Case', Report prepared for the World Bank project Support of a Monitoring and Evaluation System of the Use of European Union and Other Foreign Funds, May, Warsaw.

Bradley, J. (2003), 'Irish Development in an International Perspective', Paper presented at the conference Successes and Failures in Real Convergence, National Bank of Poland, Warsaw, 23–24 October

Bradley, J., J. Gács, A. Kangur and N. Lubenets (2004a), 'HERMIN: a Macro Model Framework for the Study of Cohesion and Transition', in J. Bradley, G. Petrakos and I. Traistaru (eds), *The Impact of Economic and Monetary Integration on Cohesion in an Enlarged European Union*, New York: Springer.

Bradley, J., A. Kangur and N. Lubenets (2004b), 'Macro Impact Evaluation of National Development Plans: Ireland and Estonia', in J. Bradley, G. Petrakos and I. Traistaru (eds), *The Impact of Economic and Monetary Integration on Cohesion in an Enlarged European Union*, New York: Springer.

Bradley, J., J. Gács, E. Morgenroth and G. Untiedt (2004c), *A Study of the Macro-economic Impact of the Reform of EU Cohesion Policy*, Report prepared for the European Commission, Directorate-General for Regional Policy, Brussels, http://europa.eu.int/comm/regional_policy/sources/docgener/studies/pdf/3cr/macro_impact.pdf.

Cecchini, P. (1988), *The European Challenge 1992, the Benefits of a Single Market*, London: Wildwood House.

Easterly, W. (2002), *The Elusive Quest for Growth: Economists' Adventures and Misadventures in the Tropics*, Cambridge, MA: MIT Press.

Ederveen, S., J. Gorter, R. de Mooij and R. Nahuis (2002a), 'Funds and Games: the Economics of European Cohesion Policy', CPB Netherlands Bureau for Economic Policy Analysis, The Hague.

Ederveen, S., H. de Groot and R. Nahuis (2002b), 'Fertile Soil for Structural Funds? a Panel Data Analysis of the Conditional Effectiveness of European Cohesion Policy', CPB Netherlands Bureau for Economic Policy Analysis, The Hague, Report No. 10, August.
Fukuyama, F. (1992), *The End of History and the Last Man*, Harmondsworth: Penguin.
Fujita, M., P. Krugman and A. Venables (1999), *The Spatial Economy: Cities, Regions, and International Trade*, Cambridge, MA: MIT Press.
Grossman, G. and E. Helpman (1991), *Innovation and Growth*, Cambridge, MA: MIT Press.
Helpman, E. and P. Krugman (1985), *Market Structure and Foreign Trade: Increasing Returns, Imperfect Competition and the International Economy*, Cambridge, MA: MIT Press
Krugman, P. (1987), 'Economic Integration in Europe: Some Conceptual Issues', in T. Padoa-Schioppa (ed.), *Efficiency, Stability and Equity*, Oxford: Oxford University Press.
Krugman, P. (1995), *Development, Geography, and Economic Theory*, Cambridge, MA: MIT Press.
Lucas, R. (1976), 'Economic Policy Evaluation: a Critique', *Supplement to Journal of Monetary Economics*, 1, 19–46.
MacSharry, R. and P. White (2000), *The Making of the Celtic Tiger*, Cork: Mercier Press.
Porter, M. (1990), *The Competitive Advantage of Nations*, London: Macmillan.
Roland, G. (2000), *Transition and Economics: Politics, Markets, and Firms*, Cambridge, MA: MIT Press.
Romer, P. (1994), 'The Origins of Endogenous Growth', *Journal of Economic Perspectives*, 8(1), 3–22.
Vernon, R. (1966), 'International Investment and International Trade in the Product Cycle', *Quarterly Journal of Economics*, May, 190–207.
Williamson, J. (1965), 'Regional Inequality and the Process of National Development: a Description of the Patterns', *Economic Development and Cultural Change*, 13/4(2), 3–84.

16
Ireland's Delayed if Spectacular Convergence

Daniel McCoy

Why is Ireland interesting?

Ireland, a small island nation on the western periphery of Continental Europe has in the space of what would appear to be a little over a decade become one of the most dynamic economies in the developed world. It has ranked consistently since the late 1990s among the top five nations of the OECD in terms of output per capita in purchasing power terms, while *The Economist* Intelligence Unit went even further in 2004, declaring Ireland to have the highest quality of life characteristics in the world. Such stellar achievement from a country that was rightly considered 'the poorest of the rich' in the 1980s, required a suitable accolade, the most used has been the zoologically improbable 'Celtic Tiger.'[1]

The Irish economy is one of the most open in the world both in terms of trade and factor of production flows. It constitutes less than 2 percent of overall output in the euro area, while its openness is reflected in the international mobility of both its labor and capital, combining strong migratory flows and high levels of foreign direct investment. A share of combined exports and imports of goods to Gross Domestic Product (GDP) of around 150 percent signals Ireland's high dependence on external trade. In recent decades the Irish economy has been transformed from one based on agriculture and traditional manufacturing to one increasingly based on the hi-tech and internationally traded services sectors. By 2004 the services sector accounted for 66 percent of employment, industry for 28 percent and agriculture for 6 percent.

Over the last decade, unprecedented economic growth has seen the level of Irish real GDP almost double. Growth, as measured by GDP, averaged 8 percent in real terms between 1994 and 2004. This remarkable growth performance throughout the late 1990s and into the start of the new millennium has led to rapid convergence of output per capita with the EU average. It has been driven by exceptionally strong growth in employment. Ireland's working population has risen from 1.2 million to 1.9 million in ten years, reducing unemployment rates from 16 percent to 4 percent of a labor force that has been boosted by the arrival of 1970s baby-boomers, increased female participation and high inward migration.

Irish living standards also have increased significantly over the last decade. The OECD has ranked Ireland fourth in the world using GDP per capita in purchasing power terms with only the US, Norway and Luxembourg ranking higher in 2003. However, it is critically important to note that the use of the GDP measure may not give the most accurate indication of living standards for Ireland.[2] Gross National Product (GNP) may give a better indication of income and hence living standards for the Irish case, as it accounts for the substantial repatriation of incomes from the large presence of multinationals based in Ireland. The difference between the two output measures is stark in the Irish case, with GNP accounting for just 83 percent of GDP in 2003.

Using this more appropriate measure Ireland's international ranking would bring it more in line with the OECD average. While Ireland's relative wealth may be flattered by the particular measure chosen, it still remains the case that it is an interesting role model for economies in transition, such as the new EU member states. In the mid-1980s, Irish output per capita was the second lowest in the EU-15 at two-thirds of the average, comparable to the other 'cohesion' countries, Portugal, Greece and Spain. Within a decade, Ireland's output per capita is ranked second highest in the EU-15 while the other cohesion countries have made relatively little headway in terms of convergence.

Ireland is interesting then because of its spectacular convergence, but it is also sanguine to reflect that the convergence itself was quite delayed. The economic story from Ireland was not always so rosy. Indeed the economic history of Ireland since its independence from the United Kingdom in 1922 was characterized more by failure throughout the last century (Lee, 1989), with the last decade a belated success. There have been many reasons advanced for Ireland's success, which, in combination, can help explain the exceptionally strong growth rates experienced. They include EU membership and access to the Single Market; Ireland's low corporation tax rate and a large multinational presence, particularly from the US; a high proportion of the population of working age; increased participation in the labor market, especially by females; a reversal of the trend of emigration toward immigration; sustained investment in education and training; coordinated social partnership agreements; and a more stable public finance position.

All of these have had a role to play no doubt, and this chapter addresses some of the underlying lessons from the Irish story. These lessons might be encapsulated with the following advice – start badly, open up and be receptive to foreign capital, avoid domestic macroeconomic policy mistakes, be business friendly, develop a shared economic consensus, get lucky and try to stay that way.

A bad beginning despite good initial conditions

Explaining Ireland's rapid convergence requires placing it in a longer-term perspective. Ireland in the 1920s, on gaining its independence from the UK, was relatively well positioned to prosper over the evolving century. As an agriculture-dominated economy, it had close proximity and reasonably free trade with the largely industrialized economy of the UK, at that time the world's largest empire. It had a common, free access labor market relationship with the UK and a fixed pegged currency arrangement. Ireland also had good administrative structures and effective legal property right arrangements in place. However, the pursuit of a strategy of self-sufficiency from the 1930s to the end of the 1950s hampered the ability of a small economy to achieve or even maintain a good standard of living.

The protectionist strategy involved bans on foreign ownership of controlling interests in domestic firms, large subsidies for inefficient firms to try to service a small and declining indigenous population and, in the mid-1930s, a trade war with the UK, which was not fully reversed until the mid-1960s, and which further hampered growth prospects. As Europe began to emerge from the disaster of the Second World War, Ireland continued to pursue dysfunctional domestic policies that resulted in a stop-go macroeconomic policy arising from a series of balance of payments crises. Although Ireland was pursuing a protectionist industrial policy, even by the end of the 1950s it was quite open to trade relative to other European countries, particularly through agriculture (Bradley, 2000). The economic failure of the 1950s, resulting in large outward migration from Ireland, fostered a national mood of despondency. The acceptance of the economic failure that a protectionist policy had brought was finally made in the latter quarter of the decade. The change in tack, which laid the antecedents of the much later success of the Irish economy was a reorientation toward being more accepting of free trade and foreign capital investment as domestic living standards would be determined by being an effective export platform.

Open up and let foreign capital in

The change in the orientation of Ireland in the late 1950s was best exemplified by the industrial strategy adopted in 1958, which began a rolling series of national economic development plans (Bradley, 2004). The restriction on foreign ownership was lifted and indeed foreign ownership was positively encouraged, with an emphasis placed upon attracting foreign direct investment (FDI). The Industrial Development Authority (IDA) was set up to seek out FDI opportunities for Ireland, armed with state-aid enticements involving grants and a zero rate corporation tax for exporting industries.

By 1961, the Irish population had been falling steadily for well over a century reaching a low then of just under 3 million persons. Employment

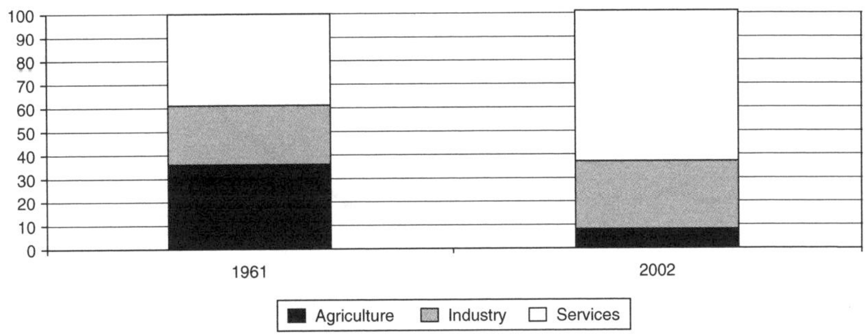

Figure 16.1: Employment share by sector in Ireland, 1961 and 2002

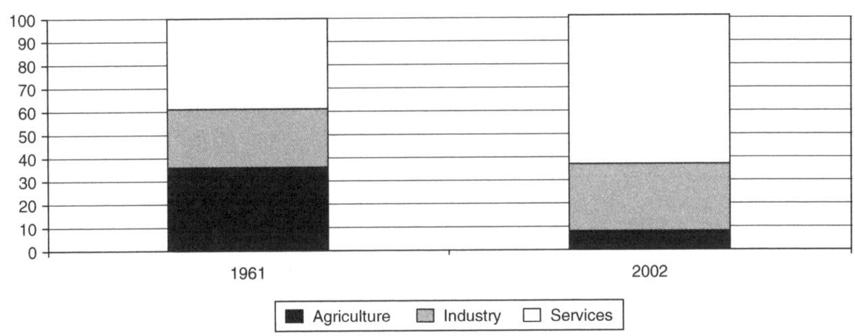

Figure 16.2: Output (GDP) share by sector in Ireland, 1961 and 2002
Source: ESRI (2003).

and output were still focused more on agriculture than on industry (see Figure 16.1 and Figure 16.2).[3] Agriculture accounted for one-third of employment and one-quarter of output in 1961, with exports being dominated by products such as live animals predominantly destined for the British market

In 1965, Ireland signed a new Anglo-Irish free trade agreement. While relationships and economic ties with the UK improved during the 1960s, the reorientation of Irish industrial policy was to help diversify Irish exports away from an overdependence on the UK. The destiny for Ireland was clearly mapped as being with mainland Europe, and both Ireland and the UK attempted unsuccessfully to join the then European Economic Community (EEC) in the mid-1960s. The orientation from that time was to get ready for eventual acceptance into the EEC in 1973 (Bradley, 2000). Throughout the 1960s, FDI into Ireland began to flow from the US, initiating a critical aspect

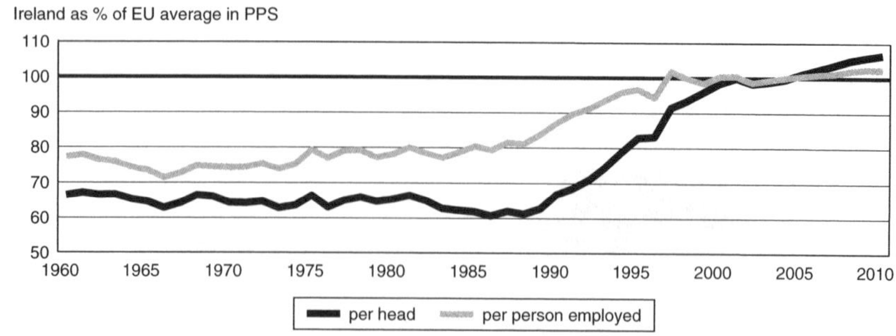

Figure 16.3: Ireland: GNP compared to EU, 1960–2010
Source: ESRI (2003).

of Ireland's subsequent success. The injection of FDI to create new industrial activities also put pressure on Ireland to raise its educational standards with the introduction in 1967 of free entry for second-level schooling. The 1960s witnessed a slowdown in emigration flows, and by the 1970s there was a considerable reversal to inward migration of mainly returning Irish people who had left over the previous two decades.

The returned migrants and the optimism imbued by the turnaround in economic fortunes that FDI and prospective EEC membership gave rise to resulted in a substantial rise in the Irish birth rate during the 1970s. These baby-boomers were to form a critical enabling factor in the success of the Irish economy in the 1990s as they entered the workforce. The combination of rising capital stock and labor, augmented by higher productivity by virtue of higher education and training levels, meant that economic growth in Ireland rose steadily from the early 1960s to the late 1970s and in turn boosted national living standards. Economic growth, however, was not sufficiently strong to bring about convergence with other European countries but it did halt the secular decline of previous decades (see Figure 16.3).

Policy mistakes retard progress, but economic consensus emerged

Membership of the EEC brought with it opportunities and threats for the Irish economy on joining in 1973. The boosts for farmers' incomes were significant and the removal of state support for industry and other capital controls had quite long lead times in contrast to recent accessions. The inevitable shake-out of industry was therefore gradual and postponed until the early part of the 1980s. The global oil shocks of the 1970s impacted negatively on the Irish economy, as elsewhere, but the low interest rate environment after the first OPEC oil price shock was used by the Irish government to borrow heavily to fund a 'dash for growth.' In addition to stimulatory fiscal policy, a decision was taken in 1979 to join the fledgling European Monetary System and thus break the link of the Irish punt to Sterling. This secured lower interest rates from the increased credibility resulting from being linked to the German mark.

The anticipated boom from lower interest rates and a more stable exchange rate, however, did not materialize in the post-second OPEC oil shock period when monetary policy was tightened throughout the Western economies. The spike in interest rates trapped Ireland, along with many Third World countries with high foreign borrowing, into a spiral of lower growth and unsustainable debt levels. The first half of the 1980s witnessed a near meltdown for the Irish economy. Growth stagnated, unemployment rates soared, emigration resumed once again, the birth rate dropped precipitously, public finances became unsustainable despite a combination of sharp expenditure reductions and increased tax burdens, which fell disproportionately on employed labor, giving cause to significant industrial unrest. The Irish punt lost value as a series of devaluations proved to be ineffective, particularly as Ireland's main trading partner, the UK, was also in a severe slump.

By the mid-1980s, while developed economies were returning to trend growth rates, Ireland remained trapped in a vicious circle of low growth, high personal taxation, high unemployment and a discouraged workforce. Public investment had been pared back substantially and the demographics of a very young population structure combined with high rates of unemployment meant that Ireland's dependency ratio of economically inactive to those employed was very high (see Figure 16.4).

By 1986, the stylized economic facts for Ireland looked rather bleak: real GDP growth was 0.4 percent, the unemployment rate was 17.1 percent, the

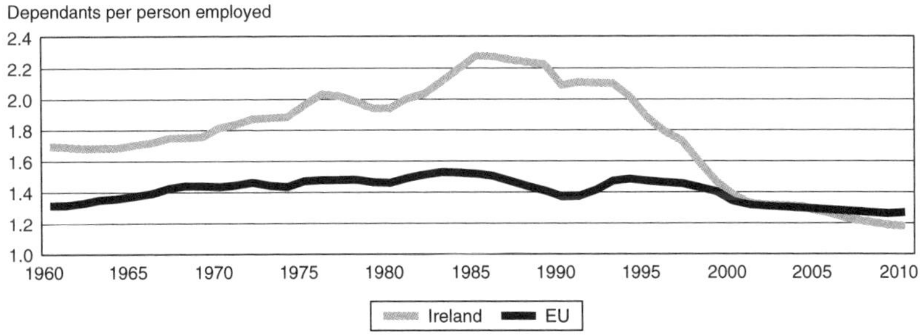

Figure 16.4: Ireland's dependency ratio, 1960–2010
Source: ESRI (2003).

government deficit was 8.3 percent and government debt was 125 percent of GDP, the deficit on the current account of the balance of payments was 3.5 percent and inflation was still high relative to trading partners at 3.8 percent as a depreciating currency quickly passed through to prices.

As in the late 1950s, Ireland had once again reached a nadir by the mid-1980s, and a consensus was forming that radical action would be required. The public finances were moving towards a sustainable position by 1987 (Honohan, 1999) but the general election of that year provided Ireland with what was effectively a national government in economic terms. The incoming administration adopted the economic policies of the outgoing government to achieve broad political support to drive through a series of substantial expenditure contractions and develop a 'Programme for National Recovery' with a centerpiece wage-deal built around the ideal of social partnership involving a tripartite arrangement comprising the government, trade unions and private sector employers. The wage deal involved agreement to accept modest nominal wage growth enhanced by direct taxation reductions in return for industrial relations peace.

The Irish economy's inflection point certainly appears to be 1987 when real GDP growth sprang back to 4.4 percent and got stronger as the decade ended. There is, however, no single explanation as to how the turnaround emerged. Social partnership is certainly one ingredient. While these deals were never fully binding, they nonetheless acted to alter expectations. Similarly the credibility gains in tackling the public finances led some commentators to view Ireland as an example of non-Keynesian impacts through expansionary fiscal contractions. Others point to a substantial devaluation within the exchange rate mechanism in 1986, which boosted competitiveness at the point when the UK economy, Ireland's largest trading partner, was having a fiscal-policy induced boom. Irish growth certainly appeared to be export-led at that juncture, lending greater credence to the 'rising tide raises all boats' interpretation. Clearly, without domestic restructuring, Ireland would not have been able to benefit from increased international demand, and the establishment of an economic consensus at that time provided conditions for catching the wave of improving international trade.

Business-friendly environment

Throughout the last near half century there has been one consistent feature of the economic consensus in Ireland: an acceptance and willingness to support business investment. Understanding this facet of the Irish economy is easier when it is recalled that Ireland traditionally had been rich in labor but poor in capital. The consistency of approach to industrial policy has never wavered since the late 1950s, with low corporation taxation being the norm even when labor taxes were quite draconian.[4] Even throughout the social partnership era from the late 1980s, the share of economic activity going to profits has risen substantially at the expense of labor without causing any great fear even among trade unions, as the growing economic pie continued to provide a win-win situation.

The consistency of industrial policy and a favorable attitude to engagement with the European Union induced US multinationals, in particular, to choose Ireland as their European base to service the expanding Single Market (Fitz Gerald, 2000). Ireland became a magnet for US firms from the late 1980s, particularly in sectors related to information and communication technology (ICT). The spectacular success of these sectors globally in the 1990s translated directly into the success of the Irish economy during that phase too.

The Celtic Tiger roars

The Irish economy was starting upon its rapid convergence by the end of the 1980s but the spectacular rates of high real output growth as set out in Figure 16.5 emerged from 1994 onwards after the growth surge had been temporarily checked by the European slowdown of the early 1990s. Ireland devalued its currency with the European Exchange Rate Mechanism (ERM) at the start of 1993 and managed a wide margin peg exchange rate policy until joining European Monetary Union (EMU) in 1999.

The decision to join the EMU was not clear-cut in the Irish case, given the UK's decision to opt out but the benefits were considered to outweigh the costs (Baker et al., 1996). The high real growth rates continued into the first few years of EMU as Irish interest rates fell significantly upon joining (Fitz Gerald, 2001).

The initial fears in Ireland in the early 1990s regarding the pick-up in growth were that it would prove to be a 'jobless recovery.' However, the Celtic Tiger performance has been as much about strong employment growth as any high productivity miracle. The contributing factors behind

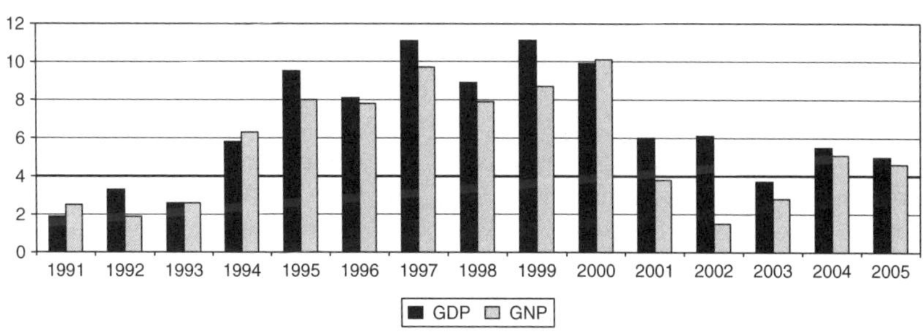

Figure 16.5: Ireland's real output growth performance, 1990–2005

the remarkable employment growth performance were natural population rise, increased female participation and net inward migration. The initial returning migrants in the 1990s were Irish nationals who had left within the previous decade, but now the returning migrants are increasingly non-nationals who have relatively higher educational attainment compared with the indigenous population (Barrett et al., 2005).

The role of EU Structural Funds is also given credit for much of Ireland's economic convergence and indeed they were significant, although not of a scale to be the full explanation. Ireland did use its EU Structural Funds wisely, but initially there were concerns that a significant proportion of the funds were invested in mobile human capital through education and training schemes. When the economy succeeded, this policy looked enlightened, but it was high risk nonetheless. EU Structural Funds encouraged Ireland to invest in its own infrastructure at a time when national confidence was low.

Lessons to learn?

The Economist (2004) referred to the 'Luck of the Irish' in a review of Ireland in late 2004. Ireland has been fortunate, as convergence is never inevitable, particularly for a small open economy (Sachs, 1997). Debate remains ongoing about what the factors that brought about the turnaround in Irish fortunes were and whether these can be replicated elsewhere. The first point to acknowledge about Ireland is its small scale, which means that some avenues taken by Ireland in the past may not be appropriate for larger economies. Krugman (1997) observes that Ireland mixes facets of a national economy where productivity will determine living standards and a regional economy where competitiveness is the key to ensuring an effective export platform.

Managing a regional economy within a monetary union limits the policy instrument choices available. The role of industrial policy becomes very important, as in the Irish case (Bradley, 1999). While good domestic economic management is not sufficient, it is necessary.[5] The sustainability of the Irish miracle attracts considerable attention, both nationally, where the focus is on whether it is a regional boom (Barry, 2002) or a mere paper phenomenon (O'Grada, 2002), and internationally by the European Commission (Cech and Macdonald, 2004, for instance).

Ireland placed a heavy emphasis on human capital development and upon selecting appropriate FDI projects. The high mobility of these factors required the courage of conviction when policies appeared to be failing, but the consistency of approach proved to be a significant factor in creating the virtuous circle of the Irish economy over the last decade. The strategy of economic development adopted in Ireland has involved the opening up of the goods and capital markets as part of the long-term process of EU integration.

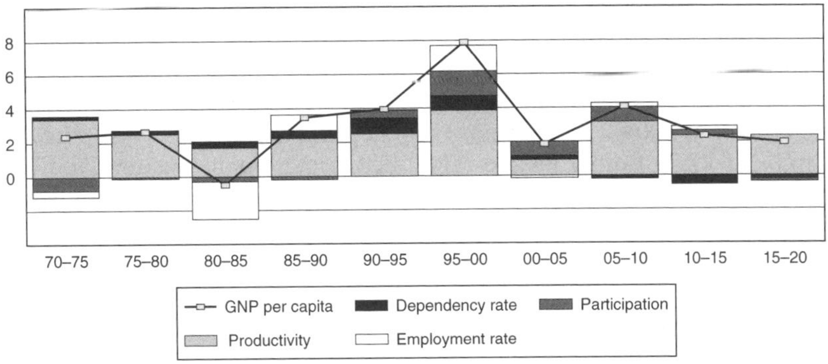

Figure 16.6: Decomposition of Irish GNP per capita growth, 1970–2020
Source: ESRI (2003).

However, there was more to Ireland's success than merely a liberalization of markets, despite the very significant role played by US multinationals in Ireland.

Figure 16.6 plots the growth contribution to GNP per capita attributable to productivity, employment, labor force participation and dependency trends. It is clear that productivity growth has been strong throughout the past thirty years, which combines the role of rising educational attainment of the labor force and the inflow of foreign direct investment. The rise in participation rates, driven by increased participation of women in the workforce, is strongly linked to the increase in investment in education as well as cultural change and improved employment prospects. At the same time, underlying demographic trends, especially with declining unemployment, have reduced the dependency ratio.

The large influx of FDI, particularly from the late 1980s, was a catalyst in the revival of the Irish economy both from agglomeration impacts and the demonstration effect to Irish staff of how the successful business model operates. The multinational sectors of the economy have exceptionally high productivity growth rates reflecting the favorable tax treatment of profits in Ireland in contrast to other regions of the EU-15. This high productivity in the traded goods sector had the potential to lead to higher wage growth in the more sheltered sectors of the economy and quickly erode competitiveness. The presence of social partnership agreements in Ireland arguably helped slow down this wage spiral spillover for much of the 1990s, allowing the economy's convergence not to be choked off too soon. By the early years of EMU membership, however, this higher wage, higher prices spillover from higher productivity in one sector to another had moved Ireland to the top of the euro area's inflation league and quite quickly to the highest price level (MacCoille and McCoy, 2002).

The challenge for Ireland now is to be worth its higher wages and prices and to deal with the increased competition from both within and outside the EU (Barry, 2004). The challenge for countries aspiring to emulate Ireland is to be lucky, but other lessons might be to open up, be business and FDI-friendly and try to form a consensus on the economic imperatives. While Irish debate revolves around whether it wants to be more like Boston or Berlin, Dublin, with its hybrid mix of the American business model with European-style social partnership might be a good benchmark for smaller, regional economies.

Notes

1. Honohan and Walsh (2003) suggest the 'Celtic Hare' as a more fitting analogy.
2. GDP measures the total output produced by factors of production located in the Irish economy. Therefore it includes the substantial profits made by foreign multinationals, but largely repatriated.
3. On partition of Ireland in 1922, industrialized activities such as shipbuilding and textiles were concentrated in Northern Ireland. The southern part of Ireland had relatively few industrial bases, brewing being a notable exception.
4. Corporation tax rates are 12.5 percent and capital gains tax rates are 20 percent, which makes them as light as expenditure taxes and lower than taxes on income in Ireland. The tax on incomes has also been reduced over the last two decades to the point where Ireland's tax and expenditure to output ratios are among the lowest in the developed economies.
5. Honohan and Walsh (2002) outline how poor economic policy choice led to Ireland's long underperformance until it was corrected during the late 1980s.

References

Baker, T., J. Fitz Gerald and P. Honohan (1996), 'Economic Implications for Ireland of EMU', Economic and Social Research Institute Policy Research Paper, No. 28, Dublin.

Barrett, A., A. Bergin and D. Duffy (2005), 'The Labour Market Characteristics and Labour Market Profile of Immigrants in Ireland', Economic and Social Research Institue Seminar Paper, 3 March, Dublin.

Barry, F. (2002), 'The Celtic Tiger Era: Delayed Convergence or Regional Boom?', *Quarterly Economic Commentary*, Summer, The Economic and Social Research Institute, Dublin.

Barry, F. (2004) 'Prospects for Ireland in an Enlarged EU', *The World Economy*, 27 (6), 829–52.

Bradley, J. (1999), 'Economic Management in Ireland Post-EMU: Policy Implications of Globalisation and Regionalisation', *Journal of the Statistical and Social Inquiry Society of Ireland*, 28 (1), 83–92.

Bradley, J. (2000), 'The Irish Economy in Comparative Perspective', in B. Nolan, P. O'Connell and C.T. Whelan (eds), *Bust to Boom? The Irish Experience of Growth and Inequality*, Dublin: Institute of Public Administration, pp. 4–27.

Bradley, J. (2004), 'Changing the Rules: How the Failures of the 1950s Forced a Transition in Economic Policy Making', *Administration*, 52 (1), Spring, 92–107.

Cech, Z. and J. Macdonald (2004), 'The "Celtic Tiger" Learns to Purr', *ECFIN Country Focus*, 1 (18), Brussels: European Commission, 1–14.

The Economist (2004), 'The Luck of the Irish: a Survey of Ireland', October.

ESRI (2003), *Medium Term Review 2003–2010*, A. Bergin, J. Cullen, D. Duffy, J. Fitz Gerald, I. Kearney, D. McCoy, Dublin: The Economic and Social Research Institute.

Fitz Gerald, J. (2000), 'The Story of Ireland's Failure – and Belated Success', in B. Nolan, P. O'Connell and C.T. Whelan (eds), *Bust to Boom? The Irish Experience of Growth and Inequality*, Dublin: Institute of Public Administration, pp. 27–57.

Fitz Gerald, J. (2001), 'Managing an Economy under EMU: the Case of Ireland', *The World Economy*, 24 (10), 1353–71.

Honohan, P. (1999), 'Fiscal Adjustment and Disinflation in Ireland: Setting the Macro Basis of Economic Recovery and Expansion', in F. Barry (ed.), *Understanding Ireland's Economic Growth*, London: Macmillan Press, pp. 75–99.

Honohan, P. and B. Walsh (2002), 'Catching Up with the Leaders: the Irish Hare', *Brookings Papers on Economic Activity*, No. 1, 1–77.

Krugman, P. (1997), 'Good News from Ireland: a Geographical Perspective', in A. Gray (ed.), *International Perspectives on the Irish Economy*, Dublin: Indecon, pp. 38–53.

MacCoille, C. and D. McCoy (2002), 'Economic Adjustment within EMU: Ireland's Experience', *Economic and Social Review*, 33 (2), 179–94.

Lee, J.J. (1989), *Ireland: 1912–1985. Politics and Society*, Cambridge: Cambridge University Press.

O'Grada, C. (2002), 'Is the Celtic Tiger a Paper Tiger?', *Quarterly Economic Commentary*, Spring, The Economic and Social Research Institute, Dublin.

Sachs, J.D. (1997), 'Ireland's Growth Strategy: Lessons for Economic Development', in A. Gray (ed.), *International Perspectives on the Irish Economy*, Dublin: Indecon, pp. 54–63.

17

Convergence and Divergence of the European Union: Are the European Economies to be 'Americanized'?

Tadeusz Kowalik

> Globalization is just another word for Americanization.
>
> Henry Kissinger[1]

> I am not proposing the Americanization of Europe but an updated European model... we need American dynamism with the European social model...
> It is not impossible to pursue both at once.
>
> José Manuel Barroso[2]

My main concern is to tackle the following problem: whether, or to what extent, the EU economies are, and should be, becoming Americanized, by adopting the US socio-economic model. Americanization means, first of all, sharply reducing the welfare state and building a flexible labor market. Current US macroeconomic policy is not part of this agenda because the US government's practice, though not its ideology, is more European than the economic policy of the EU governments and institutions. In promoting growth and combating unemployment, the Fed and the federal government use monetary and fiscal tools in a quite Keynesian way, whereas the EU governments and the European Central Bank operate within the confines of a Maastricht and Amsterdam Treaties' straitjacket.

Before tackling this problem, we have to answer a preliminary question: whether the EU is developing towards one economic system, or is rather preserving a variety of types of capitalism. In the former case, it would be pointless to treat the EU economies as one entity.

Hopes and illusion of convergence

There are two general assumptions behind EU integration. The first is a deeply rooted belief in the value of scale. The larger the common market, the more efficient it will be. From this perspective the very existence of a miniscule but rich country such as Iceland is almost impossible. The second assumption is a belief in income convergence resulting from EU policy. Enlargement, together with transfers of Structural Funds, should bring a higher rate of economic growth, higher employment and national and regional convergence. This is how Günter Verheugen encouraged new candidates to accept EU membership: 'Membership in the EU gives unlimited access to the biggest consumption market in the world; a great common market creates economic dynamism – along with growth and more workplaces... and also converging living standards in a unified Europe, through identifying areas with worse economic conditions and investing in these areas on a great scale' (Verheugen, 2001).

It is well known, however, that the Southern European economies paint a mixed picture, as their regional convergence is rather disappointing. Portugal improved its place in the rankings considerably. Similarly, Spain improved its position in the second half of the 1980s, but this process stopped in the first half of the 1990s. Greece, on the other hand, was improving its status before its accession to the EU, after that a weak divergence occurred. Only in recent years has this country's economy shown some relative improvement.

These changes were convincingly demonstrated by Boldrin and Canova (2001), who present a rather gloomy picture: 'Absent regional policies, the increase in trade of the 1950s and 1960s was associated with a fairly strong reduction in national and regional income disparities. Whereas, with regional policies in place, increasing trade within the EU was no longer accompanied by convergence in per capita income. Labour productivity kept converging, but very slowly. This is very different from, and almost opposite to, what divergence theories predict should happen' (Boldrin and Canova, 2001, p. 227).

According to Pischke (2001, p. 246), all these results contrasted with the early post-war years, as a wonderful period 'when the European economies were converging at an impressive rate of 2 per cent annually'. At that time Portugal, Spain and Greece were all catching up impressively with the more developed countries of the EU. Pischke (2001, p. 245) summarized the main conclusions of Boldring and Canova's study in the following words:

> The main message of the paper is that European regional policy is based on a growth model that implies divergence and this model directly suggests that active intervention, mainly in the form of infrastructure investment, is needed to keep poor regions from falling even farther behind. The authors conclude that there is little evidence that this model is true, and little evidence that the regional policies of the EU are effective. Instead, the basic inference from the data is that, for the most part, regions in Europe grow pretty much at the same rate, that is, neither convergence nor divergence seems to be taking place.

The only relatively backward country that entered the EU in the 1970s and that fully succeeded in catching up with the most developed EU members is Ireland. But there is wide agreement that this resulted from a combination of unique and rather unrepeatable opportunities cleverly exploited by this small English-speaking nation. It enjoyed the substantial benefit of a powerful Irish minority living in the United States of America and, what is usually forgotten, of a highly interventionist industrial policy, particularly a selective policy vis-á-vis foreign capital, supporting FDI only in the most modern branches of the economy. Ireland luckily started its unconventional industrial policy before the Maastricht Treaty was ratified and came into force. Afterwards its policy was more tolerated than supported by the EU authorities. The latest newcomers cannot expect such a degree of tolerance, unless the EU revises its policy radically.

One other remark should be added. Ireland's achievements are spectacular indeed, but are not as great as thought due to an unusually large gap between GNP and GDP. According to Dennis O'Hearn (2001, p. 83):

> Ireland is unique in Europe in the degree that its gross domestic product exceeds its gross national product because of the profits that are removed by TNCs... By 1995, they were nearly 19 per cent of GDP. In 1999, they had risen to an astounding 40 per cent of GDP... During the years 1997–1999, the rise of TNC profits was equivalent to two-thirds of economic growth... Arguably, Ireland's most important function today is as a site where US companies can shift their product into Europe, while accumulating profits in order to avoid taxation... US TNCs located in Ireland maintained profit rates in the 1990s that were five times higher than they receive elsewhere in the world.

All this poses a troublesome question of for whose benefit do the Irish work.

In conclusion, it would be difficult to accept Verheugen's over-optimistic assessment of the EU's past efforts toward regional convergence, and we see no attempts to change this policy. On the contrary, Boldrin and Canova raise a number of awkward questions. Namely, if the Union's funds were supposed to help in achieving specific goals, but the goals are not met, then maybe there are other reasons for the existence of these funds? 'Why does the EU need to "bribe" newcomers, by means of subsidies when one should expect them to be willing to pay for joining a free trade area? Why do temporary transfers and support programmes become permanent when the apparent reason for their initial establishment does not exist any more?' (Boldrin and Canova, 2001, p. 244).

In my opinion, these questions touch the very foundations of EU economic policies. One may suspect that the only function of these funds and aid programs is to limit the damage caused by the Maastricht Treaty's and the Amsterdam Pact's policies. Note that the most impressive convergence took place in Europe during the time of highly interventionist policies in the 1950s and 1960s. An implicit criticism of EU policy is the fact that the former five EFTA countries experienced quite significant convergence both among themselves and with the EU core countries, while remaining outside the EU (Ellison, 2001, p. 45).

FDI: converging or diverging?

Hopes for convergence are also based on the FDI flows to the less developed countries and regions. Jose Mencinger (2003) examined the impact of FDI on GDP growth in eight post-communist countries. His figures, reproduced in Table 17.1, show unequivocally that the correlation of FDI and GDP were opposite to what we would have expected in these countries. The higher the ratio of FDI stock to GDP, the lower the rate of growth.

The Czech Republic experienced almost the lowest GDP growth rate, but it had the highest inflow of FDI. On the other hand, Slovenia and Poland present the opposite case, a relatively small amount of FDI, but their economies performed very well in terms of GDP growth. Moreover, the Slovenian economy seems to show the most sustainable rate of growth. Hungary may claim to be an exception with the second highest inflow of FDI and the third highest growth rate.

Mencinger does not deny that the inflow of FDI can be beneficial. A good example is Ireland. Perhaps China as well, inviting foreign capital, but not as a form of mass privatization, is also a good example. Mencinger (2003, p. 62) explains the case under investigation by the character of FDI in Central European countries:

> 'Surprising' results can be explained by the distortion that FDI has had on the domestic economic environment. Namely, most of FDI in candidate countries has taken the form of acquisitions in manufacturing sector and greenfield investments in the trade sector. The proceeds from sales of firms to foreign investors increase imports of consumer's goods and cause current account deficits, which hinder growth of the short run. The acquired business units are included into production and business systems of multinationals. This might have negative 'spill-over' effects on the existing economic environment that can more than outweigh the increase of microeconomic efficiency of the acquired business units.

Contrasting this impact of FDI with the Irish experience, we may say that Ireland successfully adopted an old-fashion selective and interventionist policy, whereas the post-communist EU members relied more on a free market policy, in full accordance with the Maastricht and Amsterdam treaties.

Table 17.1: FDI inflow and GDP growth of eight new EU members' economies, in 1994–2001

Country	Growth of GDP	Standard deviation	FDI/GDP 1994	FDI/GDP 2001
Czech Republic	1.94	2.80	11.0	47.4
Estonia	2.88	5.40	9.2	38.9
Hungary	3.18	1.88	17.1	45.8
Latvia	2.10	6.72	7.6	34.9
Lithuania	0.36	7.78	0.7	23.5
Poland	4.43	1.99	4.1	21.7
Slovakia	3.53	3.04	6.1	30.3
Slovenia	3.99	0.92	9.2	18.1

Sources: EBRD, WIIW, ECE, after Mencinger (2003, tables 4 and 5).

Varieties of capitalism

Even within the old European Union, the processes of per capita income convergence have been rather slow. Changes leading to systemic convergence are still slower. In fact, there still exist significant systemic differences between the six 'veterans' of European integration. At the beginning of the 1990s Michel Albert (1994, p. 24) wrote:

> A homogeneous economic model does not exist in Europe. The British model is closer to the US one than to the German one. The Italian model, dominated by family capitalism, weakness of the state, enormous deficit of public finances and surprising vitality of small and medium companies, cannot be compared with anything, except perhaps the model of the Chinese Diaspora.[3]

These differences seem to have not decreased over the last 15–20 years, and wholesale accession of the post-communist countries only increased the diversity of capitalism within the EU.

Even before that accession, one could hardly see the EU economies as one socio-economic system. A book written by Bruno Amable, *The Diversity of Modern Capitalism* (2003), describes the variety of capitalisms within the EU. Using five criteria – product market competition, wage–labour nexus, financial sector, social protection and education – Amable distinguishes five ideal types of capitalism, four of which exist in the EU: a market based economy (the UK economy is close to this type), social-democratic economies (mostly the Scandinavian economies), continental European capitalism (mainly Germany and France), and South European capitalism. The fifth type is Asian capitalism. Moreover, in his conclusion, Amable does not predict a clear path towards successful systemic convergence. He himself would prefer 'regulated capitalism', but thinks that it is not in line with the dominant political thinking of the last decade.

Equally ambiguous conclusions follow from the studies in a book edited by Hall and Sockice (2001). Vitols's comparison of Germany and Great Britain seems to be typical: an analysis of the political process of change in institutions showed that the UK and Germany do not appear to be converging to a 'first-best' model of corporate governance. Rather the majority of key actors in both systems appears to be cognizant of the comparative advantages of their own system and striving to make incremental improvements in existing institutions rather than wholesale change and convergence toward one set of institutions.

Of course, there is a danger of homogenization forced by Brussels bureaucrats, who, by their nature, do not like variety. This can be successfully counteracted by national authorities and social movements. Michel Albert rightly stressed that the future shape of European capitalism is a matter of struggle or rivalry between the German and social-market economy and British-American capitalism: 'It will be an underground war, violent, obstinate, but partly hidden or even full of hypocrisy, just as any internal struggle within any one Church is full of hypocrisy. A struggle between brothers armed with two models . . . carrying two antagonistic kinds of logic within the same liberalism. And perhaps . . . two systems of values' (Albert, 1994, p. 26).

Many observers have criticized EU policy as too restrictive or too passive. I conceive the warning, formulated by one of the leading German-American economists, Rudiger Dornbush (2001) as touching this question particularly well:

> Public finances in the EU are linked to the requirements of the Maastricht Treaty and by their means growth cannot be stimulated. If it should turn out that revival in the USA will not be quick and significant, soon Europe will regret the Maastricht decisions, which make counter-cyclical policy impossible. The tight budget straitjacket from Maastricht, introduced to calm the fears of the German bond holder about a currency union, may now turn out to be a catastrophe.

We may say that the EU has avoided a catastrophe so far, but that its main countries were unable to counteract recession and suffered quite a serious and prolonged slowdow.

Perhaps Dornbush's wording is too narrow in explaining the roots of Maastricht's and Amsterdam's Treaties. After all, these were years of the peak of Reaganomics. But he precisely pointed to the key role of Germany in forming the foundations of the Maastricht Treaty. Hans Eichel seems to be a good pupil of Weigel, the key author of the Amsterdam Pact. When he announced his first reform package, *The Financial Times* wrote that he would do better presenting just the opposite program (Munchau, 1999). It is paradoxical that a country with the best developed social-market economy and social state has became port-parol of free market policy, which is obviously at odds with its institutional set-up.

The recent recession has shown that the EU has no common anti-cyclical policy. Moreover common rules were a glaring obstacle to such a policy in individual countries. But economic policy was extremely important. One may detest or condemn Tony Blair's foreign policy, particularly the Iraq war, but we cannot overlook the fact that the British economy escaped recession. It has a reasonable rate of growth and one of the lowest rates of unemployment in Europe, less than 5 percent. Statistical data also show that the number of children and pensioners living below the poverty line has dropped and absolute poverty has been reduced significantly. The experience of Britain shows that even moderate Keynesian policy makes a difference. Almost the same may be said about the Swedish and Danish economies, although they adopted different tools. All three of these countries performed better or much better than the eurozone as a whole, particularly as against Germany, France and Italy, which were suffering from semi-stagnation. This poses the question of when the adoption of the euro will bring visible positive results.

The existence of eurosclerosis has become almost a commonplace belief. Two Austrian scholars (Aiginger and Landesman, 2002), however, rightly argue that there are two Europes. In their opinion small countries such as Finland, Sweden, Denmark, the Netherlands and Ireland, practicing a different path of development, not only do not suffer this disease, but also 'could match US growth of output and productivity and did excel in the growth drivers' (p. 57). These countries present something like 'centers of excellence in Europe', and the authors ask whether their success leads towards a 'New European model' defined not only by exceptionally high social security, but also by investment in, and fast diffusion of, the newest technologies. In 2001–03, Finland, Sweden and Denmark were in turn ranked first among knowledge-based economies.

Aiginger and Landesman enumerated several common features shared by these countries. All of them are small Nordic countries open to world trade. Their policy is consensual, with an egalitarian touch in income policy. All have a specific, determined and socially inclusive use of information technology. High taxes go together with a very high level of welfare state provision[4]. The egalitarians are now in a comfortable situation, because they may defend a principle of equality not only as a value in itself, but as a factor of higher efficiency combined with a high degree of social security.

Is the German economy going to duplicate the American system?

Due to the special role of Germany and the German economy in the European Union, the fundamental question of convergence refers to the process of convergence of the German economy with the American economy, or submission to what Ronald Dore calls 'American-led global capitalism' at the expense of 'a good society' (Dore, 2000).

(a) Different social philosophies: individualism versus communitarianism

The fundamental division observed and discussed in the non-communist world is that between the Anglo-Saxon version of capitalism and German and Japanese, sometimes called German-Japanese, capitalism. This distinction is deeply rooted in different social philosophies. The former model is individualistic, whereas the latter one is communitarian. A detailed analysis of these philosophies has recently been proposed by two American scholars (Morrison and Wolf, 1999/2000). Some of their major conclusions are as follows.

- For the Germans, the welfare state (*Wohlfahrtsstaat*) is an outcome of a kind of social agreement between the government and the citizens. Social aid is not only accepted, but expected. Most social services are provided as rights, regardless of their cost and the income of a particular family. The state is obliged to build a social network for the common good. Communitarianism prevails over individualism. In contrast, in the United States people on welfare are seen as failures. There is a strong tendency to condemn losers. The state is perceived as an inevitable evil and the expenses of maintaining the state as a threat to individual freedom. The authors quote one of the recurring themes of Bob Dole's pre-election speeches: the scariest words in the English language are 'I am from the federal government and I am here to help you.' We know that this slogan was also used by Ronald Reagan. It is hard to imagine a European politician, even an extremely conservative one, who would use this sentence as his election slogan.
- Differences exist not only in the level of material aid aimed at reducing poverty and social pathologies, which is much higher in Germany than in the US, but also in a different method of action. The German welfare state tries to eliminate the causes of social pathology (preventive action). By contrast, social workers in the United States mainly take care of people already affected by pathology. Therefore, by nature, the German approach is more sociological and the American approach more psychological.
- Knowing the American love of individual freedom, the authors' claim that in the US an individual dependent on social aid is controlled by the

government to a greater extent than in Germany must seem surprising. The two authors explain this fact not only in terms of a different concept of the welfare state, but also by reference to German resistance to all-embracing state control, dating back to the times of fascism. As a result of the difference in approaches, the number of social care clients is much smaller in Germany than in the US, which in the authors' opinion is a direct proof of the effectiveness of preventive action.[5]

(b) Different characteristics of firms

Unfortunately, a comparison of American and German firms is not available, but Ronald Dore (2000) has contrasted the fundamental characteristics of British and Japanese firms, which, in my opinion, can be applied to the US and German enterprises (compare also Kowalik, 2005, p. 190).[6] Dore describes these two types of firms in the following way: 'the Community View of the firm as opposed to the Property View; the Entity View as opposed to the Profit Instruments View; the Corporate Membership View as opposed to the Matrix of Contracts View; the Shareholder Firm versus the Stockholder Firm. The mildest names of this opposition would be: the employee-favoring firm versus shareholder-favoring firm' (Dore, 2000, p. 26).

Some years ago many authors thought that German economy was rapidly emulating the American model. Even Michel Albert (1991, 1994), an adamant supporter of the German social market economy, regretted that the Rhine model is losing ground, although in his opinion it was socially more just and simultaneously more effective than the 'neo-American model.'

Having in mind the fragility of non-free market types of capitalism, Suzan Berger (1996, p. 12) well captured the logic of the competition between systems aiming at short-term profit maximizing and systems whose goals and resources are more socially oriented. She wrote:

> Absent a political will to sustain institutions and values that transcend efficiency and growth, no national traditions, culture, or historical legacies by themselves can restrain market forces. Seen from this perspective, even if the Japanese and German systems do better in the long run, they are vulnerable. In a competition between the long-term calculations about the uses of labour, resources, and capital characteristic of the political economies of these two countries in the post-war period and the short-term profit maximizing of Anglo-American capitalism, economic opportunism will win. When deregulation or open borders give national capitalists the chance to escape constraints on wages, working conditions, layoffs, financial speculation, mergers, or environmental protection, they will – no matter their previous involvement in social democratic neo-corporatist, or Japanese-like lifetime employment systems. Given the general decline

of the left and indeed of all those political forces in Western advanced societies that might sustain collective action on behalf of values other than competition and efficiency, market forces confront little opposition.

It is hard to predict whether a commitment by politicians and trade unionists will be strong enough to resist the invasion of Anglo-Saxon corporations. The political maneuvers of German social democracy do not give a clear answer to this question either. Before their coming to power in 1998, the pre-election declarations of German Social Democrats were ambivalent, based on a sort of dualism: some voted for the left-winger Oskar Lafontaine, others for the more centrist Gerhard Schroeder. As the new Minister of Finance, Oskar Lafontaine tried to change macroeconomic policy, his main idea was to increase global demand by increasing real wages and salaries and reducing tax burdens imposed on poorer groups. At the same time, he wanted to increase corporate income taxes, primarily paid for by the companies that destroy the natural environment. He also wanted to impose taxes on capital. He attacked the central bank, demanding that fighting unemployment and fighting inflation be treated on an equal basis.[7]

Undoubtedly, this was based on the theories and ideas of Keynesian economists, in particular Heiner Flassbeck, Lafontaine's closest aide and economic adviser. In general, however, Lafontaine's attempts at changing macroeconomic policy were unskillful, although he encouraged the governments of the other European Union states to coordinate their macroeconomic policy, which even *The Financial Times* regarded as a good idea.[8] However, without waiting for the results of any talks, he initiated actions that were badly received by business circles and the increasingly influential British Labour Party leadership.

After Lafontaine's resignation in March 1999, Schroeder returned, in a way, to a policy inspired by the Maastricht Treaty. Lafontaine's office was given to a determined monetarist, Hans Eichel. He immediately took steps to cut business taxes and dramatically reduce government expenditure, mainly on social spending, to balance the budget. His proposal for pension reform involved the establishment of a mandatory capital pillar, as in the Polish pension reform. Eichel's policy and his proposals not only gave rise to domestic protests, but also were severely criticized by *The Financial Times*: 'Mr Eichel's package is a school-book example of what fiscal policy should not be like. At the time of high unemployment and slow economic growth, he chooses strict fiscal policy... It would make much more sense to do exactly the opposite' (Munchau, 1999). The article ends with an ironic remark: 'Eichel's predecessor [Lafontaine] was not a reformer, either. At least, he understood economics.'[9]

This policy, including the joint declaration by Blair and Schroeder, published in June 1999, resulted in over half a dozen defeats for the German Social Democrats in local elections, some of them quite spectacular. Moreover, both the declaration and the policy of the government were severely criticized and the conflict with trade unions worsened. The joint manifesto was perceived as an assault on the fundamental institutions of the social-market economy and an indication of welfare state demolition.

In consequence, the authorities had to draw back from a number of intended reforms, for example, they limited the scope of the pension reform. Since that time the socio-economic policy of the government has gone in two directions. Moderate labor market liberalization is accompanied by a much more daring policy of lowering business taxes, liberalization and deregulation of the financial market and far-reaching openness to foreign competition. Deregulation and privatization of a number of industries has already begun (power sector privatization, demonopolization of Deutsche Telekom, announced privatization of the post). The *Wall Street Journal* expressed an enthusiastic opinion about this policy. Seeing Schroeder's intervention to prevent the bankruptcy of a well-known construction company, Holzmann, as an exception, added: 'What happened since then is of crucial importance... Schroeder and Eichel managed to launch free market mechanisms without attracting attention. Therefore, it seems that the policy of the current government is better for entrepreneurs than the policy of the former Chancellor Helmut Kohl' (Roth, 2000).

Nevertheless, according to *The Economist* (2000), 'There are no reasons to believe that he is ready to dismantle the system of negotiations with trade unions, which restricts competitiveness of companies so much.' It seems that Schroeder has drawn the following conclusions from the 1999 failures: give up Blair-style free market rhetoric, give up the idea of stressing the 'uniqueness' of his policy and make no more straightforward declarations of policy directions. One of the main reasons for this is the fact that, in Germany, as well as in France, liberalization, as well as the popularity of free market capitalism is limited.

Is this only tactics? The fate of the pension reform project mentioned above is an argument in favor of such an answer (after the trade union protests it was revised in a much less radical form). The same may happen to a number of other projects. One of the main reasons for this is the fact that in Germany, as well as in France, liberalization, as well as the popularity of free market capitalism is limited.[10]

A new factor, which may become decisive, is a visible erosion of the American model's appeal due to the latest recession and conflict over the Iraq war. The American economy and policy are more and more seen as 'casino capitalism' destabilizing the world economy. A sharp clash between Continental Europe and the Anglo-American coalition over 'pre-emptive wars' seems to have created a new situation. Europe, treated by some analysts as a US protectorate, is now looking for self-identity and sovereignty. Nonetheless, it is too early to say anything definite about what this means for systemic change in the European Union.

Notes

1. Quoted by S. Amin (2001, pp. 218–19).
2. Quoted by D. Bilefsky (2005).
3. This and the next passage was translated from the Polish edition by T. Kowalik.
4. A Swedish analyst (Marwaring, 2002) writes that Swedish people like to live at the cost of the state and pay high taxes.
5. It should be added that not only the German welfare state model has been maintained, with slight modifications. Also the particularly well-developed Swedish welfare state model is surviving and seems no less effective than the systems of most OECD countries. Sweden still has the highest proportion of state expenditure in GDP in the world (approximately 65 percent in 1996). Earnings and income inequalities are still small and the position of trade unions is strong. The poor and the unemployed still enjoy such ample rights that even the high unemployment of the first half of the 1990s did not cause a considerable growth of inequality or poverty (Korpi and Palme, 1997).
6. Of course, there may be some minor differences between these two pairs of firms. But we may argue that, by and large, differences between this second pair are greater than between British and Japanese firms, because American society and the socio-economic system are much more individualistic than the British one.
7. Lafontaine skillfully referred to the policy of the US Federal Reserve: the head of the Federal Reserve Alan Greenspan proved that both inflation-free growth and increase of employment are possible (Barber, 1998).
8. The paper's regular columnist wrote about it (Wolf, 1998). The editor added the following: 'Martin Wolf believes that although many of the ideas of the German Minister of Finance should be evaluated as wrong, he should be given credit for starting a debate on this issue.'
9. Because of a similar policy, Franco Modigliani called the former minister of finance, Theo Weigl, an economic ignoramus (Grzybowska, 1997).
10. *The Economist* (2000) sees these limits particularly realistically: 'Nonetheless, the faith in excluding governmental control of the European social model has its limits. As it is rightly pointed out on the Continent, advertising the British solutions is not very convincing, as on average the Germans and French are still richer than the British. The Germans, even though they have absorbed 17 million of poor East Germans, still feel rich and do not see a need to reduce their expenses. Moreover, even if the restructuring of the British economy in 1980s was successful, the success was only partial, because the productivity, even after restructuring, is still lower than that recorded in France and Germany.'

References

Albert, M. (1991), *Capitalisme contre capitalisme*, Paris: Editions du Seuil.

Albert, M. (1994), *Kapitalizm kontra kapitalizm*, Kraków: Znak.

Amable, B. (2003), *The Diversity of Modern Capitalism*, Oxford: Oxford University Press.

Amin, S. (2001), 'Ekonomia polityczna XX wieku', *Lewą Nogą*, 13.

Aiginger, K. and M. Landesman (2002), 'Comparative Economic Performance: USA versus EU', Vienna Institute for International Economic Studies Research Report no. 291, Vienna.

Barber, T. (1998), 'Schroeder Clashes with Bundesbank over Growth', *Financial Times*, 2 November.

Berger, S. (1996), 'Introduction', in S. Berger and R. Dore (eds), *National Diversity and Global Capitalism*, Ithaca and London: Cornell University Press.
Bilefsky, D. (2005), 'Barroso wants clarity from Bush', *Wall Street Journal Europe*, 18–20 February.
Boldrin, M.I. and F. Canova (2001), 'Inequality and Convergence in Europe's Regions: Reconsidering European Policies', *Economic Policy*, 32, April.
Dore, R. (2000), *Stock Market Capitalism: Welfare Capitalism*, Oxford: Oxford University Press.
Dornbush, R. (2001), 'Świat już jest w recesji', *Rzeczpospolita*, 20–21 października.
The Economist (2000), 'Blaski i cienie lewicy', quoted after Polish weekly, *Forum*, 12–14 February.
Ellison, D.L. (2001), 'CEEC Prospects for Convergence: a Theoretical and Historical Overview', in M. Dauderstädt and L. Witte (eds), *Cohesive Growth in the Enlarging Euroland*, Bonn: Friedrich-Ebert-Stiftung.
Grzybowska, K. (1997), 'Weigel jest ekonomicznym ignorantem. Bundestag wrogiem euro', *Rzeczpospolita*, 16 August.
Hall, P.E. and D. Sockice (2001), *Varieties of Capitalism*, Oxford: Oxford University Press.
Korpi, W. and K. Palme (1997), 'The Paradox of Redistribution and Strategies of Equality: Welfare State Institutions, Inequality and Poverty in the Western Countries', Institutet for Social Forsking, Stokholm.
Kowalik, T. (2005), *Systemy gospodarcze, efekty i defekty reform i zmian ustrojowych*, Warszawa: Fundacja Innowacja.
Marwaring, M. (2000), 'Cywilizacja i jakość życia', *Dziś*, no. 12, 68–9.
Mencinger, J. (2003), 'Slovenia: Alternative Economic Policies in Action', *Der Offentliche Sektor – Forschungsmemoranden*, 3–4, February, 58–63.
Morrison, J.D. and R.A. Wolf (1999/2000), 'Social Works and Social Policy in Germany and the United States', *American Studies Journal*, 44, 17–25.
Munchau, W. (1999), 'Taxing Problem', *Financial Times*, 6 July.
O'Hearn D. (2001) 'Economic Growth and Social Cohesion in Ireland', in M. Dauderstädt and L. Witte (eds), *Cohesive Growth in the Enlarging Euroland*, Bonn: Friedrich-Ebert-Stiftung.
Pischke, J.S. (2001), 'Comment', in M.I. Boldrin and F. Canova, 'Inequality and Convergence in Europe's Regions: Reconsidering European Policies', *Economic Policy*, 32, April, 205–53.
Roth, T. (2000), 'Nowe oblicze niemieckiej gospodarki', *Wall Street Journal*, quoted after Polish weekly, *Forum*, 31 January.
Wolf, M. (1998), 'Is Lafontaine half-baked?', *Financial Times*, 25 November.
Verheugen, G. (2001), Intervew in *Rzeczpospolita*, 13–14 July.
Vitols, S. (2001), 'Varieties of Corporate Governance: Comparing Germany and the EU', in P.E. Hall and D. Sockice (eds), *Varieties of Capitalism*, Oxford: Oxford University Press, pp. 337–60.

18

Political Integration and Fiscal Federalism in the American Dollar Area and Eurozone

Sławomir Bukowski

Introduction

The processes of political integration or political unification accompanying the processes of economic integration appeared in all countries in different historical periods and to a different extent. In some countries they led to the emergence of uniform systems where political and economic decisions were centralized whereas in others they led to federal structures with significant autonomy, if not independence, in the fields of fiscal policy, law formulation, and so on at the sub-national, local or regional levels.

In Western Europe the processes of economic integration, from the very beginning of the European Commonwealth, were aimed at the creation of tighter economic and political links between the integrating countries. The tradition of European federalism, rooted in antiquity and the Middle Ages and revived in different historical periods had an indisputable impact on the choice of the regional concept of economic integration. Generally, the so-called liberal concept, also known as functional or negative integration (see Tinbergen, 1964, p. 57) has been rejected. This concept assumed that, in order to have integration, it was enough to create conditions for the unrestrained operation of the market mechanism at the international level without creating supranational integrating institutions that would take over part of the national competencies in the field of politics. The concept that was adopted, institutional integration, also known as positive integration, assumes that, in order to attain integration, the participant countries must both liberate the market mechanisms at the international level and also create supranational institutions coordinating the integration processes (Tinbergen, 1964, p. 57; Sanwald and Stohler, 1959, pp. 84–9; Streeten, 1961, pp. 13–17, 55).

Calling the monetary union into life was connected with the ever stronger tendencies among European politicians, mainly from Germany, France and the Benelux countries, toward the realization of the concept of fiscal federalism and political union. It must be stressed that the emergence of the issue of fiscal federalism and political integration in political discussions in the EU is connected with the problems of the European Monetary Union as a single currency zone. The key problem here can be limited to one question: taking into account all the institutional and structural conditions of individual national economies, the mobility of productive factors, and so on, is the common monetary policy a sufficient prerequisite to assure success of the whole undertaking in an environment prone to asymmetric economic shocks?

There are many comparisons between the eurozone and American dollar area in the literature concerning the theory and realization of the European Monetary Union. These comparisons lead to different conclusions. Some economists claim that such comparisons are not quite legitimate, yet others are of the opinion that they are fully legitimate and very useful for the process of the monetary integration in Europe. The author of this chapter shares the latter opinion. The aim of this chapter is to outline the problem connected with the role of political integration and fiscal federalism in the US monetary union and European Monetary Union (EMU) and, in particular, to attempt to answer the question whether, in view of the American experience, political integration and fiscal federalism are indispensable for the success of the European Monetary Union.

Political integration and fiscal federalism

In the literature there are several definitions of political integration. Haas (1961, pp. 366–7) defines political integration as 'a process due to which political participants coming from different countries transfer their loyalties, expectations and political activity to a new (supranational) center whose institutions exert jurisdiction over the earlier existing national states.' In conformity with this definition, the ultimate effect of political integration is the emergence of a new political commonwealth that overlaps the former ones, namely national states. Lindbergh (1963) defines political integration as the sum of two processes. The first one makes the states, independently of each other, reject their own internal and foreign policies for the sake of mutual decisions in this respect or delegate them to the new common bodies. The second process includes the transfer of expectations and political activities by political groups of interest to the new, supranational political center. According to Bożyk (Bożyk and Misala, 2003, p. 184), political integration means the process of adjustment to the internal and foreign policies of the integrating countries. 'The former refers to the organization and form of the public life in which physical and legal persons participate. The latter refers to the relationships among nations and states expressed by mutual support, alliances and tolerance.'

These definitions show that political integration can be treated either as a process or as the state of things. As a process, political integration means that internal and foreign policies of individual states are becoming closer by means of such measures as consultations, coordination and agreement on policy goals, especially long-term goals. Viewing political integration as the state of things, it is possible to distinguish two basic models of the political union: the federal and the functional. The former can be described as the creation of the federal state embracing the so-far independent countries. Thus, it means that the majority of powers of the legislative, executive and administrative authorities are transferred from the national to the supranational level. The latter model means that political decisions are made at the national level, whereas the international body only coordinates mutual political undertakings. Consequently, some of the of the decisions referring to internal and foreign policies have much in common while others are autonomous decisions of individual states participating in the integrating group. What we are dealing with here is the integration of states and their policies and not a uniform state. Last but not least, eclectic solutions are possible that attempt to combine the functional model with the federal one. This can take the form of a division of powers between the supranational body and national state authorities. Political integration is treated in the literature as the effect of economic integration but also as its prerequisite at a certain higher level of the integration process (Bożyk and Misala, 2003, pp. 184–8; Haliżak, 2002, pp. 368–85).

Fiscal federalism (fiscal unification) means that the integrating countries transfer either all or part of their fiscal policy competencies to a supranational body. Thus, the body in question is in charge of public expenditures and fiscal policy instruments. If the integrating countries create a monetary union with a supranational central bank and a uniform monetary policy, then full coordination of fiscal and monetary policies is possible in order to accomplish macroeconomic goals established for the whole integrating group. What is left to the national level is the accomplishment of regional goals. National governments can achieve these goals through the use of some fiscal instruments, that is, local taxes, and coordination between the national budgets and the central budget of the integrating group (Allen and Kenen, 1990, p. 537; Bukowski, 2003, pp. 59–60). The relationship between the fiscal powers of the supranational center and those of the national governments can vary. However, the supranational center should be responsible for the macroeconomic stabilization and income redistribution (Oates, 1999). An open question is that of the division of competencies in the provision of public goods.

Theoretically three solutions can be mentioned here. In the first one, the entire fiscal policy is highly centralized at the federal government level.

Consequently, neither regions nor states have any fiscal competencies. In the second case, fiscal policy is created at the national level with few or no fiscal powers left to the supranational or federal level. In the third case, the competencies in the field of fiscal policy are equal for regional or state governments on the one hand and the state or federal government on the other hand. Only in the first or third case does fiscal federalism require political unification. In the second case there is no such need.

From the point of view of macroeconomic stabilization and income redistribution between rich and poor regions and countries, the following three types of fiscal policy can be mentioned:

- The interim provision of financial means through the capacity to borrow or repay loans from future taxes by central or regional authorities in order to finance budget expenditures for economic development or economic stabilization in a given region or country.
- Interregional, short-term transfers in order to absorb short-term economic shocks.
- Interregional transfers aiming at counteracting long-term permanent economic shocks.

As the above analysis shows, political integration and fiscal federalism are significantly intertwined. The transfer of any part of fiscal competencies to the supranational level always leads to some form of political integration and fiscal federalism. This involves not only full political integration, meaning the creation of a federal state in place of the sovereign states, but also political integration of the functional nature where national fiscal policies are coordinated, taxes are harmonized and the common budget is created, even if its size is relatively small. It must be emphasized, however, that a certain degree of fiscal federalism does not always mean the necessity of a full political union. While a certain degree of fiscal federalism can be economically justified, still, it does not mean that this is the basis for full political unification.

A single-currency zone versus fiscal federalism and political integration: theoretical analysis of the main problems

A single-currency zone consists of two or more countries/regions using a single currency. The existence of the single-currency area with a uniform monetary policy carried out by the central bank may, but does not have to be connected with the existence of a political union. It is indisputable that monetary unions may be accompanied by a certain degree of political integration, but the question is still unanswered whether this is necessary. An example here can be a monetary union of the hegemonic nature where there is one country, the leader, whose currency is adopted as the common one by other countries, and their economies are subordinated to the monetary policy carried out by the leader's central bank. In this case, the countries participating in the monetary union can retain their political sovereignty and have a fiscal policy of their own.[1]

If the processes of political and monetary integration go side by side, then the monetary union area overlaps the political union area. Both forms of integration are closely related to one another. Consider for example the cases of Germany in the period from the Congress of Vienna to the unification in 1871 and of the United States. It is worth mentioning here that, from the beginning of the integration processes, the participants' fiscal powers are significantly limited while the fiscal powers of the central authorities are extended. The limited competencies of the monetary union participants in the field of fiscal policy result in pressure for political unification. Thus, sooner or later, the development of fiscal federalism leads to political union. The situation is different when the monetary union participants are free to shape their fiscal policy, even if there are attempts at of coordination. Then, the monetary unification's stimulation of fiscal integration and political integration is negligible (Eichengreen, 1996).

A fundamental problem of a monetary union is asymmetric shocks. Participants in the monetary union with a single currency and a uniform monetary policy created by the union's autonomous central bank lose the opportunity of using monetary policy to stabilize the economy against asymmetric shocks. On the other hand, the monetary policy of the monetary union is aimed at price stabilization in the union's economy as a whole, and it cannot adjust its instruments selectively depending on the situation in particular countries. Besides, it must be stressed that particular countries' economies respond to monetary impulses differently. A uniform monetary policy has a different impact on individual economies of the monetary union. It can thus be the source of asymmetric shocks or strengthen the effects of these shocks.[2]

Thus, we can ask whether a monetary union and uniform monetary policy can function without fiscal federalism? One of the major arguments for fiscal federalism is that the uniform monetary policy concentrated at the supranational level is insufficient to stabilize the economy. Thus, it is also indispensable to transfer fiscal powers to the supranational level and to create a system of budget revenue redistribution among different countries as part of the adjustment mechanism. Many economists who contributed to the theory of the monetary union advocate the transfer of fiscal policy to the monetary union level (McKinnon, 1963, p. 717; Kenen, 1967, pp. 13–14; Snider, 1967, p.15; Grubel, 1977, p. 452). On the other hand, Mundell (2003) claims that a certain degree of fiscal policy coordination is needed in the monetary union, which does not mean that fiscal federalism must be based on subsidizing some countries. According to Mundell, economic shocks can be caused by an excessive increase in wages as a result of trade union pressure. In such circumstances, subsidies may undermine the monetary union's economy and lead to social conflict.

To make fiscal policy a good instrument of stabilization, it must be effective. Unfortunately, there are a number of limitations to its effectiveness. First of all, it is not a very flexible policy due to information, political and social reasons.[3] These reasons may make government unable to respond to asymmetric shocks in the time required, suggesting that a mix of monetary and fiscal policy would be preferable. Krugman (1995, pp. 201–2) criticizes the view that a fiscal policy created at the supranational level is indispensable in the monetary union. According to him, in the 1980s and 1990s, a majority of countries gradually stopped using fiscal policy as a tool to stimulate demand. Therefore, there is no reason to attribute too much significance to the role of fiscal policy as a stabilizer because monetary policy and the market can successfully perform this function.

Taking into account the limitations of fiscal policy, a much more important problem is the creation of the appropriate institutional environment that would enhance the role of the market as an adjustment mechanism. This requires a sufficient degree of flexibility of the market – in particular the labor market – prices and wages as well as removing the burden of high taxes from individuals and the corporate sector and undoing excessive regulation of business activities. An important role in the absorption of economic shocks is also played by financial markets and risk-sharing mechanisms.

Political union and fiscal federalism versus monetary unification: the American experience

In 1789, when the Constitution was adopted, 13 North American states created a federal country, the United States. The period of monetary unification lasted until 1913 and eventually it ended in the creation of the Federal Reserve. A political union and fiscal federalism accompanied the process of monetary integration. Fiscal federalism was based on a division of taxing power between the federal and state governments. It should be stressed here that there were no income taxes. The sources of the federal government budget revenues were excise duties, customs duties and real estate taxes. Only in 1913 was the income tax introduced and, in 1933, social insurance contributions. In the period when the US monetary union was being shaped, neither the federal nor state governments implemented an active fiscal policy based on redistribution. The situation changed only after World War I and radically in the years of the 1929–33 crisis (Rabushka, 1996, pp. 177–212). The fiscal federalism system in the US was reshaped after World War II. The US Constitution became the legal basis of this system while Keynesian theories and the welfare state concept became its doctrinal basis.

Owing to the fact that the state did not play an active role in the economy, the concentration of fiscal competencies at the federal level was of no consequence for the monetary integration processes in the United States between 1789 and 1913. Absorption of the economic shock effects, which were numerous during that period, was accomplished by market adjustment mechanisms. No monetary policy was used because there was no central bank apart for two twenty-year periods. On the other hand, political union was more important owing to the fact that the decisions related to the monetary processes were concentrated at the federal level. They concerned the introduction of the dollar (1792), creation of the state mint in Philadelphia, establishment of the official parity between gold and silver, establishment of the gold standard as the basis of the currency system, the issue of paper bank notes and the ultimate introduction of dollar bank notes exchangeable for gold as a replacement for numerous currencies and, eventually, the creation of the Federal Reserve in 1913. Thus, in view of the history of monetary unification in the US, it would be difficult to conclude that a political union and fiscal federalism are indispensable for a monetary union.

What is important, however, are contemporary experiences in this respect, first of all those that deal with the question of fiscal policy as an instrument of stabilization. The US tax system consists of two tiers: the federal, and the state and local. Despite the fact that the American economy is highly integrated, there is no harmonization between state taxes. Thus, there are significant differences in taxation between the states. Factor mobility exerts some pressure to equalize tax rates, but very few factors are perfectly mobile. What is more, the compensation for a higher tax burden is often a higher supply of public services, perceived as attractive by the population and corporate sector.

The burden of stabilization policy resides at the federal level. The federal government uses automatic stabilizers as well as discretionary policy. It is estimated that the share of automatic stabilizers in the absorption of demand-related economic shocks amounts to 8 percent and 10 percent in the case of supply-related shocks (Auerbach and Freenberg, 2000; Cohen and Follette, 2000). Another instrument for stabilization is the federal system of taxes and transfers. Within the framework of this system, income redistribution between the states is accomplished. It is estimated that the transfers, which are a response to current asymmetric shocks, compensate for about 15 percent of income. It is worth mentioning here that transfers, to a large extent, are an element of income redistribution for the purpose of equalizing the development standards in particular states and they have little to do with economic stabilization.

The American economy is characterized by relatively flexible markets, including the labor market, and a highly developed financial market. The main burden of adjustments to economic shocks falls on market mechanisms. The labor market plays a significant role, characterized by wage flexibility and mobility of the labor force between professions, sectors and regions. In the 1990s, the migration index, the ratio of migrants to the whole population of the country, between the states was 2.5 percent (HM Treasury, 2003, p. 29). Asdrubali et al. (1996) estimated that between 1981 and 1990, about 45 percent of shocks were smoothed by the capital market, 15 percent by the credit market, 15 percent by the fiscal policy of the federal government and 25 percent were not smoothed at all.

Political unification and fiscal federalism versus the monetary union: the EMU experience

In the eurozone, the issues of fiscal federalism and political unification are quite different from those in the United States. First, in the European Union only some forms of political unification appear. It is unlikely that in the immediate future there will be a transformation of the EU into a federal state. When it comes to fiscal federalism we observe a small budget at the EU level, attempts to coordinate national fiscal policies and relatively independent national fiscal policies. Thus, basically, the entire fiscal powers are at the level of the EU member states. It must be emphasized that the EU budget is the budget for the whole integrating group and not only for the Economic and Monetary Union, which includes 12 out of a total of 25 member countries. Thus, the budget policy objectives are not connected with the problems of the monetary union. The EU authorities carry out a budget policy to equalize the levels of development among member countries and regions as well as to stabilize the income of the agricultural population. The EU budget policy has nothing to do with the stabilization of economies. Moreover, the EU budget is relatively small. As Oręziak (2002, p. 7) writes: 'the relatively small EU budget (the major part of which, i.e., ca. 50 per cent is earmarked for financing the common agricultural policy) means that actually it cannot play a major role as a mechanism stabilizing the member countries economic situation in case an economic shock specific for a given country or region occurs.'

A symptom of fiscal federalism is tax harmonization, which in the EU refers to indirect taxes and some regulations related to corporate taxation (Oręziak, 2004, pp. 205–57). Indirect taxes still vary because harmonization is limited to the establishment of minimum VAT and excise duty rates. Therefore, it is doubtful whether this kind of harmonization is necessary at all. As far as direct taxes are concerned, their differentiation seems to be justified. There are non-fiscal factors that determine whether an investment location is attractive, and lower taxes can offset other locational disadvantages.

Adjustment to economic shocks is the responsibility of national fiscal policies and depends also on market mechanisms. However, one of the major problems is over-regulation and rigidity of the EU's economies. Prices and wages in the EU countries are not very flexible. Labor force mobility is relatively low and it is estimated that the mobility index for the 1990s was at the level of 0.1 percent (HM Treasury, 2003, p. 29). Hence, in the EU countries, stabilization is the responsibility of national politicians.

A relatively successful attempt of coordinating national fiscal policies is the Stabilization and Growth Pact, which was adopted by the European Council. The pact defines the rules of the EU countries' economic policy coordination and lists the requirements that must be met by the countries aspiring to join the Economic and Monetary Union (CEU, 1999, pp. 25–77). The pact strengthens some resolutions included in the treaty establishing the European Community. The EMU countries are required to avoid excessive budget deficits. It was decided that the maximum budget deficit cannot exceed 3 percent of GDP. Also, the limitation on the public debt included in the Maastricht Treaty has been repeated. It allows a maximum ratio of public debt to GDP of not more than 60 percent. The European Commission was entrusted with the surveillance of the budgetary position of individual countries. It was obliged to compare the real results to the reference value. If the budget deficit in a given country exceeds the reference value, the Commission must prepare an appropriate report. The report in question is to show whether the deficit is of permanent or temporary nature. If the Commission comes to the conclusion that the deficit is too high, it is obliged to inform the European Council. The latter is to make appropriate recommendations to the country concerned. If the country concerned fails to meet the requirements, the Council can initiate the following procedures:

- To demand the publication of additional information specified by the Council before issuing treasury bonds;
- To ask the European Bank of Investment to revise their loan policy towards the country in question;
- To put the country under an obligation to lodge a non-interest bearing deposit to the benefit of the Union in the amount proportional to the reference value surplus (this deposit contains a fixed component equal to 0.2 percent of GDP and a variable component equal to one-tenth of the excess of the deficit over the reference value of 3 percent of GDP; there is an upper limit of 0.5 percent of GDP in respect of any single deposit). This deposit is refundable as soon as the deficit falls below 3 percent of GDP;
- To impose a fine on the country concerned if, after two years the deficit continues to be excessive; the deposit will be converted irreversibly into a fine and paid to the benefit of the Union's budget.

The GSP also allows countries to avoid financial sanctions if the deficit to GDP ratio only exceeds the prescribed 3 percent for a temporary period and under exceptional circumstances. Such circumstances include a real GDP drop of at least 2 percent. In the case of an abrupt economic downturn, the Council of Europe can accept a GDP decline of 0.75 to 2 percent as exceptional. What is more, the Council of Europe monitors the budgetary situation of individual EMU countries systematically and will address recommendations to the member state concerned as early warning precautions.

Observing the rules specified in the GSP safeguards the prices and the currency against destabilization. On the other hand, it also reduces the possibilities for an active application of stabilizing fiscal policy, which limits the effectiveness of this mechanism. The problem of asymmetric shocks can be solved at the national level providing that deeper reforms are accomplished in the majority of the EMU countries. The reforms should include deregulation and create a friendly environment for the flexible functioning of markets, including labor markets.

Conclusions

The above analysis yields several conclusions based on the American experience. However, they should not be treated as absolute. Many questions require still more thorough research. The efficient functioning of the European Monetary Union does not require a political union or full fiscal federalism of the American type. Fiscal federalism, even if it were possible politically, would be a very costly undertaking, and as shown by Fatas (2003, pp. 89–91), the costs of introducing a uniform, supranational tax and transfer system for the entire Union would exceed the possible long-term benefits. Fatas also argues that the problem of asymmetric shocks will decrease on account of the higher correlation of economic cycles in the EU countries as integration grows. In any case monetary union does not have to be accompanied by fiscal redistribution. What is needed are institutional and economic reforms that would facilitate better and more flexible markets. National fiscal policies should be treated as supplementary to market adjustments. The American experience shows that the dominant role in the economic shock absorption belongs to market adjustments, provided that the markets are flexible.

Tax harmonization and, in particular, direct tax harmonization, is not a necessary condition for the effective functioning of a monetary union, as proved by the American experience. What is more, in Europe, further tax harmonization would increase the tax burden, restraining economic growth due to the dominant role that the countries with the highest tax burden and most over-regulated economies, such as Germany, France, Italy, Sweden and the Benelux countries, play in the integration processes.

Notes

1. On hegemonic monetary unions see Tavlas (1993).
2. This has been confirmed, among others, by the research into the monetary policy of the European Monetary Union. See more in Demertzis et al. (1997, pp. 199–209) and Cecchetti (1999).
3. For more on the limitations of the fiscal policy effectiveness see Bukowski (2003, p. 61) and Mortimer-Lee (2001).

References

Allen, P.R. and P.B. Kenen (1990), *Asset Markets, Exchange Rates, and Economic Integration. A Synthesis*, Cambridge: Cambridge University Press.

Asdrubali, P., B.E. Sørensen and O. Yosha (1996), 'Channels of Interstate Risk Sharing: United States 1963–1990', *Quarterly Journal of Economics*, CXI(4), SS 1081–110.

Auerbach, A.J. and D. Freenberg (2000), 'The Significance of Federal Taxes as Automatic Stabilizers', NBER Working Paper, No. 7662, April.

Bożyk, P. and J. Misala (2003), *Integracja ekonomiczna*, Warszawa: PWE.

Bukowski, S. (2003), 'Teoretyczne podstawy i realizacja unii monetarnej krajów członkowskich Wspólnot Europejskich. Szanse i zagrożenia dla Polski', Wydawnictwo Politechniki Radomskiej, Radom.

Cecchetti, S.G. (1999), 'Legal Structure, Financial Structure, and the Monetary Policy Transmission Mechanism', NBER Working Paper, No. 7151, www.nber.org/papers/w7151.

Cohen, D. and G. Follette (2000), 'The Automatic Fiscal Stabilizers: Quietly Doing Their Thing', *FRBNY Economic Policy Review*, April.

Council of the European Union (CEU) (1999), 'Legal and Political Texts Adopted by the Council of the European Union and the European Council', *The Euro and Economic Policy*, General Secretariat of The Council of The European Union, January, Brussels.

Demertzis, M., A.H. Hallet and O. Rummel (1997), 'Does a Core-Periphery Regime Make Europe into an Optimal Currency Area?', in P.J.J. Welfens (ed.), *European Monetary Union. Transition, International Impact and Policy Options*, Berlin; Heidelberg and New York: Springer-Verlag.

Eichengreen, B. (1996), 'On the Links between Monetary and Political Integration', University of California, Berkeley, www.politicalintegration/emlab.berkeley/edu/user/eichegr/research/c96–97.pdf.

Fatas, A. (2003), 'The Benefits and Costs of Creating a European Fiscal Federation', in *Submissions on EMU from Leading Academics*, EMU Study, HM Treasury, London, www.hmt.treasury.gov.uk.media18F33ad/Sussex/03 exec88.pdf.

Grubel, H.G. (1977), *International Economics*, Homewood, Illinois: Richard D. Irwin Inc.

Haas, E. (1961), 'International Integration: the European and the Universal Process', *International Organizations*, 15(3), summer, 366–92.

Haliżak, E. (2002), 'Współzależność integracji ekonomicznej i politycznej W Unii Europejskiej – przyczynek do rozważań o istocie ekonomii politycznej stosunków międzynarodowych', in E. Haliżak and S. Parzymies, *Unia Europejska. Nowy typ wspólnoty międzynarodowej, Fundacja Stosunków Międzynarodowych*, Warszawa.

Kenen, P.B. (1967), 'Toward a Supranational Monetary System', in G. Pontecorvo (ed.), *Issues in Banking and Monetary Analysis*, New York: Holt, Rinehart and Winston.

Krugman P. (1995), *Currencies and Crises*, Cambridge, MA: MIT Press.

Lindberg, L. (1963), *The Political Dynamics of European Economic Integration*, Stanford, CA: Stanford University Press.

McKinnon, R.I. (1963), 'Optimum Currency Areas', *American Economic Review*, 53, September, 717–24.

Mortimer-Lee P. (2001), 'Czy Euroland może funkcjonować przy jednej stopie procentowej?', in P. Temperton (ed.), *Euro. Wspólna waluta*, Warszawa: Feldberg, SJA.

Mundell, R. (2003), 'Mundell's Comments on EMU', in *Submissions on EMU from Leading Academics*, EMU Study, HM Treasury, London, www.hmt.treasury.gov.uk.media18F33ad/Sussex/03 exec88.pdf.

Oates, W.E. (1999), 'An Essay on Fiscal Federalism', *Journal of Economic Literature*, XXXVII (September), 1120–49.
Oręziak, L. (2004), *Finanse Unii Europejskiej*, Warszawa: Wydawnictwo Naukowe PWN.
Oręziak, L. (2002), 'Polityka budżetowa na obszarze euro (cz.I)', *Bank i Kredyt*, 6, June.
Rabushka, A. (1996), 'Od Adama Smitha do bogactwa Ameryki', Centrum im. Adama Smitha, Warszawa.
Sanwald, R.F. and J. Stohler (1959), *Economic Integration. Theoretical Assumption and Consequences of European Integration*, Princeton, NJ: Princeton University Press.
Snider, D.A. (1967), 'Optimum Adjustment Process and Currency Areas', *Essay in International Finance*, No. 62, October, Princeton, NJ: Princeton University Press.
Streeten, P. (1961), *Economic Integration. Aspects and Problems*, Leiden: A.W. Sythoff.
Tavlas, G. (1993), 'The New Theory of Optimum Currency Areas', *The World Economy*, No. 6, 663–9.
HM Treasury (2003), 'The United States as a Monetary Union', www.hmt.treasury.gov.uk. media 18F33ad/Sussex/03 exec88.pdf.
Tinbergen, J. (1964), *International Economic Integration*, Amsterdam: Elsevier.

19
Toward an Efficient Labor Market Model in the EU: To Centralize or not to Centralize

W. Stan Siebert[1]

Introduction

How centralized or corporatist should the setting of wages and working conditions be? Corporatism has been defined by Bruno and Sachs (in Calmfors and Driffel, 1988, p. 24) as: 'institutionalised negotiation, bargaining, collaboration and accord about wages and incomes policies between representatives of the major economic groupings in the society, typically labor confederations and employers' associations and often including representatives of government.'

The important point here is higher-level control of wage negotiations; should Poland follow? On the one hand, we have the strongly corporatist countries such as Austria and Sweden (Siaroff, 1999, p. 177) with strong labor and employer federations, centralized wage-setting, and strict employment protection laws. These countries have narrower income differentials, but their unemployment performance is mixed, with high unemployment duration (unemployment is concentrated on outsiders). On the other hand, we have non-corporatist countries such as the US and, to a lesser extent, the UK. These countries have shorter unemployment duration, higher employment/population ratios, but wider income differentials. Yet the attraction of corporatism for emerging capitalist countries appears to be strong, as shown, for example, by China's current program of 'tripartite consultation' (Clarke and Lee, 2003).

Moreover, there is the underlying question of whether the labor market needs special privileges for unions in collective bargaining at all; the debate over 'what do unions do?' which broke out over Freeman and Medoff's (1984) famous book, and continues today (Addison and Belfield, 2003). In this debate, the wider role of trade unions as organizers of the working class's struggle for democracy needs to be recognized (Rueschmeyer and Stephens, 1992, p. 6). There are several recent examples of unions championing democracy, from Poland to South Africa. Even so, there is always the question of managing trade unionism in case wage gains for union members come at the expense of unemployment for non-members.

The aim of this chapter is to consider how centralization or corporatism affects labor market operation. First, we will look at the evidence from OECD countries (see also Siebert, 2003). Then, we narrow the focus and concentrate on a detailed comparison (Siebert et al., 2003) of matched enterprises in France, a corporatist country, and the UK, comparatively decentralized. Finally, we will look at evidence from a sample of newly-industrializing countries (Siebert, 2001) to show the different ways trade unionism and wage-setting can develop.

OECD evidence

The famous article by Calmfors and Driffel (1988) starts with a 'hump-shaped' relationship between real wages or unemployment and centralization, as evidenced by inter-union and inter-employer cooperation in wage bargaining, which is their measure of corporatism. High centralization presumably enables 'encompassing' coalitions between employers and unions, so wages are not driven up enough to cause unemployment. Low centralization implies competitive wages, so unemployment is not an issue. Countries in the middle are worst off according to this argument.

It is true that the hump-shape relationship has not stood the test of time (OECD, 1997, p. 77), but a consensus has emerged that corporatist arrangements have definite advantages. Corporatism seems to reduce both unemployment and income inequality. The way in which corporatism seems to help unemployment is robust to the inclusion of many other variables, as Table 19.1 shows. In the table we have the total unemployment rate, the long-term unemployment rate, and the youth employment/population rate. We want to look at the long-term unemployed, and youth, because these are outsider groups particularly at risk from imposed high wages and working conditions. Beginning with the total unemployment rate column, increases in the bargaining coordination index imply a large improvement to unemployment, –0.547,[2] other things equal. As can also be seen, however, increases in union power and union collective agreement coverage have an adverse impact on unemployment. Nevertheless, as Nickell and Layard (1999, p. 3067) point out, a 100 percent unionized and collective agreement covered country, which is also fully corporatist, has a better unemployment rate than a non-corporatist, zero-union and zero-coverage country. This argument holds well for the youth employment/population and long-term unemployment variables as well, because the positive effects of bargaining coordination are strong in all cases.[3] The conclusion is that corporatism genuinely allows encompassing coalitions to develop;[4] we can have powerful unions and, at the same time, manage this power through central fora so that the power is used responsibly. Arguments such as this

However, Galtier and Gautié's (2003, p. 140) comprehensive analysis of the French system is not optimistic: they conclude that the system appears to favor the male breadwinner, that is, the high productivity, prime-age male group. Hence, French production typically has more capital and high productivity labor than the UK (see below). In France, wages and worker effort of prime-age males apparently need not adjust to offset the employment effects of high labor costs and employment protection because these effects are felt by the young and the old.

Table 19.2's middle panel shows how only a single generation, the prime-aged, works. The UK's employment rates for young and old workers are much higher than France's. Admittedly, the figures on long-term unemployment show the two countries to be almost equally bad, with long-term unemployment comprising 44–45 percent of unemployment over 1985–1990. Yet, much can lie behind an unemployment rate. The last rows of the table show that both countries have training and subsidized work programs. The French programs are large, absorbing 0.59 to 0.73 per cent of GDP, and with inflows currently equal to 9.8 per cent of the workforce, which could confuse the unemployment count. Employment figures are more reliable. Taking the 20–24 age group, we see that the employment/population ratio in France is low, 53 percent, and falling to only 36 percent. Similarly, for the over 55s in France, the employment/population ratio is low and falling from 36 to 34 percent. The implication here is that the French form of corporatism is not particularly encompassing.

Let us now turn to the detailed company comparisons, starting with Table 19.3. Each establishment in the table is a matched pair, both being subsidiaries of the same multinational. Thus, the retail pair sells the same brands of women's clothes, the motor vehicles pair makes the same engines, and the pharmaceuticals pair makes the same medical products. Therefore, the establishment pairs cannot differ much as regards quality of product.

Table 19.3's first row shows the difference in the method of pay determination as between the UK and France, which in turn feeds back into labor costs and the unskilled/skilled pay ratio. As can be seen, for all the French establishments, pay is determined by sectoral collective agreement, in line with the corporatist system discussed earlier. For the UK, pay setting is decentralized: in the manufacturing establishments, it is determined via company collective agreements, and in the UK retailing organization via the free market. Consequently, pay in the French establishments is higher than in their UK counterparts despite the high French social security taxes, which add 45–50 percent to wages. In line with the privileged position of the male breadwinner noted above, there is no evidence of the higher costs of French social security taxes being backward-shifted onto workers. The end result is higher labor costs in France for all three of our comparisons. This effect is greatest for the retailer, whose labor cost in France is £20,290, almost three times its level in the UK, £7,940.

Table 19.3: UK–France comparisons of pay, labor costs, and productivity (averages over 1992–95)

	UK			France		
	Retail	**Motor vehicles**	**Pharmaceuticals**	**Retail**	**Motor vehicles**	**Pharmaceuticals**
Pay determination	Individual	Collective agreement	Collective agreement	Industry agreement	Industry agreement	Industry agreement
Percent union	0	97	75	20	20	0
Mean pay[a] £s	7720	23,070	15,700 (15,600)[b]	12,660 (12,860)	20,270 (19,490)	16,340
Total lab. costs, £s[c]	7940[d]	26,830	17,150 (17,040)	20,290 (20,620)	29,910 (24,460)	24,100

Notes: [a] Full-time equivalent costs are converted to sterling using average market exchange rates; [b] Bracketed terms include fixed-term contract workers, where applicable; [c] The difference between pay and total labor costs is due to statutory social charges and company pension schemes.; [d] Most employees are part-time and so fall below the earnings limit for paying National Insurance taxes.
Source: Siebert et al. (2003).

High labor costs in France should lead to the substitution of capital for labor, reducing unskilled job opportunities. This reduction follows since capital and skilled labor are normally complementary, so substitution of capital for labor causes the unskilled/skilled labor ratio to fall. To judge unskilled job opportunities, the five indicators we develop from personnel records are young age, old age, tenure, prior experience, and education. These data are summarized in Table 19.4. As regards age, Table 19.4 shows that the UK establishments employ significantly greater percentages of young and inexperienced workers to make or sell the same products. Moreover, UK establishments also employ significantly more over-55s. In these results, we see confirmation at the micro level of the more equal UK youth and older worker job market reported in the aggregate in Table 19.3. As regards prior experience, there are sharp differences, the most marked being for motor vehicles. For 8.9 percent of the workforce in the UK plant, this is their first job, compared to only 0.5 percent in the French counterpart. We also see here a source of the UK establishments' generally lower productivity: inexperienced workers must be less productive. Admittedly, tenure differences are not marked. UK establishments do not exhibit the lower tenure that might be expected given the 'hire and fire' UK labor market environment. However, the French establishments use many temporary workers, who will have short tenure. Finally, as regards education, French workers tend to be more educated. In sum, as can be seen, in 12 out of 15 possible comparisons, the indication is that the UK establishments employ more unskilled labor than do their French counterparts.

Table 19.4: UK–France measures of unskilled job opportunities (samples taken 1994–95)

	Retailing			Motor vehicles			Pharmaceuticals		
	UK	Fr	UK–Fr[a]	UK	Fr	UK–Fr[a]	UK	Fr	UK–Fr[a]
Age									
% < 25yrs	50.3	35.5	+**	6.2	2.9	+**	5.3	1.5	+**
% > 55 yrs	1.3	2.1	–	18.4	3.9	+**	12.1	5.3	+**
Tenure									
% ≤ 3 yrs	80.3	55.4	+**	0	1.9	–**	3.5	3.4	+
Prior experience									
% < 1 yr	14.7	3.5	+**	8.9	0.5	+**	16.0	8.7	+**
Education									
% ≤ 12 yrs	100	100	0	95.0	74.3	+**	95.5	72.1	+**

Notes: **, * denote significance at the 5% or 10% level, with the indicated sign.
[a] t-test for significance of difference in proportion/rate.
Source: As for Table 19.3.

The policy implication is that corporatist or centralized wage-setting and employment protection need not be benign with respect to the impact on unskilled job opportunities. The lack of jobs for young and old in France (Table 19.3) can then be broadly explained by conventional economic variables such as the higher cost of unskilled workers in France, remembering that employment protection laws make employers especially choosy about hiring the unskilled. Hence, to widen job opportunities beyond the 'single generation' in France would require wider wage differentials,[8] or less employment protection, or both. Furthermore, since UK establishments are generally more unskilled-labor-intensive on all our measures, UK labor productivity must also be lower; we find it 25 to 35 percent lower in manufacturing, 50 percent in retailing. Policy-makers often worry about labor productivity, but we see here that low productivity may be no bad thing; it is the consequence of more equal access to jobs.

Evidence from newly industrializing countries

We now look at evidence from a different sample of nine countries, an emerging industrialized country group, ranging from Brazil to Turkey. This group might be of more relevance to Poland and other transition economies. We will see the same empirical regularities coming through, in particular the association of increases in union power with increases in unemployment. At the same time, in many of this group, the association of trade union power with the extension of democracy is obvious. It has been well demonstrated that democracy and economic growth are linked (Rueschmeyer and Stephens, 1992), and trade unions do their societies an undeniable service in this respect. Still, trade union power has to be managed. Each of this group of countries has its methods, more or less successful.

To analyze employment and unemployment it is easiest to start with a basic supply and demand diagram, as in Figure 19.2. Initial equilibrium is shown as point A. Unemployment (*U*) is given by the difference between employment and the potential labor force, as shown. Figure 19.2 can be used to illustrate two possibilities, one good, and one bad. Let us take the good possibility first. Here, the economy expands, for example due to foreign direct investment inflows, and the labor demand curve moves outwards from D_1 to D_2. At any given real wage, more people can be employed. The economic expansion will bring about a new equilibrium such as B, with higher real wages and employment, and lower unemployment. Secondly, there is the bad possibility. Here, trade union power forces wages upwards, with demand and supply unchanged. The result is a new equilibrium such as C, with higher real wages, but lower employment and correspondingly higher unemployment. The important point for wage-setting policy is to ensure that the good scenario emerges rather than the bad.

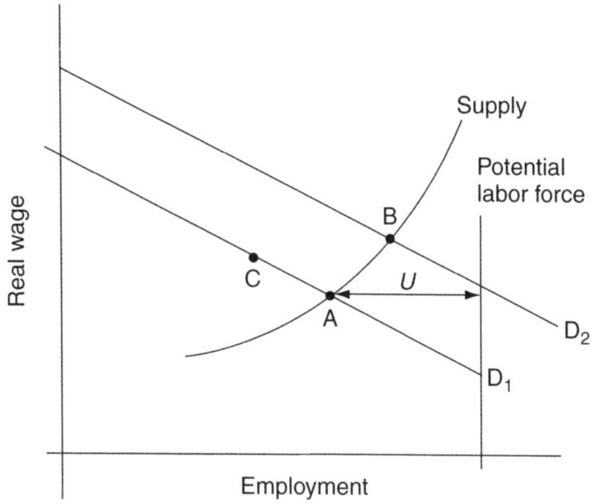

Figure 19.2: Supply and demand

Figure 19.3 and Figure 19.4 contain comparative data on unemployment, and trade union density in the nine countries, with the UK added in for interest.[9] From Figure 19.3 we see the link between trade union power and unemployment that we have already observed for the OECD sample. Countries such as Brazil and South Africa, with the largest union density increases, have also had the largest unemployment increases. It is also these countries

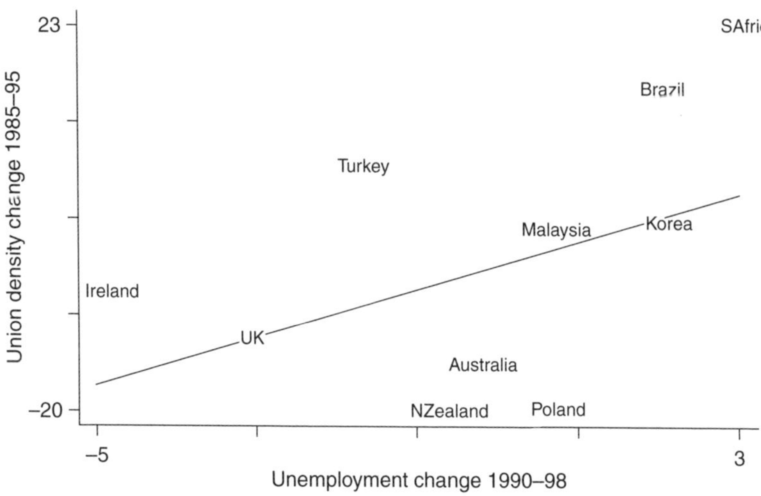

Figure 19.3: Union density increase is positively linked to unemployment increase

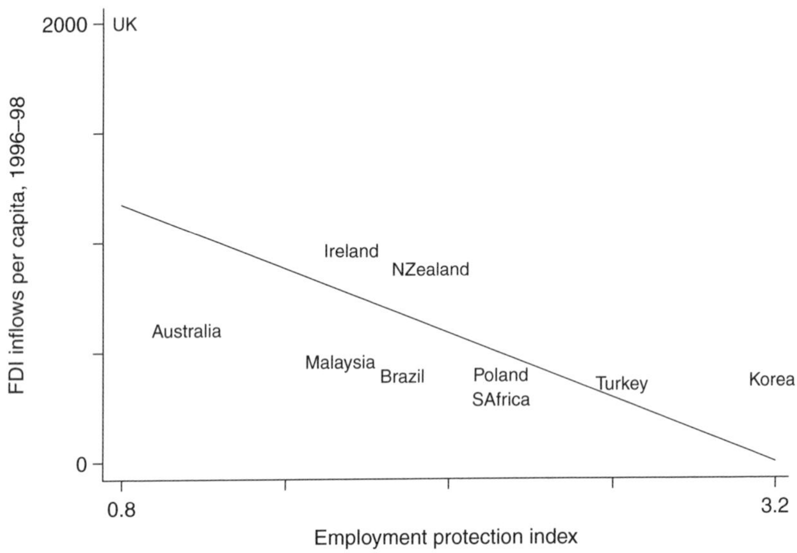

Figure 19.4: Employment protection laws reduce FDI

that have had the largest real wage increases (see Table 19.5). It is hard not to conclude that for these countries we are observing a move akin to that from A to C in Figure 19.3.

Calculations for trade union density are given in Table 19.5. We see that South Africa has had the largest increase in union density over the period 1985–95, 23 percentage points. The only country with a similar increase is Brazil, with its new 1988 pro-union Constitution. Both Brazil and South Africa, in fact, have had contemporaneous increases in union power, in real wages and in unemployment.

At the other end of the spectrum are countries that have had real wage increases linked to unemployment decreases and trade union density decreases. Such a situation would correspond to a move from A to B in Figure 19.3. Countries in this position appear to be Australia, Ireland, New Zealand and the UK. Poland could also be put in this group, since, even though its unemployment increased slightly over the period, this increase was obviously for special reasons, and the trend seems now to be downward. In all these countries, the trade union movement, while free, has been prevented from wielding undue influence by deregulation.

Employment protection legislation is also important. Such laws tend to be part of the corporatist package, but we have already seen how these laws can adversely affect outsider groups such as the long-term unemployed. Figure 19.4 shows a further way in which these laws can reduce employment;

by deterring foreign direct investment inflows (FDI). High FDI inflows are obviously important for employment because FDI inflows are a factor shifting the D curve outwards in Figure 19.2.

Conclusions

Let us look back through our tables in turn, and briefly summarize the findings. Table 19.1 showed that centralized or corporatist policies had a beneficial impact on unskilled job opportunities, other things equal. At the same time, we saw that employment protection laws, trade union strength, and taxation all had adverse effects on unskilled opportunities. A typical corporatist country is high on all these variables, implying that the net effect is adverse for the unskilled.

France is a case in point (Table 19.2), with high bargaining coordination, strict employment protection, and high taxes and very low participation of the young and the old in the workforce. Looking at our matched pairs of UK and French plants, we saw that the French policy of high taxes and strict employment protection had not resulted in lower wages in the French plants to adjust for this extra 'social wage' but higher wages, and much higher labor costs (Table 19.3). Naturally, the French plants had to secure much higher labor productivity, with the consequence that unskilled workers were shut out, with few inexperienced or uneducated workers (Table 19.4). French corporatism does not seem to have encompassed all workers. It is true that the French earnings distribution is more equal than the UK's (Table 19.2), and so is its income distribution after transfers, but happiness studies strongly suggest that jobs are more important than income.

Finally, we considered a fresh group of countries, some of which owe their new-found democracy to union organization. These countries present different approaches to the question of managing trade union power. We saw in this group of countries as well the link between union power and unemployment (Figure 19.3), paralleling the earlier OECD results (Table 19.1). The countries that experienced both a real wage and an employment increase were those that had brought about a trade union density decline (Table 19.5). Countries such as South Africa and Brazil, with union movements that increased their strength, could manage a real wage increase only at the expense of jobs. In fact, those countries with increasing union movements tended also to have strict employment protection laws, which seemed to deter FDI (Figure 19.4) and so further reduce jobs.

We began this chapter by asking how centralized or corporatist should the setting of wages and working conditions be. We have seen that centralization, by itself, seems to have beneficial effects on unemployment. However, centralization rarely comes by itself, but brings with it high taxes and employment protection legislation. It is argued that high taxes and employment protection legislation can in principle be accompanied by lower

Table 19.5: Union density and real wages

Country	Trade union density (percent of wage and salary earners)			Real wage increase 1993–98	Remarks
	1985 (2)	1995 (4)	Change 1995–1985 (4)–(2)		
Australia	50	35	–15	17	Decentralized bargaining since late 1980s
Brazil	(13–30)	44	16	25	New pro-union 1988 Constitution after years of military rule – which unions opposed
Ireland	56	49	–7	6	Deregulation following Thatcher
Korea	12	13	1	11	Democracy Declaration in 1987 after military rule – which unions opposed – but unions still restrained
Malaysia	14	13	0	19	Regime closely controls unions – banned in semiconductor industry
New Zealand	54	24	–20	3	Deregulation – Employment Contracts Act of 1991
Poland	59	39	–20	23	Fall of communism in 1990 due to union opposition – Poles are pro-capitalism
South Africa	18	41	23	120	Fall of apartheid in 1994 as a result of union power has led to union-friendly laws
Turkey	21 (25)	34 (32)	7	72	Military rule until 1982 – military still powerful, but becoming less suspicious of unions
UK	44	32	–12	15	Deregulation following Thatcher
China	67	50	–17	26	Unions changing role as free market expands – will unions become independent, and will decentralization be pursued?

Source: Siebert (2001, p. 10).

wages and/or increased worker effort, if the corporatist state is run on encompassing lines. Perhaps this ideal is achieved in Sweden or Austria. It does not seem to be the case in France. Admittedly, corporatism may also bring narrower earnings and income differentials, although this fact has not been demonstrated outside the OECD group. Happiness studies suggest that such narrowing of differentials is not worth paying for in terms of higher unemployment. However, a further democratic objective is ensuring an independent trade union movement. There seems no simple prescription for achieving this objective. Given this objective, the answer to our question, therefore, is that a decentralized setting of wages has the overwhelming benefit of opening up job opportunities for outsiders.

Notes

1. The author would like to thank Fei Peng for expert research assistance. Any errors are his own.
2. The estimated coefficients (×100) give the change in percentage points of the dependent variable. Thus, for the bargaining coordination coefficient, –0.547, a decrease in coordination from the average (4 index points) to the current UK level (2) gives a large reduction in unemployment, 109% ($= 2 \times -0.547 \times 100$).
3. For example, for the youth employment/population variable, the third column gives the combined effects of 100% coverage and full coordination (= level 6) as $100 \times -0.3 + 6 \times 7.9 = 17.4\%$ improvement in youth employment/population.
4. Teulings and Hartog (1998) argue that wage contracts are more easily varied in a corporatist world where higher-level bodies (that is joint industrial councils) can be entrusted with setting wages. Otherwise, the parties fear 'hold-up.' Higher-level bodies can then control insider power and restore competitive wage differentials. The flexibility argument is thus turned on its head. Corporatist economies are more, not less, flexible than decentralized ones.
5. For the 20 OECD country sample in Table 19.1, the simple cross-country correlation of the coordination variable with the employment protection legislation variable is 0.514**, with the tax wedge 0.527**, with union density 0.536**, and with collective agreement coverage 0.617***.
6. However, Summers et al. (1993, p. 407) warn: 'Part of the logic of socialism was that a wise government could internalize everything and so generate efficient economic outcomes. This has proved wrong, and should give pause about excessively benign views of negotiated alternatives to market solutions.'
7. See Daniel and Siebert (2004) for a model and results supporting the view that employment protection costs are higher for unskilled than skilled workers.
8. While France has a higher poverty rate than the UK (see Bazen, 2000, p. 63), consistent with lack of jobs for the unskilled, its poverty rate after transfers is lower.
9. Normally, it would be advisable in particular to analyze employment rather than unemployment figures, since employment figures are generally easier for statistical bureaus to estimate. However, in the case of Brazil, South Africa, and Turkey there are large informal or 'grey' sectors, which make employment calculations hazardous. At least unemployment rates can be estimated from sample surveys (whereas total employment cannot). Therefore, we will stick with unemployment measures.

References

Addison, J. and C. Belfield (2003), 'Union Voice', IZA Discussion Paper, No. 862, Institute for Labour Research, Bonn.

Bazen, S. (2000), 'The Impact of the Regulation of Low Wages on Inequality and Labour Market Adjustment: a Comparative Analysis', *Oxford Review of Economic Policy*, 16, 57–69.

Calmfors, L. and J. Driffel (1988), 'Bargaining Structure, Corporatism and Macroeconomic Performance', *Economic Policy*, 6, 14–61.

Clarke, S. and C.-H. Lee (2003), 'Towards a System of Tripartite Consultation in China', unpublished paper, Centre for Comparative Labour Studies, University of Warwick.

Daniel, K. and W.S. Siebert (2004), 'Does Employment Protection Reduce the Demand for Unskilled Labor?', Discussion Paper 1290, Institute for Labour Research (IZA) Bonn.

Flanagan, R. (1999), 'Macroeconomic Performance and Collective Bargaining: an International Perspective', *Journal of Economic Literature*, 37, 1150–95.

Freeman, R. and J. Medoff (1984) *What Do Unions Do?*, New York: Basic Books.

Galtier, B. and J. Gautié (2003), 'Flexibility, Stability and the Interaction between Employment Protection and Labour Market Polices in France', in P. Auer and S. Cazes (eds), *Employment Stability in an Age of Flexibility*, Geneva: International Labour Office.

Koeniger, W., M. Leonardi and L. Nunziata (2004), 'Labor Market Institutions and Wage Inequality', Discussion Paper 1295, Institute for Labour Research (IZA), Bonn.

Nickell, S. (1997), 'Unemployment and Labor Market Rigidities: Europe versus North America', *Journal of Economic Perspectives*, 11, Summer, 55–74.

Nickell, S. and R. Layard (1999), 'Labor Market Institutions and Economic Performance', in Orley Ashenfelter (ed.), *Handbook of Labor Economics*, Vol 3c, Amsterdam: Elsevier, pp. 3029–84.

OECD (1994, 1997, 1999), *OECD Employment Outlook, 1994, 1997, 1999*, Paris: OECD.

OECD (2001), *OECD Labour Market Statistics* CD-Rom, OECD, Paris.

Rueschmeyer, D. and D. Stephens (1992), *Capitalist Development and Democracy*, Oxford: Polity Press.

Siaroff, A. (1999), 'Corporatism in 24 Industrial Democracies: Meaning and Measurement', *European Journal of Political Research*, 36, 175–205.

Siebert, W.S. (2001), *Investment, Employment and South African Labour Laws: an International Comparison*, Free Market Foundation Monograph no 30, Johannesburg: Free Market Foundation, October.

Siebert, W.S. (2003), 'Notes on Labour Market Flexibility', in Rita Cheng, Richard Meadows and Roger Sugden (eds), *Urban and Regional Prosperity in a Globalised, New Economy*, Cheltenham, UK and Northampton, MA: Edward Elgar.

Siebert, W.S., J. Morton and R. Barrett (2003), 'Labouring under Different Rules: Matched Establishments in France and Britain', unpublished paper, Department of Commerce, Birmingham University.

Summers, Laurence, Jonathan Gruber and Rodrigo Vergara (1993), 'Taxation and the Structure of Labor Markets', *Quarterly Journal of Economics*, 108(2), May, 385–411.

Teulings, C. and J. Hartog (1998), *Corporatism or Competition?*, Cambridge: Cambridge University Press.

Winkelman, L. and R. Winkelman (1998), 'Why Are the Unemployed So Unhappy? Evidence from Panel Data', *Economica*, 65, 1–15.

Section 5

Economic Policy Choices in Europe: Perspective on the US Model Performance

20

Discussion by Jan Krzysztof Bielecki, John Bradley, Marshall Goldman, Stanisław Gomułka, Ruslan Khasbulatov, Andrzej K. Koźmiński, William A. Niskanen

Discussion held at the final session of the conference 'American Economic Way: Its Character, Effectiveness and Applicability' in Warsaw, 23 October 2004.

JAN KRZYSZTOF BIELECKI: Without further ado, let me start by saying how delighted I am to have the privilege to chair this panel this afternoon with so many distinguished panelists alongside me. I would also like to express my gratitude to Professor Bieńkowski, the key organizer of this conference because, for us Poles, the question regarding 'the American way' and 'the American model' has always been interesting both politically and economically. And I have jotted down a few key points that reflect or summarize the situation in Poland after accession; these once again show us that when we look at our big European neighbors, farther west, we find several economic models for which we do not care, either in Europe or particularly in Poland. Let me just recall a few recent examples, including a joint campaign to impose higher corporate tax rates on the new EU members from central Europe, so as to stem the flow of investment and, of course, jobs eastwards; or discussion in both Germany and France of a 1970s style industrial policy aimed at protecting, in fact, national champions. Sometimes they mix these up with European champions, but by European champions they mean French and German champions operating in Continental Europe. Another example is the introduction in the new European constitution of a new hurdle for countries wishing to join the euro, which, in addition to the Maastricht criteria, will be required prior to joining the eurozone. Of course, this is a mechanism in the new constitution that will allow France and Germany to pre-empt the shape of future EU cooperation. These are only a few examples that show that the discussion about the future EU model may be a departure from the model employed in Poland over the last 15 years.

For countries like us, catching up, determined to raise the standard of living of our population, the challenge is enormous. Therefore, we look to the United States, which, by the way, has a similar ratio of young entrepreneurs willing to establish their own companies. The entrepreneurial drive is quite high in Poland; according to OECD research nearly 80 percent of young Poles declare an interest in establishing their own business, while for our neighbor to the south, the Czech Republic, it is just 30 percent. I think in Germany it is around 60 percent. That shows that we have this entrepreneurial drive, and, even during the difficult days of martial law and communism, we tried to find solutions that depended quite often on our own initiatives. Therefore, we naturally and historically look at the American model and the American entrepreneurial way of development, and this leads me to the final point. I remember that when George Bush Senior came to Warsaw for the first time, he emphasized a strong bond between Poland and the United States, emphasizing that, since the Versailles Treaty, we have had this particular political liaison, special connection and good understanding. This shows that there is some substance on which to base this conference and I am therefore delighted that Professor Bieńkowski organized it for us in Warsaw. During the last two days, we have had an opportunity to review so many important issues regarding the American way. Today, we are in a bit of a difficult situation because we have Poles and non-Europeans discussing policy choices in Europe; we are short of a Continental Europe view on this panel, but, I hope, perhaps Professor Bradley will represent this Continental view. If not, then we have a second choice, which is Professor Khasbulatov, who could be the Continental component in the debate on policy choices in Europe. So, therefore if you do not mind, I will start in alphabetical order and ask you to deliver during the first round a relatively short statement. I would not use the word 'brief', because when I worked for an international organization for ten years, we had a special vocabulary, or a dictionary, that explained typical expressions used by international bureaucrats, for example if somebody says 'I will be very brief,' it meant 15 minutes [laugh]...and 'comprehensive' was even worse. Therefore, if you would be so kind Professor Bradley, and not that 'brief,' not that 'comprehensive,' then it will help us to run the panel. Professor Bradley...

JOHN BRADLEY: Thank you. I was hoping that an opening statement would not be required from us but let me just give you a few reflections on the conference so far. I am a European and I come from the periphery of Europe. A lot of Irish identity is tied up with Europe in a very important way, and I think the same applies to my Polish colleagues. And the European way is a way of consensus, of sitting around the table of 9, of 12, of 15, of 25, of 27, of maybe more. But it is a consensus arrived at within a certain context. That context has an economic dimension, it has a social dimension and it has a cultural dimension. We have largely been talking about the economic dimension, and the economic dimension is, indeed, the American way, it is the triumph of liberal market economics over central planning. So, you have the party and you go home and get up the next day and you ask, whither now? And that is my big problem with the libertarian agenda that very much dominated this conference. That now you have polarization, you have a polarized view that says the government has no role in developing the future of the country. That it is only market forces that will operate. But that is not the European way, and it is not the European Commission way and most of my work is carried out through the European Commission. I would hope that out of this conference would come perhaps a meeting of minds between the American libertarian agenda and the European social consensus model, because I think we misunderstand each other. These are not polar choices. In each of our continents, Europe and America, coalitions and consensus are arrived at, but in different ways, and, in Europe, given Europe's history, it has to be slow and tedious and our constitution cannot be like the American constitution, our political speech cannot be like the Gettysburg Address, it has to be 10,000 pages of detailed laws and regulations. I am not sure that we should have a problem with that, because you are sitting around the table talking about what is a sausage or whether British chocolate should be called chocolate. These are unifying forces. But if you polarize the debate politically within Europe, you get tension. So, what I got from this conference was a better understanding of the libertarian agenda, which of course is difficult to understand from the European perspective, but I hope our American friends in the Cato Institue and the AEI develop a greater tolerance for the needs within Europe to engage in a process of social consensus...

JAN KRZYSZTOF BIELECKI: That is it? [laugh] That is a special round of applause. However, regarding the model you have mentioned, I have to say that we were accused by our bigger neighbor to the west quite recently that we have a lack of understanding of the European model, so we Poles will not help you definitely in resolving this problem. Now let me refer to our non-European speaker, Professor Marshall Goldman...

MARSHALL GOLDMAN: Well, I have to agree, with what John just said. I think he hit it precisely. What I was going to say is that if you look at the United States there is some sense that we had enormous advantages. The advantages were that we did not have an inherited structure, we started from scratch, we did not have to worry about the landed aristocracy, which had all the privileges. So, in the United States what you wanted to do when you became an adult was not to become a landowner, what you wanted to do was to make money. And that had, to the extent that you were doing it legally, advantages. So we became a meritocracy. The meritocracy was judged again on the basis of how much you could earn, how much you could contribute. Of course in academic life that would be slightly different, but we still had different standards to measure merit.

We were more of an individualists' society, we were much less collective. Certainly the farther east you go in Europe, the more collective, the more social things become. Look at agriculture. In the United States the farmers live in a home on their own land. They do not live in a village. That emphasizes the idea of being an individual. There was a book that was very popular in the 1950s and 1960s called *The Organization Man* by William Whyte. He argued that everyone at the time wanted to be a part of an established structure, part of a larger organization. But if you look at what happened subsequently, it turns out that that book did not reflect what was going on in the United States in the 1990s, where the whole idea was to go off and start your own business, create a start up with venture capital. It was an incredible time. Unfortunately it did not last.

I have two sons, both sons who went to business school. And their aspiration was to go into business for themselves, not to go into academic life. But when I reflect on England or Europe generally and try to explain why in the United States we are more likely to go into business, it is in part because it is more socially acceptable. In England, if you wanted to rise in the hierarchy, you became a landholder aristocrat or you went into the military or to the foreign service, or to the court or to the ministry. In the United States it is not quite the same. What you are more likely to do, is go into business. Why? Well, part of the answer is that one way to advance in business is to go first to a business school and earn an MBA degree. That helps make it socially acceptable because you get a degree from the Harvard Business School or Stanford or Duke or North Carolina. So, we made going into business acceptable in a way that is, I think, not duplicated in many other societies. It is interesting, however, that if you go to Russia, you will find everybody is setting up their own little business school. So in some sense they try to duplicate what we did.

Another factor is that we have been much more tolerant of immigrants. For years we were criticized, certainly during the Soviet period because we did not absorb these immigrants, and there was racial discrimination. Well, there is racial discrimination, but looking at what is happening in Europe, by comparison, we are doing pretty well. And to the extent that we increase immigration, that brings in new blood. Not everybody succeeds, not all different groups succeed, but it keeps infusing us with something dynamic and I think that is important.

It is also true that we have less in the way of social benefits. This goes right to the point that I think that John was making. There are times when I am very critical of the fact that we do not have social benefits. If you are unemployed, you are on your own, but, at the same time, in a period when the business community is in one of its dynamic phases, it is more likely that American businessmen and women will hire new employees. We do not have to worry as much about the consequences of firing these new employees. It is difficult to generate new businesses when, if you hire somebody, you are stuck with them, because you cannot fire them. Somebody this morning said, 'that when looking at economic growth it is important not only to look at the opportunities for expansion but the opportunities for contraction.' There are times when you need to close things down because they are inefficient. Again, that is much easier to do in the United States than in Europe. In Europe, they are more sensitive. Yet, in fairness there is a trade-off. The sensitivity that precludes growth opportunities also makes available social benefits to help those who have no jobs.

Let me then just end with one other comment about the European Union. Europe is creating a market that will allow for the advantages of scale that we have always had in the United States. And indeed that is impressive. Look how easy it is now for a European to cross borders within Europe. That clearly is an important contribution. At the same time, going back to the point that John made, the disadvantage that comes with this new Union is the bureaucracy. This new structure is so bizarre. You are destroying the opportunity that exists for economies of scale. We in the United States were lucky, because we did not inherit all this. The European Union in a sense did not inherit it either; instead they are creating it. It is as if they are trying to make up for lost time, which seems bizarre. This will end up putting a stranglehold on the opportunities that exist within Europe, which takes away from the great opportunity the European Union had.

We in the United States have to worry about how we work out the balance between being socially responsible and encouraging entrepreneurship and there are times when we go too far to either extreme. At the same time, you in Europe have to worry about achieving the same balance, but with too much emphasis on social benefits and bureaucratic control. I do not consider myself a libertarian, I do believe in individualism, but not at the expense of the very poor. It is very difficult to keep a balance, but the Europeans, if they are not careful, run the risk of destroying this new opportunity that you and they have.

JAN KRZYSZTOF BIELECKI: Thank you. To keep a balance and to create jobs. Maybe we will come back to this issue a little bit later. I was nearly ready to hand over the microphone to the next speaker, but your perfect comment on business stopped me from doing so. When you mentioned that youngsters aimed to go to the best business schools and, of course, you started with Harvard and then Duke and then you named North Carolina and did not mention Wharton where I had a privilege to spend five years on the advisory board, you must understand why I make a reference to that school.

MARSHALL GOLDMAN: I am a graduate at Wharton, so forgive me... [laugh]

JAN KRZYSZTOF BIELECKI: Thank you, sounds better. We may return to Europe, Professor Gomułka.

STANISŁAW GOMUŁKA: Thank you very much, Mr Chairman. During our discussions yesterday and today, several speakers and, indeed, several members of this conference, participants, were trying to establish what is precisely the difference between the European model and the US model and what are the implications of any differences for countries like Poland. It seems to me that there is perhaps a temptation to exaggerate the differences. We should not forget that the US economy was created by Europeans. That perhaps the British model, the Anglo-Saxon model, was created in Europe. Now, however, it is true that in the first half of the last century, Europe departed from the model it established earlier. And there were two events or three events perhaps which actually made a huge impact on events on this continent, namely the First and Second World Wars and the socialist experiments in Central and Eastern Europe. If you like, three disasters. And these three disasters made a huge impact also on the way Europeans have been thinking in the second half of the twentieth century. Basically the European Union is a response to these disasters. Now, in that response the European Union has sort of, more or less, returned in part to its roots, to its more liberal roots and situation where we have less bureaucracy and fewer borders.

Now, when we think about the American model, it was emphasized by one of the speakers, we think perhaps about stability, liberal rules and private property. And let us recall that the European Union has become, basically during the last twenty years, an island of economic stability and has been much more liberal, more competitive than before. I am talking about a very considerable integration of product markets, capital markets and more privatization. So there has been a very substantial shift toward that model. It is true, however, that some differences, and important differences, remain, and it is these differences that might be perhaps the focus of attention for policy-makers in a country like Poland. Now these differences, at the moment, seem to largely concern the flexibility of the labor market and public expenditures: the labor market, which is much less competitive, much more restrictive, in Europe than in the United States, and public expenditures, which are much larger in Europe. Now, my suggestion is that for a country like Poland and, indeed, for new European Union countries, the US model should be seen as more attractive, because our concern right now is catching up, removal of the income gap between this part of Europe and Western Europe. Western Europe can afford to be less competitive as far as labor markets are concerned, where they have unemployment rates of, say 10 percent; they can afford not to work as hard as the Americans. But in Poland the situation is different and Russia is even more the case for adopting simply a strategy for faster growth. That is the basic concern of this part of the world for the next half a century. So we have to adopt reforms in the labor markets and in public expenditures simply to become more competitive, to have a better environment for new enterprises, to be a more energetic recipient of the know-how of technology, of business techniques that have been invented elsewhere. To be simply a very good student of market economics. OK, so from that perspective it seems to me that we should simply try to adopt the American way of conducting business, perhaps to a greater extent than that of the European Union, in these two areas: labor markets and public expenditures. When Poland and the other countries of Central Europe become as rich as Germany and France are, perhaps in half a century, perhaps there might be also a need to change that. But for the time being, for the next half a century, I think that substantial reforms especially in these two areas are needed. For this particular purpose: faster and more energetic catching up.

JAN KRZYSZTOF BIELECKI: OK, thank you. So, now I have a problem, because on the name cards the spelling of the surname of Professor Khasbulatov gives as the first letter 'K' and I think the more correct would be 'CH'. Am I wrong?

RUSLAN KHASBULATOV: 'KH'.

JAN KRZYSZTOF BIELECKI: If 'KH', then Professor Koźmiński will follow behind you... Anyway... Kruschev was with 'K', definitely. Professor Khasbulatov...

RUSLAN KHASBULATOV: Thank you. Thank you ladies and gentlemen. In my presentation yesterday I raised two topics. The first, the experience of the American economic way and the second, how this experience influenced Russian economics. The American experience should be used by all states of the world, because of the companies and the market economy. Russian academics always learn from American academics via translated books or in original versions, so we are always updated with the newest American economics approaches. The second issue is how we managed in Russia to establish a market economy. We associate transformation from a socialist approach into capitalism with a putsch, when the regime collapsed. At that moment, the ideas of the leaders of the Communist Party were very unpopular in Russia. And that was the right moment to introduce a new economic approach. However, I do not mean to discuss here the quarrels that happened in those days. In my opinion, we Deputies in Parliament are more experienced and educated in economics than in politics, so we were trying to put onto Russian ground the experience of Western countries. It is well known that the American economy is very specific because of its huge multinationals and we decided to build the Russian economy based on such multinationals or huge corporations. I do not know how many years such companies as General Motors or Ford were forming themselves, but I guess fifty to sixty years, sometimes one hundred. In the Russian case, it was only one day. So, if you ask Ivanow 'Who are you? What's your profession?', he might reply, 'I am a younger specialist in academics or researcher.' They would say, 'No, you are not! You are now an oligarch.' He is given a bank, corporation or factory with a huge amount of money in its accounts. I am a little bit simplifying the situation, but the meaning stays unchanged. As a result there appeared a nouveau-riche accumulation of capital, but this is not the main issue. The worst thing about the origin of Russian capitalism is that new oligarchs learned how to raise capital without knowledge, just through political connections. So that is the worst thing that the businessmen were taught during the origin of the capitalist system. It is like a genetic disease in a child that you cannot get rid of. It was the emergence of that disease I was already pointing to when I was in Parliament. We discussed not if we should go back to the communist regime. The main quarrels were about how to form a true business culture. We changed Ricardo's formula from money-production-money into money-authorities-money. That is the model that exists in Russia that I called a private bureaucratic model. The other consequence of such a model is in the social sphere. In academic environments we are raising these issues that I am going to present to you now. It is social, cultural and educational degradation. Before the reforms, the educational level and the level of living were quite high in Russia. To present you that issue I should tell you that now professors in Russia earn three times less than at the end of the 1980s. Doctors, teachers, academics are millions of people who earn much less than during the socialist regime. If you look at this issue from that point of view, you can expect whatever. You could excuse such a situation if the government did not have money. But it is already five years since huge amounts of capital started coming from the oil industry. And this capital is distributed in many areas, not in the areas that are for society. I think that Russian politics would be great if it were not distorted through the demands of society. Unfortunately, society requires some assets, however, the government cannot provide them. And the government is explaining this situation through an economic approach, for example monetary approach, that we cannot allow a budgetary deficit. But yesterday we could hear the presentation of Professor Niskanen, who said that there has been a current account deficit in America for the last three hundred years. However, Russia has huge economic power and I do not think that an adverse budgetary deficit may influence negatively our political circumstances. But we have huge trade surplus of 100 billion dollars. So we have a different situation and we cannot base our political decisions on monetarism. Today I presented my doubts that classical monetarists may not be able to exist in the twenty-first century. Nowadays, during the process of globalization and internationalization of the world, I think we should rethink the economic basis of political decisions. The world economy is not only influenced by the American economy, Chinese economy or European Union economies. Even changes in the small states in the most remote parts of the world may influence the world economy. I would like to remind you of the 1998 Russian debt crisis. It influenced very seriously capital markets of other countries. American investors started to remove their capital from Russia. In my opinion, Bretton Woods establishments are obsolete nowadays. I think we should establish some national regulatory system to run politics. Thank you very much for your attention.

JAN KRZYSZTOF BIELECKI: *Bolszoje sposibo*, Professor Khasbulatov. I would like to ask Professor Koźmiński to take the floor.

ANDRZEJ K. KOŹMIŃSKI: Thank you Mr Chairman. First of all I would like to congratulate the organizers of this conference for this exciting topic. I was tempted by it for a long time as someone who has shared his time between the US and Europe and of course comparisons are very tempting. But before I begin, first of all I want to recall the question that was formulated for panelists to address. Is the US economic experience a useful guide for economic policy choices in Europe? I want to stress the notion of guide or inspiration, because certainly copying American policies and institutions on the other side of the big pond does not make sense. The US has a very strong and very specific cultural, political and spiritual identity. It also has the size, scope and volume of economy very difficult to compare with Europe, because Europe is far from being one country and one nation and will remain so in my opinion in the foreseeable future. To stay within a reasonable time limit, I can touch upon one area of American inspiration for Europe that I personally find the most powerful and the most important. America has pioneered a new type of economy, the knowledge-based economy, and a new type of information and knowledge-based competitive advantage. In this respect, America still remains far ahead of everybody else and will probably continue to do so. In spite of the famous Lisbon declaration and huge resources, Europe is still lagging behind as far as a knowledge-based economy is concerned and will probably continue to do so. Why? And here I would like to take up Professor Gomułka's point. Can Europe afford to lag behind? And my answer is different than his. No. Because if it continues to lag behind, the European way of life will, I would say, rapidly deteriorate. But, first I would like to answer the question, why is America so successful in building a knowledge-based economy? First of all, because building a knowledge-based economy was not planned or engineered by anybody. It resulted from a spontaneous interplay of culture, market forces, individual strategies and pragmatic focused government policies on the federal, state and even local levels. Such a situation remains in sharp conflict with the European vision of all-powerful state taking care of all strategic issues. Such a vision becomes obsolete very rapidly in times of globalization, generalized uncertainty and decline of nation-states. The question remains open. Is Europe capable of abandoning its outdated, state-centered vision of economic mechanism and policy? It will probably have to do so sooner or later. Social science ideology has an important role to play here, and my question is, are they capable of changing European minds fast enough? I have my doubts about it, but of course we can hope. In American culture, science, knowledge and education occupy a very special, almost sacred position. It is perceived as a main indicator and instrument of individual and collective success. By moral obligation it is linked to individual charity. And this individual charity produced a dynamic network of private research universities as well as countless charitable foundations, generously supporting research, education, culture and science. American generosity in this field is spontaneous, not necessarily triggered by fiscal incentives, it is driven by moral obligation. Knowing American resourcefulness and inventiveness in financial matters, none of these would have emerged without benevolent action. In Europe charity is limited to helping the poor and perhaps the arts. Science and education are perceived as the state's domain and the state is obliged to support them in exchange for high taxes. This is the state of mind of Europeans. In America, the free market rewards innovation, unique skills and knowledge to an unprecedented degree. Much more than in Europe. This is due to market deregulation and a taxation system much more business-friendly than in Europe. Individual strategies are built upon these premises, and Americans are morally and socially obliged to succeed. Failure is not tolerated. Europeans are often somewhat disgusted by this rat race, as they call it. They tend to forget, however, how functional it is to promote economic growth, which finally benefits everybody. In Europe instead of a mythology of success, we have developed mythologies of compassion and solidarity. Are we ready to modify and adjust them but certainly not to completely abandon? And here I agree with Professor Bradley. It is too deeply rooted in our mentality and in our tradition and our culture. Government plays a role of harmonizing, coordinating and sometimes focusing action, action taken independently by different groups of actors. The US government can be in this respect compared to a good gardener. Watering, trimming, weeding, sometimes planting independently growing species. The best example of it is Ronald Reagan's policy of developing higher education in California. It produced the UC system, the main driver and solid foundation of California's economic prosperity. I think it is something to think about. Thank you very much.

JAN KRZYSZTOF BIELECKI: Thank you Professor Koźmiński. Let me make try to streamline and reduce the differences between both distinguished panelists, Professor Gomułka and Professor Koźmiński regarding the pace of European change and the need to change it. When Professor Koźmiński said 'rapidly,' maybe by rapidly we understand 'in the next 25–30 years.' Professor Niskanen, the floor is yours.

WILLIAM A. NISKANEN: This is a rare opportunity to have the last word on this case, it is only because my wife is not here [laugh]...

I may be the only unapologetic libertarian on the panel, but may I remind my European friends about the ancient broad and deep European roots of what they call American libertarianism. Locke, Smith, Mill, Acton, Blackstone, Cox were from Great Britain, Montesquieu, Tocqueville, Constant from France, Mises and Hayek from Austria. These are all names that are engraved in the buildings of my institute, which is named after a Roman named Cato. So our intellectual roots are in European intellectual contributions to literature and liberty. One distinctive feature of libertarians, I suppose, is that they regard liberty itself as a value. And that it should be traded off against other ends only with great caution. Now, as I said in my remarks last night, I think it is important for Europeans to recognize both the strengths and the weaknesses of the American political and economic system. Because it is an opportunity for you to learn from both those strengths and those weaknesses. And second, it is not our business to tell you how to run your own affairs, but I think that you have an opportunity to learn from our experience. My own judgment is that the greatest weakness in our political system, roughly in my lifetime, is that the federal government has acquired the potential to define its own powers. The limits on the enumerated powers of the federal government in article 1, section 8 of the Constitution have been breached for seventy years now and most of the growth of the federal state has had no constitutional authority. Now, that reflects a flaw in our constitutional design that does not provide an outside check on the abuse of the constitutional powers. That is something you should think very carefully about in your own situation, because all governments have an incentive to try to extend their own powers. And you ought to think about ways that you can limit the opportunity for them to extend their own powers by making sure that there is a check that is outside the government itself that would check the expansion of those powers.

One of the greatest strengths of the United States, in both our economy and our culture, is that we are a nation of immigrants. My grandfather was an immigrant from Finland. That is not an unusual situation. I think if I asked members of my class, almost all of them would say at least one of their grandparents were from some other country. It has given us perspectives and insight and cultural contributions from a wide variety of sources. It does mean also that you have underestimated American economic growth because conventional measures of economic growth do not include how much the immigrant improves his income in the year that he moves to the United States. So to estimate our economic growth correctly, you should either take immigrants out in the given year or you should add their income in the country which they came from before they increased their income by coming to the United States. So our immigrant population, which is quite high, has had the effect from a purely statistical point of view of underestimating the rate of our economic growth. It also turns out to be an important contributor to being able to defer the day of reckoning in our public pension plan. We have still a substantial immigrant population and increasing immigrants. That has meant that our pension problems can take longer to solve than in most of Europe.

There is a lot to like, for both Americans and Europeans, in the American model. I caution you to look carefully at the problems that have developed in the United States, in many cases in my own lifetime. Poor performance of the public schools for example, the abuse of the courts as almost an independent legislature, the abuse of the courts for redistribution purposes through the tort law. These are all things you have to worry about in your own countries even if you do not start with the kind of Anglo-Saxon legal system we have. Americans are the beneficiaries of learning from our fathers and grandfathers who came from your countries, and we can learn from you now as well. So I encourage you to learn from both our strengths and our problems and our weaknesses and on occasion our proposed solutions. Thank you.

JAN KRZYSZTOF BIELECKI: Thank you Professor. Your comments remind me of one of the most significant, in my opinion, misunderstandings of a functioning market economy between my fellow Poles and, let us say, Anglo-Saxons. Why? Because when we discuss in Poland about development and economic models, we argue quite extensively about financial aspects, monetary aspects, social aspects, but we never talk about the law. When you made a short intervention, even I might say 'brief,' because it was barely five minutes, you referred a few times to the law and to the legal system of the United States. And also it reminds me of the famous words of Margaret Thatcher, who said: 'There is no functioning market economy without honorable judges.' And this is something we observe in Poland quite deeply and painfully, that this market may be a functioning market but strongly deteriorated by the lack of sufficient rule of law and honorable judges. And discussion about our judges and prosecutors is quite extensive these days. So, we not only need economic policy and discussion on economic policy choices, but also we must understand that it is so much connected to the legal and political system of any country that wants to achieve sustainable growth.

WILLIAM A. NISKANEN: Adam Smith himself said that the market economy is very dependent on what he called 'a strong arm of the civil magistrate' to secure property rights and enforce contracts. The concern of Smith and his colleagues is that the government might be too weak to perform that important role. Now, fortunately, for the most part of the United States, that role has been well performed, often superbly, but typically well performed, but it is an essential role for the government to do well. And, as I suggested last night, we all face the fact that we are dependent upon the government to be an effective agent to secure property rights and enforce contracts, but that the government itself, in most of our countries, is the major predator. And we have to figure out somehow to resolve that dilemma, and until we do, we will never really be free men and women.

JAN KRZYSZTOF BIELECKI: That is very true and that is why the weaknesses of the institutions were also so strongly emphasized by Professor Khasbulatov when he referred to the development of the situation in Russia. But let me ask a question, because we discussed about how successful was the American model and for me the successful American model is also proven by the number of jobs. When I look for benchmarks, and if we forget about the GDP growth ratio, and we have to refer to job creation and, if I remember the figures well, according to the OECD, for the last 23 years, between 1980 and 2003 in the US roughly 48 million new jobs were established, while at the same time in Europe only 17 million. So it is a devastating difference. Having said that, let me question Professor Koźmiński's comment, who praised so nicely and eloquently the advantages of the knowledge-based economy and the revolution of the late 1990s. However, if we look at the figures regarding job creation of the last years from 1998 to 2003, Europe created many more jobs than the US did. Does this mean that the knowledge-based economy is not creating jobs or they will come later? Or is it because Europe is lagging behind in this advancement of a knowledge-based economy? I find some contradictions here because historically the argument was quite simple. Yes, we Europeans do not create jobs, but we have different social models. But, if the Europeans could prove that they have more jobs established over the last five years then it will sound even more convincing that the European model is not only better balanced but also more successful in job creation. In a country like Poland, where unemployment is nearly 20 percent, job creation arguments sound very, very important. So I would very much appreciate any comment from the panel on this issue. Professor...

MARSHALL GOLDMAN: I think that it is a good question. In the short time I have been here, the focus has been on the European Union and the US There was one short presentation on China but we have really not looked much at the role of Asia in all this. I think this should be addressed. If you look at jobs in the United States, there has been some shrinkage in the information sector, but the biggest hit has been in the traditional industries, which have lost jobs to Asia. This has to do with the difference in wage rates, and, I would suspect, looking at the data that you presented about Europe, the increase of jobs in Europe does not refer so much to Germany and France. It may refer to England and Eastern Europe. The reason for that is, again, high wage rates. If you look at Japan, Japan has also shrunk, and why? Because businesses in Japan are now moving offshore to China, Vietnam, India and even the United States. Looking at why Poland has done so well, or at least ['Not in job creation,' voice from the audience] in terms of the investment figures that Professor Balcerowicz showed this morning, it is in part because jobs are being sent from Germany and located here because of the wage rate. So Eastern Europe has benefited in the same way that Asia has benefited by attracting jobs that had been in Western Europe but have now moved to Eastern Europe. The United States is a high wage country. To some extent that is offset by the fact that the United States remains a center for innovation, so we innovate, we develop new industries, those industries then very often move offshore. Our challenge is to innovate quickly enough, so that we balance off the loss of jobs in traditional industries.

Coming from Massachusetts, I gave a course once on high technology in Massachusetts called 'Making it in Massachusetts.' This course was taught in late 1990s, and the companies we looked at included Digital Equipment and Wang Laboratories. We met with the CEOs of different companies in order to determine how they got started and why they were doing so well. Now the computer industry has all but disappeared and most of those companies are gone. Many were bought up or went bankrupt. For a time it looked like we had completely misjudged the prospects for Massachusetts and the US. But now, when you come to Boston and go to MIT you find a whole new set of industries that did not exist ten years ago. In some sense, the information industry is gone, replaced by biotechnology companies, some of which have come from Switzerland and Europe. They are focused around MIT because this is where that development is taking place. So the point is: one year it is computers, the next year it is software, and the next year it is biotechnology. Our challenge is, can we keep developing those new industries fast enough, and, if we can, that may save us, otherwise we really run the risk of long-term and far-reaching unemployment.

JAN KRZYSZTOF BIELECKI: If you do not mind, Professor Koźmiński and then . . .

ANDRZEJ K. KOŹMIŃSKI: I would just add one thing to what you said, Professor Goldman, that in a knowledge-based economy jobs are being created in the service sector. And very rapidly so. These are not necessarily well-paid jobs, however, they somehow fill the gap. As far as the low value-added industries are concerned, jobs are really being created somewhere else, abroad, because the industries are moving. And this is one of the key issues in the knowledge-based economy. Are we capable of developing new sectors fast enough, because otherwise we might have serious problems?

JAN KRZYSZTOF BIELECKI: Professor Gomułka . . .

STANISŁAW GOMUŁKA: Here I think that there is a bit of a difference between a macroeconomic approach to these matters and that of someone from a business school who looks at the question at the micro level. Now, from the macro perspective an answer to your question is much simpler. India, the population growth has been much higher than in Europe. In Europe there is almost zero population growth, in Japan zero or negative, but of course in India and China much higher. In the United States also much higher because of immigration and a higher birth rate. So, during the last 20–30 years, the United States' population increased by how much – 20–25 percent? So, obviously, the labor force increased also and therefore employment. From the macro perspective it is not the millions of new jobs created or the percentage change in the labor force that is of interest, but the rate of unemployment. That is the key thing. Whether the unemployment rate is low or high. Because when we look at unemployment rates, we remove from our analysis this question of population growth or the growth of the labor force, which varies from country to country. And from that perspective the situation in Europe is different. You have the United Kingdom and you have Holland, where you have very low unemployment rates, and we have the bulk of the Continent, France and Germany, where it is rather high, although not so high as it used to be in Spain or is now in Poland. And of course now we have the US experience, a very good experience with large flexibility of the labor market and a low unemployment rate. Now the second point is about this knowledge-based economy. This is a kind of a new phrase, but for a macroeconomist it is simply technological progress. One should not forget that innovation is nothing new, that the technological revolution we are talking about lasts more than century, two centuries. In fact, if we look at the productivity growth in the United States, it has been remarkably stable during the twentieth century. Remarkably stable. Of course, we have one revolution replaced by another revolution, one knowledge by another knowledge, so it is nothing new. There has been some increase in the growth of productivity during the last 20 years or so, 15 years in the United States, and it is not quite clear whether this is the beginning of a new trend or simply a fluctuation. With respect to that fluctuation, incidentally, it was Marx who thought that this knowledge-based economy will eventually lead to the collapse of the capitalist system, because it will lead to the destruction of jobs and the system will collapse because of the huge unemployment. Of course, we believe that the knowledge-based economy, highly innovative type of society is quite compatible with a high rate of growth of job creation and with low unemployment. What is needed is simply sufficient labor market flexibility.

JAN KRZYSZTOF BIELECKI: Can we have one more comment from the panel and then let us allow for some voices from the audience. Professor Niskanen ...

WILLIAM A. NISKANEN: Total employment in the knowledge industries is higher than it was in 1999, but it is lower than it was at the peak of 2000. We had a 7 trillion dollar loss in equity values from the collapse of the technology bubble, in many cases involving knowledge-based industries in telecommunications. So it has been a drop relative to that spring 2000 peak, but employment in the knowledge-based industries is now higher than it was in 1999. We have a net trade surplus in knowledge-based goods and services, so it is still a part of the strength of the American economy, and it is not weakening. Overall, manufacturing employment peaked in the United States in 1979 and in most of the other OECD countries before then, so manufacturing employment as a share of total employment has been dropping for some period of time and absolutely in the United States since 1979. That is not a new phenomenon, and it is much the same phenomenon as has been the case over a much longer period with agriculture. The rate of growth of productivity has been very high in manufacturing, as it has been in agriculture, and that just does not create as many jobs per dollar of output as would otherwise be the case. I think we should not look for ways of doing business and kinds of products that produce a lot of jobs per output: that is a way to be poor. We have to look just the other way around, which is by and large the outcome of the capitalist system. For all that creative destruction, we have a quite high total employment to total population ratio; we have among the lowest unemployment rates in the world. The statistic that most amazes Europeans is that half of our unemployed are re-employed within nine and a half weeks, even though unemployment insurance lasts for twenty-six weeks in the United States. So a lot of people go through the unemployment pool in the United States, but they go through and come out of it quickly and are re-employed, sometimes in the same firm, more often in different firms and in different locations.

JAN KRZYSZTOF BIELECKI: Thank you. That was a very good observation, because I think in our countries unemployment usually lasts for some years. I see that we have a speaker from the floor... Professor Kowalik, yes?

TADEUSZ KOWALIK: Professor Gomułka made some comparisons of growth, and it was the United States and Europe he mentioned, I would say rather conveniently for two reasons: Europe has a less flexible labor market, and much higher redistribution, higher spending. How would you explain this phenomenon: that all five Scandinavian countries have the highest level of spending, the highest level of the welfare state, the highest level of taxation and simultaneously three of them, first was Finland, second was Sweden, the third was Denmark, are on the top of the list of, if you do not like knowledge-based economy, then most modern technically, scientifically economies? How would you explain that, because the labor market in all those countries is much more rigid than in other European countries? And this leads me to another question. I was worried that you were talking about Europe as almost as homogeneous as the United States, whereas the European Union itself is very much diversified. Diversified, having different social and economic systems. About one I was talking, these are Scandinavian countries, and differences between the Scandinavian countries and England or even Spain are bigger that between Europe and the United States. And perhaps I would like, since Mr Chairman you were not only chairing but taking part in the discussion, and during last ten years you studied the euro, and you were prime minister, and it may happen that you will be prime minister again, so I would like to direct this question to you. Entering the euro, are we facing a choice of socio-economic system or not? Or are you happy with this conventional answer that we shall have a very Polish economy, or shall we have a socio-economic system such as the European Union? The last word is connected with the teachings of Nobel Prize winner James Meade. He was defending the right of experimenting in systemic matters. He was afraid of one united Europe. I am also against. I am in favor of a kind of cooperation of different nations, not of unified Europe as one socio-economic system. I wonder what is your opinion.

JAN KRZYSZTOF BIELECKI: Thank you very much Professor Kowalik. So we have a few questions. Let me address them first, then Professor Gomułka and maybe Professor Niskanen can support your comment, because the question refers to the so-called Scandinavian model, and he may still feel it, as some remnants of his childhood.

STANISŁAW GOMUŁKA: Yes, I feel that I am not really able to comment on what happened in the Scandinavian countries. I have not studied development there, and I am not sure whether the facts which have been mentioned here are correct or not and what have been the changes in policies and so on and how to explain them, I am afraid I am unable actually to respond in a sensible way to your interesting question.

JAN KRZYSZTOF BIELECKI: OK, so we need support from the panel... Professor Niskanen...

WILLIAM A. NISKANEN: I have been puzzled for a long time about how Sweden does as well as it does. I think what happened to Britain is Lady Thatcher, and that has made all the difference to the competitiveness of Britain and the much superior economic performance since her days, even under a Labour government.

MARSHALL GOLDMAN: I think your points are very important, and I would not question the data, I think it is correct, and, indeed, if you look at the measures of competitiveness just prepared by the World Economic Forum, the Scandinavian countries are at the top, Finland is also number one in terms of the least corrupt, which also has something to do with its long-standing traditions. In the case of Finland, I think the data are very dependent on one corporation, and that is Nokia. If you remove Nokia from the equation, I do not think you would find that the country would be so competitive. You know Phillips has some impact in that region as well, but I think in the case of Finland it really has to do with one company.

I do want to go back to something that someone said earlier. Marx said that knowledge industries would lead to unemployment and the collapse of the system. Well, in some sense it is doing that, but what Marx neglected to realize was that some of those jobs would also be moved offshore. He did not allow for that. If you look at total world employment, it is going up. It is just that it is not as high as it used to be in the United States.

JAN KRZYSZTOF BIELECKI: Thank you, Professor Bradley, please...

JOHN BRADLEY: One of the characteristics that Poles share with the Irish is they are obsessed with history, and when you look at Scandinavia, I think you have to look at it both in historic context and in a short-term context. I once looked at migration rates in the late nineteenth century, expressed as the proportion of the population of the country and there were only four countries in Europe that had highly significant out-migration rates: Ireland, of course, but also Sweden, Denmark and Norway. Now, their societies adjusted and they became successful and what they show I think is that the libertarian model of the economy is capable of multiple solutions, it is a non-convex set. But what it also shows you if you look at the shorter term is that the Scandinavian model may be a useful one, and one based on a concept of society. And when you look at Scandinavia you see a societal influence on those countries. But we live in a really harsh world where globalization provides nowhere to hide. Even America is suffering from globalization as low-waged manufacturing jobs move to other parts of NAFTA and elsewhere. And of course, this is where the Scandinavian model is vulnerable and therefore is not a suitable model for a country like Ireland or a country like Poland. Because it develops rigidities, it developes collusive coalitions, and when there are big technological changes and Asia develops and activity moves offshore you face problems. These Scandinavian countries are well off, prosperous, stable societies, but they can sometimes become very vulnerable. So I think the Scandinavian model does show that economic success does not necessarily have to follow the American libertarian model and its economic implementation but it also shows that any model has difficulties.

JAN KRZYSZTOF BIELECKI: Thank you, Professor. I have an experience of the last twenty years, or twenty-five, but I remember going back to actually my poor memory... When I arrived in Norway for the first time in the early 1970s to attend a course at the university of Oslo, I remember how this country was struggling and how many jokes were popular in Scandinavia about poor Norwegians, stupid Norwegians. Much more than the famous Polish jokes in the United States. And I remember what expectations they had at that time regarding the North Sea oil, particularly in the Ecofisk field exploration and how money coming from it then improved the standard of living.

And, if we look at the nineteenth century literature, living in Norway was not a paradise whatsoever. Therefore, I think it is better to take the Scandinavian model more precisely by particular country than to say that this is a Scandinavian model. There was the Swedish model, but to me Sweden was only lagging slightly behind Switzerland in providing Hitler's army with guns, ammunition and all those beautiful weapons that created fantastic world opportunities [public laugh]. That means, as Professor Bradley correctly indicated, that this wealth creation should be taken into its historic context. So, Professor Niskanen, a short statement please and then Professor Ćwikliński – I saw he raised the flag twenty-five minutes ago...

WILLIAM A. NISKANEN: May I suggest that the societies that are most vulnerable are not those that allow change but those that try to restrict change. Those that try to restrict loss of jobs in particular firms, locations, regions, industries or occupations, that is the solution for poverty. And we have to allow change to maintain the opportunity to create wealth and for each of us to use our comparative advantage.

JAN KRZYSZTOF BIELECKI: OK, thank you Professor, and Professor Ćwikliński please.

HENRYK ĆWIKLIŃSKI: A few very short remarks. I think Mr Bielecki's response to Professor Kowalik was maybe extreme, but very good. Before discussing how to divide a new value we need a discussion of how to produce it. This example was extreme, but we have to discuss what should be the legal system of effective production. I would say, and this is the second remark, what everybody knows here, where does the world economy come from? From the ancient Greeks. 'Oikos' means house, 'nomos' it means law. So we should discuss, I refer to the subject mentioned before, we should discuss the legal institutions that allow effective production. Only then it will make sense to discuss how to divide it. Thank you.

JAN KRZYSZTOF BIELECKI: Thank you and Professor, Koźmiński – the floor is yours...

ANDRZEJ K. KOŹMIŃSKI: I can easily understand that Professor Gomułka could not explain the Scandinavian phenomenon because it cannot be explained on macroeconomic grounds. The explanation lies in microeconomics and in business. Very simply, Scandinavian economies are the most internationalized ones. This reminds me a story of the Vikings. What the Vikings did, they were going abroad, plundering everybody and taking the wealth back home. And if you look into some practices of some Scandinavian companies, that reminds me of the Vikings' style. Very clearly. Asea Brown Bovery and IKEA and many, many others are doing exactly that. And then they go back home with accumulated wealth and redistribute it equally among all the needy people. And this is, in my opinion, the Scandinavian model [applause and laughter].

JAN KRZYSZTOF BIELECKI: I cannot refrain at this stage from saying that our Polish Solidarity model of development and wealth creation was very different. So, Professor Niskanen...

WILLIAM A. NISKANEN: The question was asked about the legal system which best contributes to the economy. The central feature of the legal system of prosperity and freedom is self-ownership. That means you have the right to determine what you do yourself, but you have no automatic claim on the output or services of other people. It is self-ownership that precludes slavery, precludes an obligation to the state, it precludes obligation to other people, but it gives you the right to conduct your activities in any way that you choose, short of harming other people. That is the central feature of the legal system that is essential to both liberty and prosperity.

JAN KRZYSZTOF BIELECKI: If we do not have any more questions...yes, there are a few more voices from the floor...I am sorry, I do not recognize you...I thought that I know everybody in the audience...

CLIFFORD BATES: Clifford Bates from the Warsaw University, American Studies Center. The legal system, I think, is a fundamental ground of the American model. The Anglo-Saxon legal system in one sense differs from the Continental Europe legal system which explains fundamental differences in not only economics, but also in policy-making and regulation. In the American legal system, law is an effective means to regulate society in ways that in European systems would require bureaucracies, massive bureaucracies to deal with issues such as sexual discrimination, workplace, occupation, health and safety issues, contract violations, so forth and so on. There are many areas of competition, consumer rights and other matters where Americans go to the courts to get redress for their grievances. And enforcement of rules and norms is done through self regulation. Yes, you have government regulations, but the fear is not of the bureaucrat but the fear is of the legal judgment wiping you out. So I think one of the fundamental ways in which adopting the American model may be problematic in this part of the world is that they do not have the legal system to deal with these things in the same way Americans can deal with them. So, the model may be great, the ideas may be wonderful but the problem here is that the legal environment cannot accommodate it.

JAN KRZYSZTOF BIELECKI: That means that we are not only exhausted but we are punctual. We were asked to end at 3:45 and we are approaching that exact time... Yes, Professor Gomułka is exhausted [laugh]. Anyway, if I may entertain you a little bit longer, let me record the visit to Poland in 1991, so many, many years ago... of Margaret Thatcher, who over dinner said to me 'You guys have altogether too many parties in Poland. And there is only room for two parties in a well-run country: the capitalist party and the socialist party.' Professor Niskanen said that private ownership is for him the most important factor of a good system. The problem at present in Poland is that according to the last round of voting of the Polish parliament, we had 400 MPs voting for a socialist solution and 60 with some hesitation voted for a capitalist solution. This proves that we are not only heading towards a Scandinavian model but toward a strict European model, a good German model, which gives me enormous optimism that after these slightly academic discussions, we return to our roots, good European roots and tomorrow we will start building a brilliant European future. Thank you very much. [applause]

WOJCIECH BIEŃKOWSKI: I will not take more than three minutes to conclude, because in the book that is going to be the outcome of the conference, both in Polish and printed in Poland, published in Poland, but also the version of it that will deal with the applicability of the American model to European and post-communist countries that is to be published abroad we will have the real summary of the discussion and you will all have the opportunity to judge the value of what has been contributed during the conference. So, it will not be that there will be a ceremony or something to lengthen these concluding remarks. Let me start by just saying that this round table, this plenary session, was really a wonderful one, and I would like to thank all the participants of this round table and prime minister Jan Krzysztof Bielecki in particular, because it was here, today that we had both the values, the arguments, the data, but of course the sense of humor and his perspective, which is really needed if we want to change our economic policy and advance. We have been just kind of flying, we have wings and have the perspective, and all the wisdom and all this we could find just during this plenary session led by prime minister Bielecki. Also, we just again say 'thank you' to Radek Sikorski, who is representing the American Enterprise Institute, the co-organizer of the conference. I would like to stress that it was really thanks to the National Bank of Poland, and the great support of Leszek Balcerowicz and his team that we are able to accomplish what we have accomplished and thank you all of the participants and the sponsors and the people who attended the conference, so thank you, thank you very much. Good bye. [applause].

Conclusions

John Maynard Keynes was once a strong believer in the classical approach to economics, but, during the economic crises of 1928–33 and because of the mistakes in monetary and foreign trade policy made by governments of the leading countries, he changed his mind and that change led him to develop some new ideas. When he was approached by Montagu Norman, Governor of the Bank of England, who asked him why he had changed his mind so dramatically, Keynes gave this well known reply, 'When circumstances change I change my views, what do you do sir?'

Paradoxically we in Europe, that is, in Continental Europe, are facing a similar dilemma, a change in circumstances that forces a rethinking of views. But now it is intellectually the reverse of Keynes's shift in the 1920s. Now it is not only the political and economic leaders in Europe that face this need for a new paradigm, the same challenge is being faced in Africa, Asia, South and Central America. Economists and policy-makers throughout the world face the same challenge: how do we help guide our respective countries to successfully benefit from globalization? Doing so may require the restructuring of their ideas on economic policy to reflect the changed environment created by globalization.

In the case of Continental Europe, one possible rethinking of assumptions might be a re-evaluation of the benefits of the so-called 'Anglo-Saxon' model. All the evidence, as shown by statistical data, clearly points out that those nations that utilize such so-called 'Anglo-Saxon' ideas of the free market, transparency, individual rights, and the rule of law perform better than those whose ideas are deeply rooted in welfare economies or a belief in the positive benefits of extensive intervention by state actors. The economic performance of the US since Ronald Reagan's presidency, or the United Kingdom's performance since Margaret Thatcher's 'revolution' or those of Ireland, New Zealand, Australia or Chile, show that, by redirecting economic policy toward classical or neoclassical principles, the economies of these countries have started to perform better, whereas countries that maintain large unreformed welfare economies or retain extensive state intervention seem either to face prolonged economic slowdowns or declines. The data clearly indicate that today, especially in a globalized economy without barriers, classical economics appears to work better and bring better results.

The greater the independence of people from state control, either regarding their fiscal obligations (that is, high taxes) or excessive and burdensome regulatory regimes, allows them to more successfully navigate the global economy. Because the emerging global environment allows for greater opportunities for entrepreneurship, economic policies must be conducive to these new circumstances. The evidence presented in this volume shows that the solutions we should seek are ultimately similar to those initiated by Ronald Reagan.

We see it as very important that among the leading political, social and economic actors in Europe, there is confusion not only about how to bring about economic growth, lower unemployment and greater efficiency and competitiveness, but also about the importance of these factors in creating the high standard of living they desire for their countrymen. One form of denial is the reluctance to admit the superior performance of the so-called 'Anglo-Saxon' model of economic policy. All too often, such a model is described as 'American,' which in the context of current European thinking suggests something not necessary pleasant nor desirable. Too many people, among the decision-makers and intellectuals perceive 'American' as something negative, ranging from simplistic Hollywood movies, McDonalds' food or so-called outright imperialistic undertakings such as Vietnam or Iraq. Such a hostility, so often found in Europe, to things American seems quite odd, in that the basic ideas that so underpin the American economic system come from European thinkers such as Montesquieu, Locke, Hume, Smith, Say and the other numerous, but lesser known, founders of the great European tradition of classical liberalism. The American model is very much a product created in Europe. The originally 'American' thing about it was that America unreservedly implemented it. Yes, the environment of America was more hospitable to the introduction of these European ideas because the environment of America had no existing feudal barriers nor pre-existing state and social structures that would protect or privilege certain sectors or groups and prevent the full implementation of these ideals. Europe has tended to deliver good ideas conducive to economic prosperity, especially those developed by eighteenth and nineteenth-century European economists such as Adam Smith, David Ricardo, and John Stuart Mill, but it has too often failed to trust them sufficiently to make effective use of them.

Although Keynes remains a profound and important economic thinker, he has now been effectively challenged by Friedrich Hayek, whose ideas were implemented by Margaret Thatcher, giving Europe an example of how a nation can effectively escape from the trap of a welfare economy and reawakening the possibilities of liberal policies that create superior economic performance. But for her, better economic performance was not an end in itself, but rather a means to improve the standard of living and increase the economic opportunities across the board for all Britons, thus making the British model she championed sustainable. The bottom line of these arguments is that Europe already had and has superior ideas conducive to economic efficiency and competitiveness. So one need not call them American. However, there is still not enough political will in Europe, especially in Continental Europe, to implement these 'European' ideas. Returning to the older European ideas of Locke, Montesquieu and Smith, as demonstrated by US economic performance over 200 years and especially since Reagan's reaffirmation of it, is the best way for not only Continental Europe, but also for the post-communist countries and other countries desiring to stay competitive in a globalized world. Keynes was right – when circumstances change, our ideas must change also.

Index

Acton, John Emerich Edward Dalberg-, 12–25, 245
American
colonies, 6, 17, 20
Constitution, *see* Constitution (American)
dream, 29
economy, 30, 40, 44, 48, 60, 74, 104, 106, 114, 199, 202, 211, 241, 242, 249
model, 104–13, 125, 126, 132, 170, 200, 202, 235, 236, 240, 246, 247, 254, 255, 257
social thought, 28
Revolution, 23
Anglo-Saxon
legal system, 246, 254
model, 170–2, 174, 177, 240
Armenia, 87–93, 95, 97, 99
Austria, 86, 158, 161, 198, 217, 231, 254

Belgium, 158, 159, 161
Bill of Rights, 7, 9, 10
Bulgaria, 87–93, 95, 97, 99
Bush, George W., 5, 10, 59, 67, 69–78,

capital
foreign, 60, 181, 182, 194, 195
formation, 54
human, 88, 89, 155, 157, 162–5, 167, 172–5, 188
investment, 60, 75
market, 111, 148, 188, 212, 240, 242
physical, 165
stock, 60, 184
substitution for labor, 225
Carter, Jimmy, 56, 57
Chile, 86–8, 91–3, 97, 256
China, 89, 90, 94, 98, 115, 137–51, 195, 217, 230, 247, 248
Clinton, William J., 57, 61, 64–8
Cohesion Funds, 165
communism, 14, 53, 86
communist system, 86, 87
Constitution (American), 5–10, 12, 18, 20, 23–5, 44–9, 105, 210, 245
Constitution (European), 235
corruption, 7, 37, 105, 112, 118, 124, 127, 174
Czech Republic, 87–94, 102, 115, 121, 133, 139, 146, 195, 196, 236

Declaration of Independence, 5, 6, 20, 23
Denmark, 158, 159, 161, 175, 198, 250, 252
deregulation, 57, 58, 70, 77, 163–5, 200, 202, 214, 228, 230, 244

economic
convergence, 165, 188
growth, 12, 53, 59–61, 64, 66, 67, 71, 72, 76, 89, 91, 95, 96, 111, 122, 137, 143, 155, 160–2, 164, 180, 184, 193, 194, 201, 214, 226, 239, 244, 245, 257
transition, 137
Economic and Monetary Union (EMU, also European Monetary Union), 187, 189, 206, 212–14
education, 36, 38, 66, 74–6, 86, 88, 89, 107, 121, 126, 157, 164, 181, 184, 188, 189, 196, 225, 244
employment
demand, 111
protection, 158, 159, 162–4, 217, 219–23, 226, 228–31
rates, 156–9, 164, 166, 223
security (labor security), 73, 105
England, 6, 12, 16–18, 20, 21, 25, 30, 45, 238, 247, 250, 256
entrepreneurship, 29, 30, 36, 85, 87, 111, 125, 131, 133, 164, 165, 239, 257
Estonia, 87, 90, 178, 196

Europe, 8, 12, 16, 17, 19, 39, 44, 45, 53, 61, 92, 106, 107, 109–12, 114, 115, 121, 125, 126, 128, 133, 136, 148, 157, 164, 171, 173, 174, 180, 182, 183, 192–8, 202, 205, 206, 213, 214, 233, 235–41, 243–5, 247–52, 254, 256–8
European Commission, 167, 173, 188, 213
European Council, 166, 167, 213
European social model, 163, 166, 192
European Union, 98, 107, 110, 113, 115, 122, 126, 133, 149, 153, 155–68, 170–7, 180, 181, 184, 187–90, 192–203, 206, 212–14, 217–31, 235, 239–42, 247, 250, 251
expenditure
  budget, 145, 208
  defense (military), 86, 90, 107
  government, 9, 97, 107, 162, 201
  public, 160, 173, 175, 207, 240, 241
  social (welfare), 145, 148

federal government, 5, 8, 9, 24, 25, 46, 55, 57, 66, 76, 105, 107, 192, 199, 207, 208, 210–12, 245
Federalist Paper, 8
financial assets, 60, 85
financial crisis, 36
financial institutions, 41, 95, 109, 110
Finland, 61, 158, 161, 198, 245, 250, 251
foreign direct investment (FDI), 74, 90–2, 143, 176, 180, 182–4, 188–90, 194–6, 226, 228, 229
France, 8, 16, 18, 28, 41, 45, 109, 159, 168, 175, 177, 197, 198, 202, 206, 214, 218, 221–5, 226, 229–31, 235, 241, 245, 247, 249
French Revolution, 20, 21
Friedman, Milton, 8, 60

Galbraith, John Kenneth, 32
Germany, 16, 61, 86, 110, 158, 161, 173, 177, 197–202, 206, 209, 214, 235, 236, 241, 247, 249
globalization, 122, 192, 242, 243, 252, 256
government
  budget, 10, 210
  central, 24, 45, 144
  federal, *see* federal government
  intervention, 126, 138, 140
  limited, 7, 14, 16
  national, 45–8, 168, 186, 207
  programs, 55, 56, 77, 78, 108
  revenue, 60
  self-, 12, 15, 17, 18
  services, 77, 107
  share of GDP, 110
  size (scale) and scope, 6, 10
  weak, 138, 139
Great Britain, 13, 21, 159, 197, 245
Great Depression, 10, 54, 61
Greece, 15, 16, 87, 88, 91–3, 97, 158, 159, 161, 173, 181, 193

Hamilton, Alexander, 6, 8, 9, 40, 46
health, 65, 77, 86, 88, 92, 96, 106–8, 120, 121, 254
Hobbes, Thomas, 28
Hungary, 86–93, 95, 97, 99, 115, 133, 146, 195, 196

income tax, 9, 58–61, 66, 72, 73, 157, 158, 201, 210
inflation, 6, 7, 54–6, 59–61, 64, 67, 89–91, 99, 101, 106, 186, 190, 201, 219
information and communication technologies (ICT), 162, 163, 166, 167, 187
infrastructure
  economic, 47
  institutional, 110
  market, 121
  physical, 112, 172, 173–5
  social, 121
  spending, 64
  transport (transportation), 47, 166
investment
  business, 186
  greenfield, 195
  infrastructure, 193
  aid, 173, 175
  behavior, 59
  funds, 139
  public, 64, 112, 160, 173–5
  state-directed, 54
  wasteful, 90
Ireland, 88, 93, 97, 110, 158, 159, 161, 168, 171, 173, 174, 177, 178, 180–90, 194–6, 198, 227, 228, 230, 252, 256
Italy, 16, 158, 159, 161, 168, 198, 214

Jay, John, 8
Jefferson, Thomas, 23
job security, 86, 164

Kazakhstan, 88, 90–3, 97, 99
Keynes, John Maynard, 256–8
Keynesian, 53–5, 69, 115, 122, 186, 192, 198, 201, 210
knowledge-based economy, 155, 162, 243, 247–50

labor
 force, 9, 90, 164, 181, 189, 211, 212, 222, 226, 227, 249
 market, 9, 30, 36, 40, 47, 99, 105, 106, 111, 141, 155, 156, 158–60, 162–4, 167, 181, 182, 192, 202, 210, 211, 214, 217–31, 240, 241, 249, 250
 productivity, 91, 156, 226, 229
 security, *see* employment security
 utilization, 156, 162, 163
Latvia, 87, 88, 90–3, 95, 97, 99, 196
liberalization, 54, 62, 87, 95, 96, 98–102, 110, 122, 141, 142, 149, 170, 172, 189, 202
Lisbon Strategy, 155–68
Lithuania, 87, 88, 90–3, 95, 97, 99, 196
living standards, 90, 125, 128, 133, 177, 181, 182, 184, 188, 193
Locke, John, 5, 17, 28, 245, 257, 258
Luxembourg, 181

Maastricht Treaty, 194, 197, 198, 201, 213
Madison, James, 8, 46
market-oriented reforms, 87, 94, 95, 96, 98, 102
Medicare tax, 65
Mexico, 47, 86–8, 91–3, 129
Mill, John Stuart, 245, 257
Mises, Ludvig von, 245
Moldova, 87, 89–95, 97, 99
monetarism, 122, 242
Montesquieu, Charles-Louis de Secondat, 245, 257, 258

NAFTA, 62, 67, 252
Netherlands, 158, 161, 168, 175, 198
Norway, 61, 157, 181, 252, 253

Poland, 9, 53, 54, 85–93, 95, 97, 99, 100, 102, 104–12, 115, 121, 133, 146, 177, 195, 196, 217, 227–30, 235, 236, 240, 241, 246, 247, 249, 252, 255
Portugal, 158, 161, 173, 181, 193
private property, 7, 100, 105, 115–17, 125, 128, 131, 132, 137, 240
privatization, 70, 77, 85, 95, 96, 98, 100–2, 110–12, 117, 137–9, 141–3, 145, 148, 149, 170, 195, 202, 240
product markets, 158, 162–4, 240
property rights, 47, 48, 70, 75, 104, 105, 111, 112, 132, 133, 137–9, 141–3, 246
public
 consumption, 159, 160, 162, 165
 culture, 125, 127, 128, 130–3
 debt, 111, 213
 finance, 165, 181
 finances, 173, 185, 186
 good, 177
 goods, 86, 126, 132, 140, 175, 207
 health, 92, 120, 121
 investment, 64, 112, 160, 173–5
 sector, 111, 112, 173, 175
 service, 15
 spending, 159–61, 165, 167

Reagan, Ronald, 58–62, 69, 70–5, 77–9, 199, 244, 256–8
redistribution, 142, 160, 207–11, 214, 246, 250
rent
 granting, 126, 130, 131
 seeking, 100, 131, 143
research and development, 112, 155, 163, 166, 167
Revolutionary War, 6–9
Roosevelt, Franklin D., 55, 58
Rousseau, Jean-Jacques, 28
Russia, 67, 87–99, 102, 108, 114–33, 139, 141, 143, 150, 238, 240–3, 247

Scandinavian model, 251–5
Schumpeter, Joseph, 38, 140
Slovakia, 87–93, 95, 97, 99, 115, 196
Slovenia, 90–3, 95, 97, 99, 195, 196
Smith, Adam, 29, 30, 57, 104, 125, 126, 245, 246, 257, 258

social
  cohesion, 155, 162, 166
  contract, 28, 127
  engineering, 7, 54
  good, 30
  mobility, 31, 39
  policy, 44, 70, 73, 75, 123
  security, 9, 66, 68, 70, 72, 75, 77, 111, 145, 155, 158, 163, 164, 167, 198, 223
  welfare, 28, 61, 125, 126, 133, 145
  mobility, 31, 39
socialism, 53, 54, 115, 119, 122, 123
socialist economy, 53, 99, 102
Spain, 6, 18, 20, 45, 86, 158, 159, 161, 173, 181, 193, 249, 250
state-owned enterprises, 85, 86, 111, 112, 138, 142, 144
Structural Funds, 168, 171, 173–5, 177, 179, 188, 193
Sweden, 33, 61, 158, 161, 175, 198, 214, 217, 221, 231, 250–3

tax
  burdens, 185, 201
  cuts, 58–61, 69, 71–3, 78
  excise, 65
  labor (imposed on), 157, 162, 186, 220
  liability, 59, 60
  policy, 47, 60, 61, 71
  rate, 58, 61, 63, 65, 107, 108, 158, 181
  rates, 58–61, 66, 73, 110, 158, 164, 211, 235
  revenue, 59, 108, 160
taxation, 16, 17, 21, 46, 66, 72, 78, 173, 185, 186, 194, 211, 212, 220, 229, 244, 250
technology, 36, 74, 91, 106, 131, 166, 177, 187, 198, 240, 248, 249
Thailand, 86–8, 92, 93, 97
Tocqueville, Alexis de, 13, 31, 38–40, 42, 109, 111, 113, 245
trade unions, 186, 187, 202, 217, 226–31
transition countries (economies), 83, 90, 92, 93, 95–7, 181, 137–49, 177, 226

Ukraine, 87, 90, 91, 92, 93, 97, 99
unemployment, 54, 55, 61, 64, 74, 91, 105, 107, 128, 130, 144, 145, 156, 157, 159, 160, 163, 181, 185, 189, 192, 198, 201, 217–23, 226–31, 240, 247–50, 252, 257
United Kingdom (UK), 102, 110, 158, 161, 181, 177, 182, 183, 185–7, 196, 197, 217–19, 221–30, 249, 256

welfare state, 61, 77, 86, 125, 157, 160, 162, 163, 192, 198–200, 202, 210, 250
Wilson, Woodrow, 5, 10